TERROR AND TRIUMPH

THE 2002 EDWARD CADBURY LECTURES
UNIVERSITY OF BIRMINGHAM, UNITED KINGDOM

TERROR AND TRIUMPH

The Nature of Black Religion

ANTHONY B. PINN

FORTRESS PRESS

Minneapolis

TERROR AND TRIUMPH
The Nature of Black Religion

Cover and book design: Zan Ceeley
Cover art: Jacob Lawrence, "A Foothold on the Rocks," 1967, egg tempera on hardboard, 30 x 24 in. Private Collection. Artwork copyright 2002 Gwendolyn Knight Lawrence, courtesy of the Jacob and Gwendolyn Lawrence Foundation. Used by permission.
Author photo by C. J. © C. J.
Lyrics on p. 144 copyright 1968 Wynwood Music Co. Inc. Used by permission.

Library of Congress Cataloging-in-Publication Data
Pinn, Anthony B.
     Terror and triumph : the nature of Black religion / Anthony B. Pinn.
        p. cm.
     Includes bibliographical references and index.
     ISBN 0-8006-3601-5 (pbk. : alk. paper)
        1. African Americans—Religion. 2. United States—Church history.
     I. Title.
     BR563.N4 P495 2003
     200'.89'96073—dc21   2002152636

Manufactured in the U.S.A.
07   06   05   04   03   1   2   3   4   5   6   7   8   9   10

To Dr. Charles Long,
Dr. Gordon Kaufman,
and the Ancestors

CONTENTS

◇◇◇◇

PART ONE ◇ CONSTRUCTING TERROR

PART TWO ⟡ WAGING WAR

PART THREE ◇ SEEKING TRIUMPH

PREFACE

◇◇◇◇

What does it mean to be black and religious in the United States? What is the nature of black religion? How does one speak about and investigate what appear to be multiple manifestations of black religion? What is the *religion* in black religion? That is, what is it that makes black religion distinctive and distinguishable as a modality of experience?

This book represents my response to these questions, all of which stem from my earlier writings. Earlier I attempted to give some shape to my understanding of the *diversity* of black religion through descriptive presentations of the varieties of black religion, including at least one unlikely category—black humanism.[1] In presenting these traditions and their theological frameworks, my goal was to challenge monolithic and myopic depictions of religious experience in black communities, depictions that take the path of least resistance by framing all discussion in terms of the Black Church. Although the Black Church has dominated the religious landscape of black America, other traditions are nonetheless present and have played important roles in the lives of many. My objective, however, in the following pages is more ambitious than a description of the various forms of religion found within black communities. The questions I posed earlier call for more than this. In fact, they push for a more general study of black religion, one that gives more precise attention to the very nature and meaning of black religion. Through the development of an interdisciplinary approach, I seek to articulate a vision of black religion's nature and meaning—in terms of both its primary structure and its historical manifestations in the institutions and movements—such as the Christian churches and the Nation of Islam—that typically come to mind when black religion is mentioned. What I mean by such ideas as religion's basic structure and historical manifestations of religion will, I hope, become clear.

My writings up to this point made addressing the issues contained in this volume mandatory. For instance, my effort to rethink the black religion "canon" begs the question of religion's nature.[2] What does it mean to be religious? What distinguishes religious experience from other forms of experience? What is the nature of religion if it is not confined to the Christian faith? How does one study religion conceived in the broad terms generated by my book *Varieties of African American Religious Experience?* In this volume, I address these questions in a way that I hope extends the important theoretical and methodological work started by Charles Long several decades ago—a way of looking at the manner in which religion grows from the inside out.

Readers will note that the arrangement of the chapters seeks to make clear the necessary move from data to theory. That is, experience or "raw" material informs the theory and method of study. Therefore, the first chapter, the introductory essay, begins this project by briefly discussing the existential and ontological challenges of the enslavement process. Chapter 1 provides the necessary intellectual context for understanding the treatment of black bodies presented in the next two chapters. In chapters 2 and 3, the making of the "negro" is extended to a discussion of acts of violence, what I call rituals of reference, used to keep Africans and their descendants within their proper place. Chapters 4 and 5 address an important question: how did Africans respond to the terror, dread, and anxiety produced by the slave system and these rituals of reference? I suggest that black religion as manifested by the Black Church and the Nation of Islam, for example, is the primary response to this existential and ontological dread or terror. In chapter 6, I discuss the ways in which religion so understood has been studied. But is there more to religion than these historically defined modes of reaction? In chapter 7, I respond in the affirmative. Yes, these institutions and movements represent the historical context for a more central reality. The Black Church, the Nation of Islam, and other expressions of African American religion are manifestations of a more basic impulse; and this basic impulse—what I will define as the quest, or feeling, for complex subjectivity—is the central nature or core of black religion. The final chapter addresses key issues associated with the theory of religion I promote in chapter 7.

While I believe this book provides important and in many cases unique perspectives on the nature and meaning of black religion, only readers can assess the usefulness of the text. And although I am responsible for any shortcomings, many people helped to make this book possible. With this in mind, I am grateful to the faculty of the University of Birmingham's Department of Theology—particularly Professors Markus Vinzent, Emmanuel Lartey, Isabel Wollaston, and Robert Beckford—and the Division of Historical Studies, particularly Professor John Haldon, who extended the invitation to deliver the Edward Cadbury Lectures. Conversation with John Hick and Anthony Reddie also proved helpful. I am also grateful to the other members of the University of Birmingham community who made the time my wife and I spent in Birmingham so enjoyable.

I also thank my wife, C.J., because her support of my work and patience with my moodiness are a display of pure grace and love. I am indebted to her for her encouragement and vision, without which this and other projects would be far less meaningful.

Fortress Press has always supported my work, and I appreciate the encouragement and patience demonstrated by Michael West as well as Zan Ceeley and the other folks in Minneapolis. Macalester College's provost made arrangements that allowed time to complete the writing of this book, and the Religious Studies Department allowed me to rethink my schedule in important ways. I am particularly grateful to Allen Callahan, who read the manuscript, raised important questions and possibilities, and encouraged my take on the study of religion. Thank you. And of course, I thank the students in my courses during the spring 2002 semester—Religion 43-01, Religion 53-01, African American Studies 10-01—for their encouragement and enthusiastic response to many ideas presented in this volume. Their questions and comments on early presentations of the book's major themes were greatly appreciated. Other folks from the Macalester campus have been extremely supportive: thank you to Richard Ammons, Ahmed Samatar, Robbie Seals, and Ramon Rentas for welcomed breaks from work to enjoy conversation over a good meal or a game of pool. I am also grateful to Peter Paris and the members of the Pan-African Seminar, who, over the course of our time in Ghana and Kenya, helped me to think through important themes and potential pitfalls. In particular, Katie Cannon encouraged and critiqued my work on the body in ways that helped me revise my conceptual framework. I also thank Phyllis Weiner for her help with my thought on and appreciation for modern art.

Charles Long and Gordon Kaufman, to whom this volume is dedicated, have inspired and challenged me to think beyond the easy categories, and I am grateful for their work and support of my efforts.

1

"LOOK, A NEGRO!"

How the New World African
Became an Object of History

What is black religion? To answer this question, I explore the unique circumstances and history of black people in the United States. I identify a common quest and shared meaning in the rich variety of religious expressions that black religion manifests.

Although the Black Church has dominated the religious landscape of black America, other traditions are nonetheless present and have played roles in black life. As historian of religions Charles Long states in an often-quoted passage, "The Christian faith provided a language for the meaning of religion, but not all the religious meanings of the black communities were encompassed by the Christian forms of religion."[1] In other words, while the Black Church has held a prominent place, it is only one of many available modes of religious expression. The Nation of Islam and other traditions add a richness to the religious sensibilities of black Americans. In other works, I have outlined the content of some forms of religion that thrive within black communities. However, my objective here is to locate in the 400-year odyssey of black people in America and in the variety of their religious expressions and practices and institutions[2] a common core—the heart and soul of black religious life.

Drawing from a number of disciplines, in this volume I seek to articulate a vision of black religion's nature and meaning in terms of both its primary structure and its historical manifestations in institutions and movements that typically come to mind when black religion is mentioned. But I must note at this point that attention to the historical manifestation of religion is here focused on the Black Church and the Nation of Islam. This should not be taken as an explicit (or even implicit) suggestion that only these two forms merit attention, or that only these two modes of religious expression really count. I believe my earlier work demonstrates my interest in a full range of experiences of religion in black communities. However, in pointing to these two traditions, and by extension the presence of Christianity and Islam in more general terms, I am able to give attention to the forms of religious experience that in terms of popular imagination and memorable rhetoric, for good or ill, dominate the black American landscape.[3]

To provide a description of black religion, it is necessary to set the stage in sociohistorical terms. This first chapter does so through a brief discussion of the initial rationale for the African presence in North America, with a particular focus on the United States.[4] Attention to the images, language, and attitudes that served to define the nature of the African as an object of history is important. It surfaces the underlying philosophical and ideological workings that inform the slave trade. Although there are other ways to develop such a discussion, I frame it in terms of white supremacy and its ramifications. The primary concern here is the description of ideas, ideals, and an aesthetic that constitute the workings of white supremacy as well as a description of this process with respect to the creation of the "negro" within what becomes the United States.[5]

Framing the Initial Contact

Cornel West has argued that a "normative gaze" or ideal of beauty, exhibited in the human form depicted in classical Greek art, came to be seen as superior during the age of exploration. By the 1600s, this theory of ideal form was applied in natural history as a way of categorizing and ranking races. The closer a race was in appearance to the Greek body, the nearer that race was to the ideal. It takes little imagination to realize that Africans, depicted as dark-skinned, having typically thicker lips, broader noses, and more coarse hair, were far from this ideal form. By implication, Africans were inferior in beauty to Europeans, who more closely resembled this subjective ideal. The discipline of physiognomy connected physical attributes and character by arguing that "a beautiful face, beautiful body, beautiful nature, beautiful character, and beautiful soul were inseparable."[6] During the eighteenth century, phrenology (the reading of skull shapes) argued for a connection between the size of the skull and the depth of character. Although these disciplines said more about the likes and dislikes, idiosyncrasies and biases, of investigators than about humanity, they held sway over popular and academic attitudes. What is more, pseudosciences like phrenology gave these assessments legitimacy, an ontological and biological grounding, and thereby provided authority for racist depictions of Africans as by nature less than fully human.[7]

While the genealogy of racism offered by Cornel West is insightful, a more historically detailed account of the development of racism is given by Winthrop Jordan. And while West and Jordan may disagree on some points, they both understand racism as a modern invention. According to Jordan, ocean voyages under way at the dawn of the modern period brought the differences between groups of people into full view and fueled increased interest in making sense of the differences. With respect to the English in particular, recognition of Africans was made first in soft ways through literature that referred to Ethiopians. Later, following the sixteenth century, after the English broke the Venetian monopoly on foreign trade, direct and rapid contact with Africans began to occur.[8] English settlements in Africa beginning in 1631 and the activities of the Royal African Company, chartered in the 1670s, brought the English and Africans into close and sustained contact. But this contact did not entail the proscription of Africans as inferior.[9] While travelers noted differences in color, they did not frame them in terms of problematic sensibilities and assumptions. Concerning this, Jordan says, "Englishmen actually described Negroes as black—an exaggerated term which in itself suggests that negros' complexion had powerful impact upon their perceptions. Even the peoples of northern Africa seemed so dark that Englishmen tended to call them 'black' and let further refinements go by the board. Blackness became so generally associated with Africa that every African seemed a black man."[10] When cultural and geographic distinctions were made between north Africans and west Africans, the overwhelming preoccupation remained skin. While differing shades could be noted, Africans remained defined by color.

The African as a "Problem": Phase One

This nonjudgmental response to the African's blackness was not to be sustained. The English popular imagination was too loaded with negative color symbolism for nonprejudiced difference to remain the norm. In other words, the color black was associated with "baseness and evil, a sign of danger and repulsion. . . . White and black connoted purity and filthiness, virginity and sin, virtue and baseness, beauty and ugliness, beneficence and evil, God and the devil."[11] Related to this negative color symbolism, Jordan concludes that, as of the eighteenth century, the African's different color was connected to a different nature that rendered the African ugly and flawed in character. And so for the English, whose idea of beauty depended upon paleness, Africans represented a people unattractive and odd in their practices. Differentiated from the English, Africans became the "Other." Africans during this period were often used as a measuring stick by which the English assessed themselves and their society, both in religious and mundane terms.[12] At its worst, differences in appearance, social habits, and cultural production were interpreted in ways that painted Africans as barbaric and of less value. The African as a scientific, social, cultural, philosophical, and physical problem persisted and intensified as English involvement in the slave trade grew during the eighteenth century.

A desire emerged to understand the African's place in the created order in keeping with the scriptural depiction of one source or one creation. In Genesis 1:25-27 we find the following words:

> And God made the beast of the earth after his kind, and cattle after their kind, and every thing that creepeth upon the earth after his kind: and God saw that it was good. And God said, Let us make man in our image, after our likeness: and let them have dominion over the fish of the sea, and over the fowl of the air, and over the cattle, and over all the earth, and over every creeping thing that creepeth upon the earth. So God created man in his own image, in the image of God created he him; male and female created he them.[13]

Also in Genesis, however, is a second account of creation. Genesis 2:7-8, 18-25, reads:

> And the Lord God formed man of the dust of the ground, and breathed into his nostrils the breath of life; and man became a living soul. And the Lord God planted a garden eastward in Eden; and there he put the man whom he had formed. . . . And the Lord God said, It is not good that the man should be alone: I will make him an help meet for him. And out of the ground the Lord God formed every beast of the field and every fowl of the air; and brought them unto Adam to see what he would call them: and whatsoever Adam called every living creature, that was the name thereof. And Adam gave names to all cattle, and

to the fowl of the air, and to every beast of the field; but for
Adam there was not found an help meet for him. And the Lord
God caused a deep sleep to fall upon Adam, and he slept: and
he took one of his ribs, and closed up the flesh instead thereof;
And the rib, which the Lord God had taken from man, made
he a woman, and brought her unto the man. And Adam said,
this is now bone of my bones, and flesh of my flesh: she shall be
called Woman, because she was taken out of Man. Therefore
shall a man leave his father and his mother, and shall cleave
unto his wife: and they shall be one flesh. And they were both
naked, the man and his wife, and were not ashamed.[14]

This story suggested the theological framework or parameter for
defining the nature and character of Africans. In short, Scripture
required that English Christians begin their thinking on Africans
with an understanding that Africans had the same creator. Yet they
were at least physically and culturally different, and this difference
had to be accounted for. As we shall see, a sense of shared creation
did not prohibit a ranking within the created order, one in which
Africans were much lower than Europeans.[15] Contained in this assertion is the ground for a theory of white supremacy that would take
various forms but, according to historian George Fredrickson, always
include at least the following assertions: "Blacks are physically, intel-
lectually, and temperamentally different from whites. Blacks are also
inferior to whites in at least some of the fundamental qualities
wherein the races differ, especially in intelligence and in the tem-
peramental basis of enterprise or initiative. Such differences and dif-
ferentials are either permanent or subject to change only by a very
slow process of development or evolution."[16] Theorizing further,
some argued that the color of the African was a consequence of close
proximity to the sun. Yet this notion did not hold, since Europeans
moved into similar areas without permanent change in pigment.
Furthermore, based on this argument, one would assume that taking
Africans out of the sun would eventually result in a permanent shift
in skin color from dark to white, the assumed natural color of

humanity. But this did not happen. Such naturalistic explanations proved faulty.

Others seeking an explanation of the African's blackness turned to Scripture and found what seemed both a theologically and a philosophically reasonable argument, one that buttressed the physical evidence provided by the scientific community. Genesis 9:20-22, 24–25 contained the answer within the story of Noah and the cursing of Ham and his son: "Noah was the first tiller of the soil. He planted a vineyard; and he drank of the wine, and became drunk, and lay uncovered in his tent. And Ham, the father of Canaan, saw the nakedness of his father, and told his two brothers outside. . . . When Noah awoke from his wine and knew what his youngest son [Ham] had done to him, he said, 'Cursed be Canaan; a slave of slaves shall he be to his brother.'"[17]

The failure of Africans to be beautiful, Christian, and English, or in more general terms civilized, had to be explained, and this biblical story tendered an acceptable explanation. One can raise questions concerning why a biblical text addressing a labor arrangement (and one not based on physiological ranking), as opposed to physiological distinctions between races, was found so useful in attempting to understand the differences between Europeans and Africans. Still, regardless of how faulty one may find the logic, this passage held sway, and it has been massively influential since then.

It is possible, but unlikely, that a hierarchy of being could develop without the intent of degrading certain groups. But, as we shall see, degradation is exactly what took place, and this spectrum of status was used to map out social relationships. As England's role in the "New World" increased, and a slave trade was devised to meet its labor demands, theological rationales offered useful justification for growing economic and social arrangements in the colonies.

It is true that an effort was initially made to use European servants and Native Americans as a labor force. Indentured servants actually provided an important labor pool for colonists, although the financial benefits for servants were minor and the ability to progress socially was limited. While distinctions were made between free colonists and servants, the differences resided primarily in cultural, social, and economic opportunity and access. In some cases, freed servants left with a trade and perhaps a bit of land, and one might assume servants would be exposed to the workings of the Christian faith. More importantly, free colonists and servants might have different levels of "refinement," but they were considered ontologically of the same substance as their employers. For example, servants were not Indians. The latter were assumed barbaric and prone to all types of despicable activities. The New World was considered a new Canaan set aside for colonists, yet it was not without its perils, including the "heathen" who called it home. Prior to the war of the late seventeenth century, there was a general interest on the part of New England colonies to avoid harming Indians. In fact, colonists who did harm them often suffered legal recourse.[18] Colonists of course assumed that their laws, based on the word of the Christian God, superseded any laws and customs of the Indians.[19] Furthermore, regulations that on the surface protected Indians did not entail strong positive feelings toward them. Various wars waged between the Puritans and the Indians testify to that. Furthermore, it was not uncommon for Indian prisoners of war and debtors to fall into the existing system of indentured servitude.[20] Still, in the long run, indentured servitude proved an unreliable and costly form of labor. And when European servants and Indians proved problematic, hope was held out for the African slave trade as a source of an easily distinguished and capable labor force.[21]

The African as a "Problem": Phase Two, or Slavery

Historical studies of slavery clearly indicate that Europeans did not invent the institution. One can trace it back to the Greeks and other early civilizations. Europeans, however, during the age of exploration, certainly perfected its racial, psychological, social, and political mechanics and structures. As John Hope Franklin insightfully argues, the Renaissance and the Commercial Revolution in Europe made perfection of such a longstanding arrangement possible because the former ushered in a sense of freedom entailing the welfare of both the soul and the body. What is most profound and tragic about this freedom is the manner in which it was denied to those without means. And the economic means necessary for this philosophical position were made available through the shift from feudalism to a town-based commerce secured through capital. While making impressive claims, a strong moral consciousness was not the hallmark of freedom and commerce emerging during the modern period. For example, Portugal and Spain decided early that African goods and bodies could play an important role in the further development of their economies and overall well-being. As early as the mid-1400s, these two countries were importing both goods and bodies, and with the exploration of the so-called New World, the labor of Africans would only increase in value.[22] Hence, the enslavement of Africans was more than a century old when England got into the business in the 1600s.

The first Africans—also called Negroes or Negars—were brought to Virginia in 1619. Before the mid-1600s, Africans in North American colonies were few and they worked under arrangements similar to European servants. It was not until England participated in the slave trade on a larger scale that Africans began to serve for life in extremely large numbers. When the Royal African Company held a monopoly on England's slave trade (in the 1670s through the late 1680s), it transported roughly 5,000 slaves per year to the English colonies. After this monopoly, the number of slaves moved by the English radically increased, with such cities as Bristol and Liverpool accounting for more than 18,000 slaves transported annually.[23] Although there were enslaved Africans in New England representing roughly 10 percent of the population by 1775, the bulk of this forced labor was on the tobacco and rice plantations of the South, where slaves represented a much larger percentage of the overall population. The Carolinas were particularly aggressive in bringing slavery into the territory. For example, in 1633 colonists were given at least ten acres of land for each slave entering the colony and, within a short period of time, the number of slaves equaled that of colonists—only to exceed it by 1715.[24] According to estimates, by the end of the eighteenth century there were fewer than 1 million slaves; but before the nineteenth century was four decades old the slave population had grown to better than 2 million. Although the importation of Africans was outlawed in 1808, the number of slaves had grown, with the epicenter in Virginia, to almost 4 million by 1860.[25]

Prior to the massive influx of slaves to North America, there seemed no real need beyond character assassination and arguments of natural inferiority to justify the purchase of Africans. Winthrop Jordan provides insight into this arrangement: "The English errand into Africa was not a new or a perfect community but a business trip. No hope was entertained for civilizing the Negros' steaming continent, and Englishmen lacked compelling reason to develop a program for remodeling the African natives. The most compelling necessity was that of pressing forward the business of buying Negroes from other Negroes. It was not until the slave trade came to require justification, in the eighteenth century, that some Englishmen found special reason to lay emphasis on the Negros' savagery."[26]

While Africans were often referred to as beastlike in behavior, the notion of one creation, discussed earlier, prevented these depictions from going so far as to say that Africans were *completely* nonhuman. That remained the case until the Enlightenment, which brought increased attention to the so-called scientific analysis and classification of the human as a physical being, as opposed to the earlier, more theological analysis of the human as defined by relationship to God. As the arguments concerning the status or nature of the African developed in the early eighteenth century, they tended to revolve around the idea of the African as a different kind of human or perhaps not fully human.[27] And so, the initial enslavement of Africans revolved most clearly around cultural difference perceived as strangeness and the vulnerability entailed by this depiction. Although the color black was often associated with negative images of sin, this, according to historian George Fredrickson, does not suggest that the enslavement of

Africans was initially premised on personification of negative color symbolism. In fact, Fredrickson writes, "this distaste for blackness was not unanimous" because there is "some evidence of a countercurrent of admiration for African physical beauty, and some of the early English and Dutch observers of Africa and Africans mentioned color only casually or in passing before commenting extensively on cultural traits."[28] Nonetheless, "among Englishmen there was indeed a vague prejudice against blacks even before the first colonists set foot in North America. As a result of early contacts with Africa, Englishmen tended to associate blackness with savagery, heathenism, and general failure to conform to European standards of civilization and propriety."[29] With an economic need and a readily available source of cheap labor, preexisting prejudices and stereotypes may not have created a desire to enslave Africans but they certainly made this action more palatable over time.

By the mid–seventeenth century, the differentiation of black bodies, with all the implied psychosocial and cultural implications, was bolstered by theological argument and solidified by legal restrictions. For example, it was understood that baptism might pose a problem with respect to the black labor force: does baptism confer humanity and brotherhood and thereby prevent perpetual bondage? Virginia's answer came in 1667 when it was decided that "the conferring of baptisme doth not alter the condition of the person as to his bondage or freedome." Maryland's regulations governing slaves were just as strict, as evidenced by a 1663 regulation that sought to make all Africans in the colony slaves and to apply this same status to all children born to Africans at any time. Ultimately, this law failed; it was softened to allow for the freedom of black children born to white women and to free black women. Colonies farther south also enacted laws to solidify the dominance of white colonists over enslaved Africans by requiring the latter to carry passes when off plantations and by giving whites permission to search Africans for passes and weapons. Georgia, which had been established as free from slavery, found it necessary to remove this restriction in 1750 and to develop laws—drawn heavily from South Carolina laws—to regulate the person and activities of enslaved Africans.[30] Laws, or Slave Codes, in all of the slave states pointed to the same assumption: slaves were less than fully human, a form of property—both as body and as labor—over which whites had clear rights that needed protection.

Slavery and Dehumanization

What we have, then, in North America is a growing dehumanization of blacks based on numerous factors, including socioeconomic need and psychological comfort, which gave shape to a sense of white supremacy and black inferiority. With time, the justifications for slavery come to include color and physical features. Whites and blacks could be easily differentiated based on these, and when the need for a strong and consistent labor force developed before the eighteenth century, color and physical features became a useful basis for enslavement. Economic, social, cultural, physical, and philosophical considerations came together and resulted in the advocation of chattel slavery as the inherent lot of black people.

Some argue that a fully formed racist ideology did not develop in North America until the nineteenth century, when slaveholders were confronted with efforts to enfranchise blacks. Then, at the end of the nineteenth century, this ideology became more rigorous through the application of theories of evolution and natural selection and the desperate effort to keep the recently freed blacks in their proper place. Yet it is clear that racism and white supremacy were in place much earlier than this. By referring to an "earlier" and a "later" articulation, we are simply distinguishing between racism and white supremacy in rough draft and as a completed project. In either case, blacks were considered of lesser value and questionable humanity.

I must acknowledge that studies such as the one I am pursuing here are frustrated by a lack of information concerning the early years of chattel slavery in the North American colonies. For example, little available information survives from Africans during this period concerning their impressions of the system. Yet it is clear that by the time slavery was firmly in place, years before hereditary servitude became normative in 1775, the nature and character of enslaved Africans had become debased. If they were not already considered less human, the complete loss of liberty, or self-determination, inherent in slavery was considered the same as a loss of humanity. Slaves became property in human form. Thus, slaveholders could "send them to the fields at younger ages, . . . deny them automatic existence as inherent members of the community, . . . tighten the bonds on their personal and civil freedom, and correspondingly . . . loosen the traditional restraints on the master's freedom to deal with his human property as he saw fit."[31] Language and color symbolism gave force to the differences between colonists with liberty and those without liberty. With increasing regularity, colonists referred to slaves as blacks and Africans (as opposed to Negroes or savages). And they referred to themselves as Christian, English, and free or white.[32] It is clear that as the slave system developed and matured, the use of complexion as the marker and justification for enslavement (that is, the loss of liberty) became more entrenched. Slaves, in short, were those who were black and therefore strange creatures. The idea here is a tricky one. It is not that Africans were always considered animals—nonhuman in this sense—but that a consistent assumption existed that blacks should have a restricted and determined identity. One can question whether colonists believed enslaved Africans were actual beasts, but one thing is certain: Africans were determined fully by their chattel status. Slavery entailed a system of relations and experience—direct and violent—namelessness and invisibility, personal violations of many kinds and dishonor that whites were not subjected to.[33] In essence, slavery became the answer to all questions concerning the African, and it settled decisively any questions about their humanity. It spoke to their nature and their status. For example, James Henry Hammonds, a pro-slavery spokesperson from South Carolina, in 1858 says this concerning the nature of the black: "In all social systems there must be a class to do the menial duties, to perform the drudgery of life. That is a class requiring but a low order of intellect and but little skill. Its requisites are vigor, docility, fidelity. . . . Fortunately for the South we have found a race adapted to that purpose to her hand. . . . We do not think that whites should be slaves either by law or necessity. Our slaves are black, of another, inferior race."[34]

Our understanding might benefit from additional attention to this point to demonstrate what it meant to develop the negro as a New World being who is confronted by an absurd social arrangement.[35] North America as a geographic and cultural space had been conquered, and with the subjugation of the Native American and the creation of the negro, "occupation of land culminated in the occupation of psyches."[36] Enslavement and life as chattel placed restrictions on those of African descent, restrictions aptly characterized by sociologist Orlando Patterson. According to Patterson, in his work on slavery and social death, slavery involves enslaved persons' status as property, insofar as they are allowed to live in exchange for their service and identity. This exchange was usually necessitated because of debt or war. But slave traders tapped into and modified this system, long in existence in Africa as well as other parts of the world, by exchanging goods for people.[37] The concept of property, however, does not fully capture the dynamics at play, since power relations and claims do not denote a specific grouping of beings. As Patterson argues, "Any person, beggar or king, can be the object of a property relation. Slaves are not different in this respect." If this terminology is employed, he continues, "we must show not simply that slaves are a category of persons treated as property objects, but . . . that they are a subcategory of human property objects." A more concrete and contemporary partial analogy involves athletes, who are sold from one team to another on a regular basis. Even amateur athletes on the collegiate level in the United States, Patterson argues, undergo a similar process when coaches and admissions officers offer parents education for their children in exchange for athletic services, and by extension for their physical bodies, which perform the services. Recent reports suggest this is purely a business arrangement in that many collegiate athletes in the United States are pushed through college courses in order to retain their work on sports fields, regardless of their performance in the classroom. In such cases, student athletes are valued for the activity of their physical bodies without regard to their intellectual growth. In short, they are viewed as property for exchange. Most of us would have a difficult time thinking of professional and amateur athletes as slaves, in part because they retain honor and recognition of value as persons within the public realm. These figures, unlike enslaved Africans, retain their status as subjects of property exchange, whereas enslaved Africans could only exist as objects of property exchange or as a lower and less-than-fully-human being.[38] Put another way, "the slave is not recognized and thus lacks both objective confirmation and subjective certainty of his human worth. The master elevates himself and is elevated to human life; the slave is reduced and reduces himself to animal life."[39]

Rather than simply an arrangement of people as property or beings without legal personality, Patterson argues, slavery is better defined as a form of social death, which entails alienation and strangeness vis-à-vis the dominant society. Enslaved Africans were defined by blackness and by their bondage because, to quote George Fredrickson, "these two aspects of the situation could coexist, reinforcing each other by creating a disposition to defend slavery because it was simultaneously the basis of concrete economic and social privilege for a class of Southerners and the institutional underpinning for a psychologically satisfying sense of racial superiority."[40] The enslaved African had no social existence, no existence as a subject of history, outside that of the master. And the master's social status and place within society were constituted in part by his or her relationship to chattel. Furthermore, even free whites who did not own slaves developed their sense of being in response to chattel. They did not own much property, and they did not belong to the most desirable spheres of society; but at least they were not black and they were not slaves. This was also the thinking during the years of indentured white servitude because, according to Abbot Emerson Smith, "whether property or not, indentured servants were Christian and

they were white. . . . The right of servants to sue in court, the fact that
their evidence was accepted in other suits exactly as that of freemen,
unless they were transported felons, their right to hold property, and
their duty in some colonies to serve in the militia, indicated plainly
the great differences in status between an indentured servant and a
slave."[41] The benefit to whites with little property is important in
maintaining the social system because such a large portion of whites
in North America fit this category. For example, according to H.
Hoetink, "in the fifteen states comprising the South in 1860, only 3
percent of the white population belonged to the genuine planter
class (those with more than twenty slaves), and a very considerable
part of the white population lived in economic circumstances similar to those of the free blacks."[42]

Slavery's power lies in the eradication of Africans as subjects and
the manner in which the enslaved African is re-created in the context of the New World as an object, depersonalized, a nonbeing. As
such, enslaved Africans occupied a strange space in that they existed
outside the recognized boundaries of human community while also
being a necessary part of that same community—as a workforce and
as the reality against which whiteness was defined. These factors,
when combined with physical darkness, resulted in the state of social
death that defines slavery and the slave. Slaves had the physical form
of the human but because of their social death possessed none of the
attributes, rights, and liberties associated with being human.[43] How
this status, or lack of status, was transferred to children born of slaves
is also important here because, although the United States imported
a small percentage of the New World's Africans, it was able to
increase the number of slaves held through "breeding."

Nonhuman status was expressed in a variety of ways, all meant to
reinforce to the African and to larger society the distinction between
persons with honor—white people—and blacks as property. Slaveholders believed that maintaining this boundary between persons
and their black property was necessary to maintain their social world
and avoid chaos, and this feeling only intensified when slaveholders
were confronted with abolitionist demands for an end to the slave

system. The rationale for opposing abolition was usually expressed through two competing and rather contradictory depictions of slaves. On one hand, slaves were considered dangerous, subhuman predators who would destroy white community if they were not kept in their place through force. On the other hand, slaves were often described as childlike creatures who were irresponsible and untrustworthy but harmless if handled properly. In the words of George Fredrickson, "The notion that bestial savagery constituted the basic Negro character and that the loyal 'sambo' figure was a social product of slavery served to channel genuine fears and anxieties by suggesting a program of preventive action. . . . As a slave he was lovable, but as a freedman he would be a monster."[44] But the glamour of recognized humanity implied by this statement is quickly tied to a nature that is more "animal" than human. George S. Sawyer, a slaveholder from the deep South, argued that slavery is the natural state of the black and, when treated properly, the slave is content: "The very many instances of remarkable fidelity and attachment to their masters, a characteristic quite common among them, are founded not so much upon any high intellectual and refined sentiment of gratitude, as upon instinctive impulse, possessed to an even higher degree by some of the canine species."[45] Defining the slave by status as property is only adequate if it is also argued that the slave is not conceived as being a person in the same sense as the master. Likewise, the notion of the enslaved African as simply one without "legal personality" is inadequate in that laws and codes meant to restrict and punish rebellion by slaves speak to a sense of recognition of personhood within the law.[46] For example, the fear of rebellion was widespread after 1832 in part because of the uprisings led by such figures as Denmark Vesey (South Carolina, 1822) and Nat Turner (Virginia, 1831). In addition to these plots, slaves also demonstrated rebellion in a more localized and covert manner through work slowdowns, destruction of equipment, and in some cases the poisoning of masters and mistresses. Such activities, when discovered, were aggressively dealt with, and measures were taken to prevent such problems. These measures included night patrols by whites to keep blacks from wandering around and gathering after dark. Again, such precautions imply a recognition of a fundamental quest for autonomy that marks humanity.

As slave narratives, diary accounts, slave owner's manuals, and state laws suggest, slaves guilty of crimes—including laziness, running away, and disrespect—suffered a variety of punishments. Many states prohibited maiming or killing of slaves done with malice, but who was to prevent such things? Most slave owners who used deadly punishment suffered only loss of property and no legal reprimand. It is also through punishment that we gain a strong sense of how ideas of Africans as a weird likeness to both animal and humans were played out. According to former slave Vinnie Busby:

> "One ob de cruelest things I ever seen done to a slave wuz done by my Master. He wanted to punish one ob de slaves what had done some 'em dat he didn't lak, a kinda stubborn one. He took dat darkie an' hitched him to a plow an' plowed him jes' lak a hors. He beat him an' jerked him 'bout 'till he got all bloody an' sore, but ole Marse he kept right on day after day. Finally de buzzards went to flyin' over 'em. . . . Dem buzzards kept a flyin' an' old Marse kept on a plowin him 'till one day he died."[47]

This and countless other episodes like it brought into graphic relief the imposed identity of the slave as beast—half human, half animal—whose value is limited to its ability to achieve the will and secure the pleasure of the slave owner, even if doing so entails mutilation and death. Slaves were considered somewhat human as a pragmatic move when it benefited and helped to secure the existing social, economic, and philosophical grounding of society. This, of course, is a restricted sense of personhood in that it only recognizes enslaved Africans and holds them accountable as persons with respect to so-called crimes that threaten the social ordering of North American life. Along with this restricted or overdetermined identity

came restrictions on movement, independent thought, and relationships. Life became defined by prohibitions, as opposed to a wide
range of life options and opportunity. Ronald Segal highlights this
point when saying: "Slaves were property with a difference. Unlike
real estate or furniture, they were capable of expressing discontent
with their owners or their treatment. It was fear of just such expression that promoted successive punitive laws."[48] The bottom line is
clear: the dehumanization of Africans was not a smooth process, but
it was inevitable. Although it was a difficult tension to hold—slaves
as both property and persons—the New World enterprise came to
depend on it to stabilize and legitimize the slave trade.[49]

The questions concerning personhood and the tension between
images of blacks as dangerous animals and as reliable and loyal
childlike creatures took a new form after the emancipation of the
slaves in 1863. What had kept blacks in line was constant supervision and discipline by whites. But, once the blacks were free from
such supervision, the southern popular imagination assumed that
they would go wild and destroy life as southern whites knew it. As
one might anticipate, the image of the black as a dangerous beast
became more dominant. After the death of the slave system, the
"Peculiar Institution," it was no longer necessary to justify enslavement through an appeal to the childlike, needy character of blacks.
Rather, with the social world developed by white supremacy in
jeopardy, it became important to present images of blacks as a
threat. This depiction, however, could not stand alone. As blacks
began to strengthen demands for full inclusion in society, it
became necessary to present them also as bumbling fools incapable of full participation in the life of society. Whether considered
a beastly threat or a relatively harmless buffoon, the dominant perspective meant a fixed identity for blacks and a continued primary
concern among whites with the economic gain achievable through
the abuse of black bodies. In this sense, blacks remained objects of
history.

Dehumanization and Postslavery America

Finally, I cannot resist bringing my reflections on the identity of the New World African into a larger context by briefly addressing some of the psychological and social ramifications of slavery in the twentieth century. The title of this chapter refers to this. "Look, a Negro!" is drawn from the work of Frantz Fanon, whose analysis of the struggle for liberation by Africans remains vital reading for those interested in the nature and psychological consequences of oppression. Writing on the African context, in *Black Skin, White Masks*, Fanon used his training in psychiatry to reflect on the effects of racism on the black psyche. When describing his work, Fanon states that it "represents the sum of the experiences and observations of seven years; regardless of the area I have studied, one things has struck me: The Negro enslaved by his inferiority, the white man enslaved by his superiority alike behave in accordance with anuretic orientation."[50] This relationship of assumed inferiority and proclaimed superiority resulted in certain depictions of blacks as having "no culture, no civilization, no 'long historical past.'"[51] Blacks become an oddity, a "something," an object.[52] There is a preoccupation with the black body as a marker of "something," as the storehouse for the fears, anxieties, stories, phobias, and desires of whites. In this way, according to Fanon, blacks remain overdetermined or fixed in historical time and space. It accounts for the manner in which blacks are restricted and deprived of the ability to transcend their circumstances. To the contrary their very being is said to be captured by their context. At one point, this situation is symbolically summed up by the proclamation of a young child: "Look, a Negro!" This remark points to the otherness of the black within the context of a world defined by white superiority. In the words of Fanon, "I am being dissected under white eyes, the only real eyes. I am fixed. Having adjusted their microtomies, they objectively cut away slices of my reality. I am laid bare. I feel, I see in those white faces that it is not a new man who has come in, but a new kind of man, a new genus. Why, it's a Negro!"[53]

In the context of the United States, Howard Thurman, the twentieth-century scholar whose volumes on religion provide sharp insights into the nature and purpose of religious life, points to the manner in which the objectification of blacks rules out basic elements of humanity, such as autonomy or a certain "givenness." Blacks, then, are incapable of creating history because they are merely the raw material from which history is forged. Blacks, in a sense, become zombielike in that they are assumed incapable of creativity or feeling; their worth is strictly defined in terms of service rendered. Thurman, like Fanon, recognizes the manner in which blacks have not defined themselves through reflection but rather have been defined by others for the benefit and security of others. In an autobiographical note, Thurman gives a reminder of this status provided by a young girl. He writes:

> When I was a boy I earned money in the fall of the year by raking leaves in the yard of a white family. I did this in the afternoon, after school. In this family there was a little girl about six or seven years old. She delighted in following me around the yard as I worked. One of her insistences was to scatter the piles of leaves in order to find a particular shape to show me. Each time it meant that I had to do my raking all over again. Despite my urging she refused to stop what she was doing. Finally I told her that I would report her to her father when he came home. This was a real threat to her because she stood in great fear of her father. She stopped, looked at me in anger, took a straight pin out of her pinafore, ran up to me and stuck me with the pin on the back of my hand. I pulled back my hand and exclaimed, "Ouch! Have you lost your mind?" Whereupon she said in utter astonishment, "That did not hurt you—you can't feel."[54]

This young child had already learned a social assumption: humans have feelings with which we must concern ourselves. You, Howard Thurman, are a Negro. You are not human as whites are human. Hence, you have no feelings.

While the language and imagery are forceful in the autobiographical accounts of Fanon and Thurman, none has expressed better the nature of this dehumanization or "thingafication" than novelist and Pulitzer Prize winner Alice Walker. Like Fanon, Walker demonstrates how this dehumanization affects the internal dimensions of the black person's being and fosters an embrace of the standards and perceptions developed by white supremacist depictions of blacks. Both Fanon and Walker point to the manner in which many blacks internalize this "otherness" and espouse a "white-as-superior" attitude. We briefly note one of Walker's novels for an example. In her controversial novel *The Color Purple*, the main character is described by her husband in a way that captures the essence of this objectification. Fed up with Mr., the name given her husband, Celie plans to leave. In response to this, Mr. says: "Look at you. You black, you pore, you ugly, you a woman. Goddam, he say, you nothing at all."[55]

This nagging "otherness," being "nothing at all," this overdetermined identity prescribed to blacks is presented in all its horribleness by writer Richard Wright in his autobiographical text, titled *Black Boy*. In a section early in the book, Wright describes the presence of black prisoners in a way that works the language of their "less-than" status with the air of normality that marks the psyche of America. He says:

> Yet I edged cautiously toward the steps of the house, holding myself ready to run if they should prove to be more violent than they appeared. The strange elephants were a few feet from me now and I saw that their faces were like the faces of men! I stared, my mind trying to adjust memory to reality. What kind of men were these? I saw that there were two lines of creatures that looked like men on either side of the road; that there were a few white faces and a great many black faces. I saw that the whites faces were the faces of white men and they were dressed in ordinary clothing; but the black faces were men wearing what seemed to me to be elephant's clothing. As the strange

animals came abreast of me I saw that the legs of the black animals were held together by irons and that their arms were
linked with heavy chains that clanked softly and musically as
they moved. The black creatures were digging a shallow ditch
on each side of the road, working silently, grunting as they
lifted spades of earth and flung them into the middle of the
roadway.[56]

At first glance, one might assume this passage represents the active
imagination of a young child. Yet, when one is mindful that the sentences and their meaning have been actively crafted by a professional writer seeking to present a certain message in his protest
novels, it becomes clear that the depiction of blacks as animal-like is
intentional and related to the world in which Richard Wright the
adult lives. Seen in this way, Wright's commentary is in keeping with
the other depictions here in which blacks are not quite human but
have merit or reality to the extent that they perform tasks and to the
degree that acknowledgment of their existence benefits the larger
society.[57]

The compelling imagery offered by these and other writers is
given academic voice by such figures as Cornel West, who writes:
"The notion that black people are human beings is a relatively new
discovery in the modern West. The idea of black equality in beauty,
culture, and intellectual capacity remains problematic. . . . The Afro-
American encounter with the modern world has been shaped first
and foremost by the doctrine of white supremacy, which is embodied in institutional practices and enacted in everyday folkways under
varying circumstances and evolving conditions."[58]

PART ONE

CONSTRUCTING TERROR

2

"HOW MUCH FOR A YOUNG BUCK?"

Slave Auction and Identity

Perception of the African as property, we have seen, was owed to physical differences that eventually gave rise to an assumed difference in character and capability. Historical, psychological, legal, and social mechanisms were put in place to safeguard this inferiority of the African and superiority of the European. In short, the ideological and structural arguments for African inferiority resulted in the creation of the "negro." The ramifications of this process were "embodied in institutional practices and enacted in everyday folkways under varying circumstances and evolving conditions."[1]

What practices did enslavers use to reinforce or display this dehumanization? At what point did enslaved Africans most feel this dehumanization? According to much of the available literature on slavery in the Americas, the importance given to the Middle Passage would suggest it is the answer to these questions.[2] No one sensitive to the historical facts of the Middle Passage—beginning with the actual capture of Africans, including the barracoon (or dungeon) experience, and concluding with the ocean voyage—can deny the way it shaped the Americas and such ideas connected to notions of identity and being as citizenship, nationality, the "foreigner," and the "other." This re-creation of identity and being is presented by historian Michael Gomez as a matter of symbolic death and rebirth: "The Middle Passage was a birth canal, launching a prolonged struggle between slave holder and enslaved over rights of definition. . . . But the Middle Passage was also a death canal, baptismal waters of a different kind. At the very least, the African died to what was and to what could have been. The experience would leave an indelible impression upon the African's soul, long remembered by sons and daughters. It is the memory of ultimate rupture. . . . The Middle Passage was one of the New World's most crucial and formative phases."[3]

Gomez's perspective echoes that provided by historian Nathan Irvin Huggins some twenty years earlier. Huggins, while giving more attention to the period of capture and confinement in dungeons, argues that the Middle Passage meant a rupture in time and caused an existential and ontological shift that would forever change enslaved Africans and their descendants. Prior to the Middle Passage, Africans judged their value based upon community and connections to strong forces both visible and invisible; but with this rupture, the African's value was truncated. Transformation from person to property, a thing, took place. In Huggins's words: "Two edges of the slave trade—the rupture of the African from the social tissue that held all meaning for him and his conversion into a marketable object—cut the deepest and touched each to the quick. All other horrors attending to the trade were merely external and superficial cruelties. With luck they might abate in time or be mitigated by circumstances. But these two shocks reverberated to the very foundation of the African's being, changing forever the framework of his life. Thus, those few who suffered these shocks but somehow managed to escape the Atlantic crossing were so altered by the experiences, so set adrift, that they could never find their way back into the world from which they had been torn."[4]

Slavery and the Business of Production

First concerned with an abundance of natural resources such as gold, Europeans made their way to the western coast of Africa as early as the fifteenth century. Although a slave trade was established on the eastern coast of Africa, west Africa was primarily targeted for trade in natural goods. Some countries initially refused to consider trade in Africans; for example, neither England nor its colonies considered such trade a necessary move. Accordingly, it was not uncommon to hear remarks like the following from English traders who dealt with Africa: "We were a people who did not deal in any such commodities, neither did we buy or sell one another, or any that had our own shapes."[5] For some time, despite attacks by pirates and interlopers, Spain and Portugal were able to control the Atlantic and the trade in goods and slaves. However, economic opportunities in both Africa and the New World converged through the potential utility of African labor and increased the aggressive participation of other nations in trading goods (for example, gum, wax, ivory, gold, woods, and hides) and black bodies. The consequence was an extension of slave trading from the east coast of Africa to the west coast where it stretched from Senegal to Angola, and from Mozambique to Madagascar in the east.[6] Adventurer John Hawkins from England, for example, tried his hand at this business after "being, among other particulars, assured that Negroes were very good merchandise . . . and that [a] store of Negroes might easily be had."[7] Cities such as Bristol and Liverpool made tremendous inroads, carrying tens of thousands of slaves to North American colonies, including Maryland and Virginia.

As many scholars note, slavery was a well-known enterprise in Africa, based largely on prisoners of war, debtors, and those who broke a community's legal and moral codes.[8] Europeans easily tapped into this existing system while also extending it—that is, the slave trade to the New World was not fed simply through trade of beads, alcohol, cotton textiles, and other products for bodies secured from African leaders and African traders; Europeans also undertook raids and kidnappings to feed the colonies' appetite for black flesh. Accordingly, as Edward Reynolds notes, "enough people were enslaved by this method to cause apprehension among populations. The fear of being kidnapped often led to Africans travelling in large armed groups."[9] Once captured or sold into slavery, they were eventually walked hundreds of kilometers to the coast, if taken from interior regions. Along this journey, those traveling from the interior were often used as domestics or field hands. Slaves who survived this walk and proved fit enough for sale were stored in barracoons, possibly for months, until forced onto ships in preparation for the voyage.[10] Barracoons were various types of storage areas, with the most makeshift being outdoor pens similar to those used to control pigs and other animals. On the opposite end of the spectrum were those built into castles or forts along the coast, such as Elmina, which was built by the Portuguese in Ghana during the fifteenth century and controlled by the English in the nineteenth century. While such structures were elaborate, their holding areas were small, dark, and poorly ventilated. They were filled to capacity with black bodies, which quickly became covered with filth; injuries were common as captured Africans fought over the food tossed to them. In addition, female slaves were always in danger of rape by traders and officers. Those who succumbed to the conditions were left in the barracoon to decompose into a covering for the brick floor.

Many traders had to move along the coast collecting slaves until their ships were filled. Hence, completely loading a ship could take as long as three months in addition to the several months slaves might spend in the journey to the coast and in confinement awaiting ships. Although England, for example, established regulations that limited the number of slaves carried based on ship size, the potential for profits often resulted in captains altering their records so they could stow more than the legal number of slaves. And while the procedure used to fill ships differed—slaves either taken from one port or collected from a number of locations—the confirmation of a slave's quality was consistent. The surgeon employed for the voyage made "a careful manipulation on the chief muscles, joints, armpits and groins . . . to assure soundness. The mouth, too, was inspected, and if a tooth was missing, it was noted as a defect liable to deduction. Eyes, voice, lungs, fingers, and toes were not forgotten."[11] Surgeons were not the only ones who engaged in these inspections. For example, Captain Richard Willing employed an overseer who "handled the naked blacks from head to foot, squeezing their joints and muscles, twisting their arms and legs, and examining teeth, eyes, and chest, and pinching breasts and groins without mercy. . . . [They] were made to jump, cry out, lie down, and roll, and hold their breath for a long time."[12] Slaves who did not pass inspection were returned to their traders, who beat the slaves for their unsatisfactory performance. In some cases, a slave's inability to bring in revenue was cause for death.

The Middle Passage

In preparation for the journey, captured Africans would have their heads shaved and their flesh branded with the owner's initials or coat of arms.[13] Either shortly before reaching the slave ship or upon arrival, their clothing was removed to make it easier to keep their bodies clean. Once transported by smaller vessels to the ship, males were chained to prevent rebellious activities and escape attempts. They were held below deck and confined to a small space that limited movement. On some ships, women and children were left on deck because it was assumed they posed little threat of violence. But in other cases, they too were held below. In the darkness of the hold, ventilation was limited and sanitation difficult to maintain. But to keep them in somewhat good health, captains would bring the slaves on deck to allow the hold to be cleaned and disinfected as well as to provide space for feeding. On many ships, slaves were fed an array of beans, yams, plantain, and other cheap goods. In addition, exercise was considered important in order to maintain the slaves' health and muscle tone and to bring a good price once in the colonies. As one might imagine, Africans taken from the familiarity of their families and homes were not in the mood for a good workout. Hence, slave traders forced them to dance under the threat of punishment.

Similar punishment was also threatened for those who refused to eat or otherwise maintain their well-being. Finally, great care had to be exercised to prevent slaves from committing suicide by jumping overboard or, more commonly, starving themselves. For example, a slave refusing to eat might have his or her mouth forced open with a mechanism designed for the task or burned for stronger cases of resistance. Such feedings often resulted in broken teeth and choking. In addition to the hardships endured by all, women on these ships were often victims of rape by the crew and captain. Ultimately, efforts to maintain the health of slaves during the voyage were insufficient, given the conditions fostered by confinement. Olaudah Equiano, or Gustavus Vassa as he was also called, was captured into slavery and, in 1789, published his autobiography, which sheds light on these conditions. He writes:

> The closeness of the place, and the heat of the climate, added to the number in the ship, which was so crowded that each had scarcely room to turn himself, almost suffocated us. This produced copious perspirations, so that the air soon became unfit for respiration, from a variety of loathsome smells, and brought on a sickness among the slaves, of which many died, thus falling victims to the improvident, avarice, as I may call it, of their purchasers. This wretched situation was again aggravated by the galling of the chains, now become insupportable; and the filth of the necessary tubs, into which the children often fell, and were almost suffocated. The shrieks of the women, and the groans of the dying, rendered the whole a scene of horror almost inconceivable.[14]

Those whose usefulness was compromised by severe illness, and those who died during the voyage, were thrown overboard. While it is difficult to know how many Africans—for reasons of illness, abuse, malnutrition, rebellion, and melancholy—died during the course of the slave trade, it is fair to say that a loss of roughly 10 percent per voyage was considered significant but not uncommon. Captains who lost this percentage of their cargo would attempt to conceal the number in order to maintain their profit margin. Taken as a whole, the Atlantic slave trade, over the course of four centuries, brought roughly 11 million black bodies to the Americas.

The high point for the arrival of slaves in North America was late spring to the end of the summer. During this season, over the course of the slave trade, 500,000 slaves disembarked. Although prominent locations changed over time, slaves touched North American soil for the first time in ports stretching along the East Coast from New England to the Gulf of Mexico, with Charleston, South Carolina, foremost.

There is no doubt the Middle Passage was full of dread and humiliation, an experience that helped shape the sense of being as property or object synonymous with status as slave. What one captain says concerning the dread of Barbados would certainly ring true for slavery in other portions of the New World, including North America: "The negroes are so willful and loth to leave their own country, that they have often leap'd out of the canoes, boat and ship, into the sea, and kept under water till they were drowned to avoid being taken up and saved by our own boats, which pursued them; they having a more dreadful apprehension of Barbadoes than we have of hell."[15] As dreadful as this experience was, does the Middle Passage provide the full answer to the questions stated earlier: What practices did enslavers use to reinforce or display this dehumanization? At what point did enslaved Africans most feel this dehumanization? Does the Middle Passage mark the only, or at least the best, cipher of the slaves' re-creation? Is it with the Middle Passage that slaves are made, once and for all, aware of their reality as an object of history?

The Other "Middle Passage"

While it provides an important perspective on these questions, the Middle Passage alone does not furnish the complete answer.[16] This is because it was not an experience unique to Africans. While it is true that Africans' relationship to this event is unique in that they alone undertook this voyage as chattel, Europeans also experienced a similar sense of disorientation as part of the voyage. For example, the crew, although free, found the voyage horrific because the food supply was problematic; when trips were prolonged, their rations were reduced. According to historian Edward Reynolds, "it was common for sailors to beg rations from the slaves." And those sailors who became too sick to work were often refused their rations.[17] Beyond problems with food, sailors also spent their nights on deck, exposed to the elements.

In addition, Europeans making the voyage to the Americas were often kidnapped or otherwise tricked into indentured servitude. The journey for these white servants from Europe to North America would have been harsh and would have shared some elements found in the Africans' experience of the Middle Passage. Undoubtedly, allotment of space, health challenges, and loss of family and community ties were troubling for both white indentured servants and black slaves. Both, in this sense, were forced into a type of existential absurdity. Although I believe there is merit to this argument, I am unwilling to push the point beyond a brief example: the threat of mutiny from frustrated whites often resulted in their being restricted to spaces below deck and only being allowed above deck for short periods.[18] This would have certainly resulted in illness through confinement as well as psychological hardship similar to—*but less intense and of a different grade*—than that faced by Africans making the voyage. This point is also addressed by Patricia Romero, who writes: "The horrors to which the Africans were subjected cannot be explained in terms of those experienced by the indentured servants, since the indentured were at least of the same culture as their masters. But the general conditions of travel were much the same for white indentured servants as they were for slaves in transit from Africa. This should not be taken to mean that slaves were well treated, but that European social attitudes toward inferiors were such that harshness and cruelty were practiced with little or no regard for race or culture. The ships transporting indentured servants were similar to those used to carry slaves."[19]

Note Romero's unwillingness to render synonymous the experience of these two groups. The cultural sameness of white indentured servants, crews, and masters is significant in that it prevented the terror of certain thoughts and expectations. For example, white indentured servants made no reports of fearing cannibalism on the part of other whites. Yet, for enslaved Africans entering a foreign cultural context that began with the ships, it was a common dread that captors would eat them or would sell them to be eaten by others. Equiano sheds light on this fear: "I was now persuaded that I had gotten into a world of bad spirits, and that they were going to kill me. . . . I asked . . . if we were not to be eaten by those white men with horrible looks, red faces, and loose hair." He continues, "I therefore wished much to be from amongst them, for I expected they would sacrifice me: but my wishes were vain; for we were so quartered that it was impossible for any of us to make our escape."[20]

The Middle Passage was not a consciously constructed tool by which to forge and enforce a particular existential and ontological reality. While the amenities could have been better, it was the only way of traveling to the Americas. Thus, because white sailors and indentured servants encounter, although on a much smaller scale and as *persons*, some conditions faced by slaves, it is worthwhile to look for other elements of the slave system that frame and reify the identity of the negro. I quoted Michael Gomez earlier to show how the Middle Passage is commonly described by historians. Here I turn again to Gomez because of his inference that the identity re-creation (and by extension the most telling enforcement of that identity) actually is incomplete with respect to the Middle Passage. Regarding slaves, he writes: "Whoever he was prior to boarding the slaver, something inside began to stir, giving him a glimpse of what he was to become. . . . Rites of passage were well understood in Africa, and the Middle Passage certainly qualified as one of the most challenging. As a consequence, those who bonded were taking *the first faltering steps* in the direction of redefinition."[21] Some might suggest that the Middle Passage and "seasoning"—a reference to the period of preparation for the slave's new sociocultural, labor, and geographic environment—represent the logical response to the question of psychological and existential recognition of difference as dehumanization. Through seasoning, the realities of the slave's status as object are given cultural and social arrangement. Yet this status is not perfected, so to speak, in the mind of the slave through this process. I acknowledge the importance of seasoning, yet I believe that what it entails is too dependent on location and the temperament of the owner to qualify (even when combined with the Middle Passage) as the best marker of dehumanization realized. In fact, there is reason to believe that slaves in Virginia, for example, were not seasoned but were placed immediately in the fields. In other areas, new slaves were broken in by older slaves, using less severe forms of punishment—such as restrictions on food—as incentives to learn English and their new station in life. Some slaves, particularly in the deep South, experienced a more physically forceful seasoning process. But ultimately, because there was great variation in seasoning from region to region, it proves an insufficient response to the questions posed earlier.

Slave Auctions: Peddling Flesh

Having argued against the Middle Passage and seasoning, I suggest that slave auctions (and private sales) provide the best answer to the earlier questions. It is the identity forged through these activities that reinforces or gives labor-based consequences to the seasoning period. And, auctions or private sales are the ultimate goal of the Middle Passage: the latter is not an end in itself. Furthermore, while the nature of the seasoning process depends on region and particular owners, the testimony of slavers, former slaves, and observers suggests that auctions were fairly similar regardless of region. Therefore, the Middle Passage and slave auctions taken together best enforce slave status and mark the moment when the slave most completely feels his or her status as nonbeing. The former is an apt description of the power play connoting the encounter between Africans and Europeans, in which both have a degree of agency. But this process is only completed with the auction block, at which point Africans are transformed into chattel, and the dynamics between the European and the African become best described as the politics of domination. At this point, the effort to objectify, to disfigure or transfix the body, is complete.

When ships arrived at port, slaves were prepared for auction. Equiano says this concerning the selling of slaves in Barbados:

> We were conducted immediately to the merchant's yard, where we were all pent up together like so many sheep in a fold, without regard to sex or age. . . . We were not many days in the merchant's custody before we were sold after their usual manner, which is this: On a signal given (as the beat of a drum) the buyers rush at once into the yard where the slaves are confined, and make choice of that parcel they like best. The noise and clamour with which this is attended, and the eagerness visible in the countenance of the buyers, serve not a little to increase the apprehensions of the terrified Africans, who may well be supposed to consider them as the ministers of that destruction to which they think themselves devoted. In this manner, without scrupple, are relations and friends separated, most of them never to see each other again. . . . Why are parents to lose their children, brothers their sisters, or husbands their wives? Surely this is a new refinement in cruelty, which, while it has no advantage to atone for it, thus aggravates distress, and address fresh horrors even to the wretchedness of slavery.[22]

The mechanics of the trade did not vary greatly from the Caribbean to North America. In fact, as we shall see, what Equiano recounts in his autobiography is similar to the portrait of the trade presented by those brought directly to North America, as well as by those who experienced the interstate (or internal) trade.

The growth in the slave population from roughly 500,000
imported Africans to the millions present in the various states by the
mid–nineteenth century points to the illegal slave trade conducted
for some time after the official withdrawal from the practice in 1808.
More significant for this growth in population, however, is the
importance of trading bred slaves. While the international slave
trade was highly profitable and continued to feed the United States
through 1807, the internal trade in American-born slaves developed
possibly as early as the first decades of the 1700s and mounted in
importance with the abolition of the international trade.[23] As the
United States expanded, the interstate or internal trade in slaves
became a key source of labor for the new territories, while trade
within particular states also remained vital. According to one historian, "the calling out for slaves for their new lands was inevitable on
the part of many settlers advancing and spreading out in the South-
west. The increase of slaves in Tennessee from not quite 3,500 in
1790 to more than 13,500 in 1800, and in Kentucky from 12,500 to
more than 40,000 must have involved such trading." Some studies
claim that Virginia alone accounted for the trade of almost 300,000
slaves between 1830 and 1860. In all, well over 500,000 slaves
moved between the states from 1820 to 1860.[24]

This interstate trade was vital for maintaining the sociopolitical
and economic welfare and identity of North America. Periods of discontent and disapproval did little more than temporarily villainize
traders, never bringing the internal trade into serious question. Even
those who felt uncomfortable with it had to recognize its cultural
and economic weight. It accounted for roughly $150 million in rev-
enue in just a couple of years before the emancipation proclamation
(1859–1860). Such a figure suggests that the internal trade generated more money for slaveholders than did the production of crops.[25]
For example, in locations such as Virginia, the trade in slaves rivaled
tobacco as the dominant source of income. In fact, politicians in Virginia, when considering the merits of the slave system and whether
to maintain it, had to recognize that "slave-rearing was a common
means of profit and that traders and other buyers annually took thou-

sands of Virginia slaves to distant States. . . . The exportation [aver-
aged] 8,500 [from roughly 1811 to 1832]." Virginians could not
ignore the fact that it was an "increasing practice in parts of Virginia
to rear slaves for market."[26] Virginia was not alone; major markets
were found all along the coast (New Orleans, Louisiana; Wilming-
ton, North Carolina; Natchez, Mississippi) in order to accommodate
trade and to make it convenient for purchasers who would have to
transport their chattel back to plantations or to another auction. Nor
was there a lack of activity in the North. In fact, northern ports
played a significant role in the movement of slaves south up to 1820,
in part because northern states were in the process of ending their
participation in the slave system. Yet southerners feared bringing
slaves from the north might foster several unsavory developments,
including (1) decreased market value of slaves already in the South
and increased debt taken on by southern planters forced to deal with
higher prices in the slave market; (2) a change in the nature of the
North's relationship with the slave system that might reduce alliances
between the North and the South; (3) the fear that northern-bred
slaves might spread discontent because of their exposure to northern
ideas of "freedom."

Even states that were supposedly closed to the internal slave
trade could not prevent the influx of chattel. Frederick Bancroft
writes: "As these prohibitions did not attempt to prevent the traders
with their gangs from passing through the 'closed' states, there was
many a well-improved opportunity to sell secretly for cash. And as
there was rarely a 'closed' state without having one or more 'open'
states as neighbors, the traders easily did business across forbidden
borders." Furthermore, these short-lived regulations were not
without loopholes; for example, laws did not restrict individuals
from transporting slaves for personal use. Economic concerns combined with an inability to actually enforce a prohibition against the
interstate slave trade resulted in such states as North Carolina (in
1818), Tennessee (in 1855), and Mississippi (in 1846) removing
restrictions except those affecting slaves who had been convicted
of crimes.[27]

In this internal trade—via railroad, on foot, or by ship—slaves were sold by either private arrangement or public notice, in small gatherings or at auctions of close to 1,000 bodies. In either case, the existential and ontological ramifications were the same. The weeks or months it could take to sell an entire shipment of slaves arriving by boat meant prolonged anxiety and uncertainty for the slaves. When combined with the conditions of transport, the implications are clear. As with the Middle Passage, slaves were chained and otherwise confined to prevent suicides and rebellion. For those forced to walk lengthy distances to auction, the following was not an uncommon scene: "The women were tied together with a rope about their necks, like a halter, while the men wore iron collars, fastened to a chain about one hundred feet long, and were also handcuffed. The men in double file went ahead and the women followed in the same order. . . . At the end of the day all, without being relieved of their collars, handcuffs, chains or ropes, lay down on the bare floor, the men on one side of the room and the women on the other."[28] Traders, agents, and merchants dealing in more than a few slaves for sale often kept them housed in public jails, slave pens, or other facilities rented for the purpose. Throughout the central areas of cities like Richmond, Virginia, such facilities were available for a small fee; in more rural areas—where much of the trade took place—other similar arrangements were made. In these enclosures, slaves were often held by chains attached to iron rings in the floor and were whipped to break their spirits.[29]

Private sales were preferred because it required no advertising and no need to identify sellers and purchasers by name. When private sales were not arranged, traders prepared slaves for public auction. For auctions, notice was made in the local newspaper, with information on the date and location as well as the characteristics of the chattel. An 1834 advertisement placed in Maryland read: "Cash for Negroes. The subscribers wish to purchase a number of likely young Negroes of both sexes, from the ages of twelve to 30 years; for such they will give the highest cash prices. Persons wishing to dispose of their slaves will do well to call . . . at Mr. Reese's hotel in Centreville who will attend immediately their calls; or a line addressed to him will meet with prompt attention."[30]

Whereas many argue that small children were not traded and that owners made every effort to keep families together, it is more likely that children of all ages were sold and that, with rare exception, little attention—all slave states considered—was given to keeping families together. Hopelessly romanticized notions of deep concern for slaves aside, the underlying motivation for slave owners was profit. And during the peak of the interstate trade, young children could bring high prices, as much as $2,000 in some markets. Slave testimony points to this practice: "Many children have been taken away, suckling babies sometimes away from their mothers and carried to Mississippi."[31] At times, rather than having a set price based on features or characteristics, young slaves were sold by the pound—yet another sign of the slave's identity as object. In some cases when the price for very young children was in dispute, they were given to purchasers as a bonus.

In preparation for sale, older slaves had their gray hairs removed or dyed. All slaves had their skins oiled to highlight muscles and cover scars and bruises, and they were dressed in better clothing so they would look healthy. Sales typically took place in warehouses with slaves paraded along a stage or raised area to promote better viewing. When properly advertised, auctions could bring hundreds of interested planters and agents from large and small farms. In both private and public sales, the apparent health of the chattel was most important and was usually guaranteed by the seller, although sellers knew that once purchased it would be difficult for buyers from far away to press for retribution. Recognizing the difficulty associated with recouping loss, those bidding on slaves gave great care to inspection. As one slave recounts:

> The slaves are put in stalls like the pens used for cattle—a man
> and his wife with a child on each arm. And there's a curtain,
> sometimes just a sheet over the front of the stall, so the bidders
> can't see the "stock" too soon. The over-seer's standin' just

outside with a big blacksnake whip and a pepperbox pistol in his belt. Across the square a little piece, there's a big platform with steps leadin' to it. Then, they pulls up the curtain, and the bidders is crowdin' around. Them in back can't see, so the overseer drives the slaves out to the platform. . . . They have white gloves there, and one of the bidders takes a pair of gloves and rubs his fingers over a man's teeth, and he says to the overseer, "You call this buck twenty years old? Why there's cup worms in his teeth. He's forty year old, if he's a day."[32]

Potential purchasers took great care to inspect slaves first through a series of questions asked as the slave moved to the front of the platform: What is your age? Are you in good health? Why is your master selling you? Are you a hard worker? Not trusting the answers received, potential purchasers also undertook more thorough inspections. According to Frederick Bancroft, once the slaves were stripped of clothing that got in the way, "hands were opened and shut and looked at inside and out. Arms and legs were felt to decide whether slaves were muscular and regular. Backs and buttocks were scrutinized for the welts that heavy blows with a whip usually left. Necks were rubbed or pinched to detect any soreness or lumps. Jaws were grasped, fingers were run into . . . the teeth and gums could be seen. . . . If there was any suspicion that one eye might not be good, a strange hand was clapped over the other and the slave was asked what object was held before him. The hearing was likewise tested. All such inquires were made with equal freedom whether the slave was man, woman, boy or girl."[33] While inspections were bad enough, forms of abuse suffered by slaves, both female and male, often took odd turns that further emphasized the slaves' debased status. According to one slave who spent a month in a market: "Monkeys would play with us and see if any boogies was in our heads. They would do pretty well if they found any, but if they didn't they would slap us."[34] No indication is given in this account that the monkeys were reprimanded or that any attempt was made to restrict this activity: slaves were at the mercy of all.

For more thorough inspections, female slaves were examined in private quarters to determine the number of offspring already produced and to assess their ability to produce additional children. Those involved in the trade were interested in female slaves who were healthy enough to bear children but were careful to make certain that this ability had not been abused by a prior owner. Sexual exploitation of female slaves was not limited to explicit breeding with blacks; many whites purchased so-called "fancy girls" for their own sexual use. Girls who proved unsatisfactory for this use, because of strong resistance or other reasons, could be returned to the agent, from whom they faced severe punishment. The use of some slaves for sexual purposes points to a dual status for the slave.[35] That is, while being transformed into objects, this overdetermined status was not consistently applied; slaves were often fitted with a limited form of subjectivity. This was noted in chapter 1 with respect to an assumed agency on the part of slaves attested to in regulations and laws dealing with punishment for criminal activity. Here we see this circumscribed subjectivity articulated in terms of the ability to provide socially accepted sexual arrangements and pleasure. In either case—objectivity or circumscribed subjectivity—the slave auction's intended effect is one of negation of true humanity.

Slaves were forced to dance, jump, and perform other acts to demonstrate their good health and general good disposition. As former slave James Martin describes these acts of agility: "The overseer yells, 'Tom or Jason, show the bidders how you walk.' Then, the slaves step across the platform, and the biddin' starts. At these slave auctions, the overseer yells, 'say, you bucks and wenches, get in your hole. Come out here.' Then, he makes 'em hop, he makes 'em trot, he makes 'em jump. 'How much,' he yells, 'for this buck? A thousand? Eleven hundred?' . . . Then, the bidders make offers accordin' to size and build."[36] Some observers assumed jumping and dancing on the block meant slaves were happy to be sold, and in fact some slaves would brag about the price they brought as an implicit recognition of their talents and abilities. Others approached the auction with a measured hope that being sold would bring better conditions and kinder circumstances. However, slaves also recognized that failure to present themselves as healthy and happy would result in whippings and other punishment. According to former slave Charles Crawley: "Some refused to be sold. By dat, I mean, 'cried.' Lord! Lord! I done seen dem young 'uns fought and kick like crazy folks: Child it wuz pitiful to see 'em. Den dey would handcuff an' beat 'em unmerciful. I don' like to talk 'bout back dar. . . . It brun' a sad feelin' up me."[37] Faked contentment was simply another sign of coercion by slave traders and slave holders. Slaves at auction had a choice, said fugitive slave John Brown: "If we did not dance to his fiddle, we used to have to do so to his whip, so no wonder we used our legs handsomely."[38]

The continuous fear of punishment and the hope for a situation better than the previous one might account for the gaiety of those who undertook the journey to new plantations, a journey described by one observer as follows: "A band or at least a drum and fife would be called into requisition, and perhaps a little rum be judiciously distributed to heighten the spirits of his sable property, and the neighbors would gather in to see the departure. First of all one or two closely covered wagons would file out of the 'barracoon,' containing the rebellious and unwilling, in handcuffs and chains. After them the rest dressed in comfortable attire, perhaps dancing and laughing, as if they were going on a holiday excursion. At the edge of the town . . . the pageant faded away, and the curious crowd who had come to witness the scene returned to their homes."[39]

The dehumanizing implications of this treatment were not lost on slaves, one of whom describes the experience in these terms: "I was raised right here in Tennessee till I was eleven year old; then Major Ellison bought me and carried me to Mississippi. I didn't want to go. They 'zamine you just like they do a horse: they look at your teeth, and pull your eyelids back and look at your eyes, and feel you just like you was a horse." The auction block left no doubt that slaves did not own their own bodies.[40] Because of the slave's imposed identity as object, traders and purchasers did not consider it inappropriate to sell horses, pigs, and other creatures during the same auctions. The philosophical perspective was straightforward: slaves and

horses were of the same constitution—creatures inferior to white
humanity. Thus, the callousness with which one might expect the
sale of a horse to be described was also applied to the sale of slaves. A
letter written in 1853 to a Z. B. Oakes from A. J. McElveen provides
an example: "I am offered today a woman 25 or 28 years old . . . tol-
erable likely. . . . Good field hand. . . . She is well formed and Stout
built. . . . Sound and harty. . . . her teeth a little defective. . . . I can
bye her for $750 . . . I think the market might afford the price."[41]

Some slaves constructed ways of dissuading potential purchasers.
For instance, in spite of the danger, it was not uncommon for slaves
to promise trouble on the plantation and to threaten the aborting or
infanticide of children if purchased. Others would simply complain
of having various illnesses to lessen buyers' interest. Still others tried
to make arrangements for sale to particular persons. This was the case
for Marie Perkins, who writes the following to her husband: "Dear
Husband . . . I write you a letter to let you know of my distress. . . . My
master has sold Albert to a trader on Monday court day and myself
and other children is for sale also and I want you to let [me] hear from
you very soon before next court if you can. . . . I don't know when . . .
I don't want you to wait till Christmas. . . . I want you to tell Dr.
Hamilton your master if either will buy me they can attend to it now
and then I can go afterwards. . . . I don't want a trader to get me."[42]

While Marie Perkins and others in similar circumstances sought
particular whites as new masters, others appealed to family members
to raise the funds necessary to buy their freedom. Stephen Penbroke
provides an example of this. In 1854, he wrote the following to his
brother, James W. C. Pennington: "[Mr. Grove] told me I might
return [to Washington County, Maryland] if you would give him his
price. Do, my dear brother, make arrangements, and that at once, for
my relief. Oh, do make them; I will work daily when I get there to
pay you back. If you only knew my situation and my feelings you
would not wait one moment. Act promptly, as I will have to be sold
to the South. My two sons were sold to the drivers. I am confined
to my room with irons on."[43] Slaveholders held no illusions concerning slaves' aversion to being traded, and in order to safeguard their

property, owners frequently did not mention the pending sale until shortly before it was to take place. Even then, slaves were closely guarded until time for the sale.

Slave Trading and Social Arrangements

Slave trading was a dirty but profitable business. At various times and in various locations, agents working for trading companies were frowned upon.[44] According to one account published in 1860, traders were "preeminent in villainy and a greedy love of filthy lucre stands the hard-hearted negro traders. . . . Some of them, we do not doubt, are conscientious men, but the number is few. Although honest and honorable when they first go into the business, the natural result of their calling seems to corrupt them; for they usually have to deal with the most refractory and brutal of the slave population. . . . [He] is outwardly a coarse, ill-bred person, provincial in speech and manners." This perspective is present much earlier than 1860, as evidenced by a document written in 1818: "Several wretches, whose hearts must be as black as the skins of the unfortunate beings who constitute their inhuman traffic, have for several days been impudently prowling about the streets . . . with labels on their hats exhibiting in conspicuous characters the words 'Cash for negroes.'"[45]

There is no doubt that some critics of traders were also critics of the slave system. Careful attention to the statements of contempt presented above brings into question the social standing of these agents, but also telling is the description of slaves as "inhuman traffic" at worse and as childlike beings at best. It is understood that the job and the merchandise handled resulted in slack morals and ethics, and thereby the degraded social status of traders had more to do with class arrangements and distinctions than with *intrinsic* qualities. Clearly, this critique of the agent was not of necessity an abolitionist appeal to the humanity of slaves; it questioned tactics of the trade, not the objectification of Africans. Many recognized it as a nasty but necessary business. The criticism seems, in short, more

rhetorical than anything, particularly considering that several prominent slave merchants and captains went on to impressive positions of
public importance. For example, Philip Livingston, of New York,
traded slaves prior to signing the Declaration of Independence and
establishing a professorship of theology at Yale University. And "Captain Jim" de Wolf, of Bristol, Rhode Island, became a U.S. senator
after years of trading slaves.[46]

Slave Auctions and Historical Displacement: Objects Defined

Through the auction—whether public or private—the enslaved
experienced a rupture that affected perceptions of the world and the
African's place in it: the enslaved African no longer makes history
but is the raw material others use to shape history. This is more than
an historical dislocation or displacement; it is the very definition of
the enslaved African as object, while on the other hand, it affirms the
superior status of whites. As one historian notes, the "shared com-
munion in the rites of the slave market—the looking, stripping,
touching, bantering, and evaluating—white men confirmed their
commonality with the other men with whom they inspected the
slaves."[47] All dimensions of the auction considered, this event
marked Africans as both existentially and ontologically inferior. The
forced recognition of status promoted a sense of dread or terror.

It does not take much imagination to recognize the traumatic
experience the auction block entailed—separation from family,
intrusive inspections, and travel to new regions of the country and
unfamiliar environments. Reuben Madison's situation points to this:
"Bout four years after their marriage, she and one of the children,
aged eight months, were sold without his knowledge, and transported to a distant Spanish territory, and with so much secrecy, that
he had no opportunity even to bid her a last farewell. 'This,' said
he, 'was the severest trial of my life. . . . I mourned and cried, and
would not be comforted."[48] Madison Jefferson makes a similar claim:

"We have a dread constantly on our minds . . . for we don't know how long master may keep us, nor into whose hands we may fall."[49] In another account, Rosa Barnwell describes the threat of auction this way: "The trader was all around, the slave-pens at hand, and we did not know what time any of us might be in it. Then there were the rice-swamps, and the sugar and cotton plantations; we had them held before us as terrors, by our masters and mistresses, all our lives. We knew about them all; and when a friend was carried off, why, it was the same as death."[50] One last example is drawn from an interview with Tabb Cross and Lewis Smith in 1861, in which the following words are found: "The continual dread of this separation of husband and wife, parents and children, by sale, which may arise from the improvidence, misfortune, death, or other accident in life, happening to the owner, is inseparable from a state of slavery. It may happen at any moment, and is one of the greatest miseries hanging over the head of the slave. His life is spent in the fear of it. The slave may forget his hunger, bad food, hard work, lashes, but he finds no relief from the ever-threatening evil of separation."[51]

Slave Auctions as Ritual of Reference

This terror results from how the auction block strips away early self-perceptions and meaning, imposing in their place "otherness" and historical irrelevance. Dread or terror in this sense is profound in that it forces the slave to confront his or her helplessness, isolation from the familiar, and submersion in absurdity. But this dread is not restricted to the individual; rather, the slave auction had implications on the communal level in that it had something to do with a despised otherness attached to both black individuals and the larger black community. There is a tension between individual and community with respect to this dread. It is a loss of humanity held in common by all blacks and addressed on the level of both the individual who stands on the auction block and the community that experiences the individual's loss as its own.

Having provided a brief description of the Middle Passage and the slave auction, I now would like to make more explicit the importance of the auction block for our study of black religion's nature and meaning. My argument is simple and straightforward. The status imposed on enslaved Africans—as objects of history—requires actions such as auctions to reinforce this status. Therefore, slave auctions were a ritual by which the slave system enforced and celebrated the dehumanization of Africans. I refer to this ritual as a ritual of reference: it is repeated, systematic activity conducted in carefully selected locations that is intended to reinforce the enslaved's status as object. The intensity of such rituals stems from the symbolic involvement of the enslaved in the process. Slavery as a major shift in being requires ritual expression that gives select behaviors their legitimacy and strength, or their power. It is through this ritualizing that the slave's status is given social force and meaning because it makes explicit the re-creation of the slave as a "thing." Auctions, as a ritual of reference, are important in that they made explicit through humiliation—and elaborate through display—the nonbeing of the African and the existential superiority of the European. The auction becomes something of a ceremony through which the making of the negro as historical material is accomplished. It is through the display of the black body on the auction block that the African in the New World became a new substance. Auctioneers and traders touched and manipulated black flesh in ways repeated with meticulous precision day after day; through this touch and accompanying liturgy—the language of the trade—black bodies lose their humanity and are disfigured or transformed into tools or toys, humanlike "things" without will or desires needing consideration.

Through this ritualized manipulation of African bodies, new social arrangements complete with existential and ontological ground rules are put in place. It is at this point, through this ritual of reference, that the African is finally made fully aware of his or her new relationship to the world.[52] This ritual meant objectification for slaves; it symbolized domination and subjectivity for whites who participated in it both directly and indirectly. Blacks became interchangeable commodities for exchange and distortion with little penalty and without the ethical issues that are present in human-to-human relations. What is more, they were expected during this ritual to act as if they enjoyed the process. Dancing, singing, and moving around the auction block annihilated the slave's autonomy and dignity while downplaying the violent nature of the ritual. In an odd twist, violence was often used to make invisible the horror of the ritual. As James Curry writes in his reflections on slavery: "I wish some of your people could see a drove of men, women and children driven away to the south. Husbands and wives, parents and children torn from each other. Oh? The weeping, the most dreadful weeping and howling! And I has no effect at all upon the hearts of the oppressors. They will only curse them, and whip them to make them still."[53] The invisibility of misery and distress is furthered through the presentation of the slaves in new clothing, with their hair combed and skin oiled. Fixing up slaves for auction was a necessary component of the ritual of reference, which is concerned with destroying the humanity of the slave while giving the impression slaves were content with the new arrangement. Slavery, and the slave auction in particular, removes the liberty to address and reject discomfort. The auction and its ontological destruction entail an acquired attempt to make the enslaved appreciate and enjoy their plight.

This ritual was a festive time for whites, a celebration of their subjectivity and dominance that could not be dampened by uncooperative chattel. Prospective buyers were often accompanied by their spouses, who dressed in their finest clothing and used the auction as an opportunity to socialize, while traders distributed alcohol and engaged those gathered in conversation.[54] Social understandings, once the ritual of reference was complete, were defined in terms of white happiness and contentment; all conversation related to the "being" of the slave was measured against the necessary increase of white happiness. As Saidiya Hartman remarks: "The simulation of consent in the context of extreme domination was an orchestration intent upon making the captive body speak the master's truth as well as disproving the suffering of the enslaved. Thus a key aspect of the manifold uses of the body was its facility as a weapon used against the enslaved."[55] In a sense, this ritual of reference marks the slave as possessed in a dual sense: whites *own* black bodies and, because negroes are tools for the achievement of white desire, whites *inhabit* black bodies. "The dissolute uses of slave property," according to Hartman, "came to define the identity of the captive and hence the nature of the negro. . . . Indeed, there was no relation to blackness outside the terms of this use of, entitlement to, and occupation of the captive body."[56]

With the auction complete, the being of blacks is truncated. It is no longer connected to community, liberty, and the power to shape history. Rather, it is confined to the cash value of flesh. Importance is no longer attached to realities that extend beyond the body, because Africans and their New World descendants have no meaning, no relevance beyond their physical form. This is what Frantz Fanon captures in the exclamation "Look, a Negro!" True, blacks had bodies before this exclamation and the history that gives the body its impact. The auction block does not create black bodies in this sense. Yet, the power of the ritual of reference is the ability to re-create the African as nothing but a body—a raw material—a zombie made by powerful acts.

The auction block as a ritual of reference promotes a form of terror and dread that best captures the reinforcing of status as historical object before the twentieth century. As will be discussed in chapter 4 and 5, this terror or dread is connected to the nature and meaning of black religion. But before discussing this connection, reinforcement of objectification after the emancipation of slaves must be addressed. That is, the auction block is the best example of a ritual of reference during the period of slavery; yet the effort to dehumanize the slaves' descendants continues, and a new process is necessary for accomplishing this goal.

3

ROPE NECKTIES

Lynching and Identity

While the Middle Passage was a horrific event, taken alone it does not fully mark the enforcement of status as "thing," a status aptly described by novelist Richard Wright in considering the colonist's relationship to the slave: "Like a miner using a pick or a carpenter using a saw, they bent the will of others to their own. Lives to them were tools and weapons to be wielded against a hostile land and climate."[1] The previous chapter described slave auctions as a ritual of reference by means of which the identity of slaves as objects of history was given its most extreme affirmation. Identity was truncated as blacks became mere instruments of another's whims, pleasure, and labor, and the slave auction, time on the block, instilled a sense of terror and dread. After the Civil War and the demise of the slave system, the maintenance of this truncated identity required whites to institute other rituals of reference. In this chapter, I explore lynching in the nineteenth and twentieth centuries as a widespread form of mob activity geared toward enforcing black identity as object.

The Price of Freedom

On January 1, 1863, the institution of slavery ended when President Abraham Lincoln proclaimed that "all persons held as slaves within any State, or designated part of the State, the people whereof shall be in rebellion against the United States, shall be then, thence forward, and forever free."[2] Two years later, in 1865, the Civil War ended with the pro-slavery Confederate forces defeated.[3] Ex-slaves chronicled the defeat of southern forces in songs containing lyrics that speak to their hoped-for change in status:

> Tain't no mo' sellin' today,
> Tain't no mo' hirin' today,
> Tain't no pullin' off shirts today,
> Its stomp down freedom today.
> Stomp it down![4]

Others sang words extolling the dominance of the northern troops over the southern forces and the destruction of the "good ol' South":

> One foot one way, one foot the other way,
> One foot all aroun'.
> So big that he couldn't cut a figure
> An' he couldn' go a half way roun'.
> Ole master, run away, and set them darky free
> For you mus' be think
> They kingdom a-comin'
> The hour of Jubilee.[5]

As these songs creatively suggest, North America was forced to rethink the relationship between blacks and whites. The sociopolitical, economic, religious, and overall cultural self-understanding of whites had been based for centuries on the dehumanization of blacks. But blacks were now free and were no longer legally obligated to serve as tools for the pleasure and labor of whites. Their social death was over, and whites and blacks were forced in a relatively short period of time to make sense of these existential changes. The world, and its logic, had been turned on its head. History, as constructed for well over two centuries, was no more; the relationship between what had been the subjects and objects of history was radically altered by the president's proclamation and the defeat of the Confederate forces. Whites maintained an interest in keeping their position of dominance—the subjects or shapers of history. But this could no longer be done through the proscription of blacks as nonbeings. Or, could it?

The period of Reconstruction, 1865–1877, was meant to facilitate the incorporation of blacks into the life of the nation through military presence, the Freedmen's Bureau, and the force of law. Schools developed; blacks were given the vote and entered politics; free labor was a thing of the past; and social restrictions were softened. These political changes gave the illusion of a country ready for a radical transformation of its practices and policies. But to the contrary, the nation's preparation for the recently freed left much to be desired. In many cases, lacking resources and know-how, blacks were forced off property. Some did take advantage of educational opportunities, and community leaders, particularly ministers, attempted to extend their influence through political office; however, most ex-slaves found themselves without shelter or suitable job prospects. Added to this was the hostility of whites who were opposed to changing their socioeconomic relationship with blacks and who attempted to impose their will through new legislation referred to as Black Codes. Explicitly discriminatory, these codes focused on three areas: (1) restrictions on the mobility of blacks; (2) limitations on the ability of blacks to secure land and other economic resources; and (3) maintenance of social decorum through fining blacks for improper gestures and conversation in the presence of whites. According to these codes, in South Carolina, for example, former slaves were not allowed to hold any job besides farmer or house servant unless they were willing to pay a substantial tax. The goal of such legislation was clearly the disenfranchisement of blacks.[6] By 1877, Reconstruction had come to an end, and a massive action to restore the basic social order—"the old South"—had begun.

Disenfranchisement and Movement

Troubles for black farmers attempting to forge a living mounted early as the boll weevil, an insect that devoured crops, as well as flooding along some southern stretches of the Mississippi River made land difficult to work. Even when natural disasters did not threaten crops and black farmers were able to prosper, danger only increased. White farmers resented their success and took action to retard their work. More subtle forms of this action included forcing blacks to sell their land or abandon it to avoid violence. In more severe instances, black farmers, and often their families, were killed. Those holding jobs in mills, for example, also faced similar hostility; many black workers were beaten or killed for daring to collect and keep their paychecks. There seemed no way for enterprising blacks to succeed, a situation that motivated many to forsake their hopes for a new life in the rural South. Some former slaves suggested that blacks would never receive justice in the United States and should therefore emigrate to Africa, their true home. According to Henry McNeal Turner, a bishop in the African Methodist Episcopal Church and one of the major advocates of emigration: "There is no more doubt in my mind that we have ultimately to return to Africa than there is of the existence of a God; and the sooner we begin to recognize that fact and prepare for it, the better it will be for us as a people. We there have a country unsurpassed in productive and mineral resources, and we have some two hundred millions of our kindred there in moral and spiritual blindness. The four millions of us in this country are at school, learning the doctrines of Christianity and the elements of civil government. And as soon as we are educated sufficiently to assume control of our vast ancestral domain, we will hear the voice of a mysterious Providence, saying 'Return to the land of your fathers.'"[7]

The appeal of the Back-to-Africa Movement was limited, and it would further weaken with the death of its most noted advocate, Henry Turner, in 1915. More appealing—despite some opposition from black community leaders, including ministers who feared the loss of church members and resources—was the possibility of

moving out of the rural South into northern and southern cities as
well as western territories. Intense discrimination initiated this large-
scale migration of blacks, which began in the late nineteenth century and lasted through almost the mid–twentieth century. The
motivation for this massive shift in population distribution—referred
to as the Great Migration—was expressed in song:

> Times is gittin' might ha'd,
> Money gittin' might scace;
> Soon's I sell my cot'n 'n co'n,
> I'se gwine tuh leave dis place.[8]

Another tune proclaimed:

> The time is coming and it won't be long,
> You'll get up some morning, and you'll find me gone.[9]

Stories of job opportunities and social freedom abounded, including stories of advantages gained through migration, of high salaries
available in factories and in employment as domestics. But these stories described rare situations, situations of the lucky few who beat the
odds. According to historian Milton Sernett: "Though southern
cities, magnet like, drew blacks off the land, they were not oases of
opportunity. Rural migrants clung to the bottom rungs of the economic and social ladder."[10] The situation in the North was described
by Reverend Reverdy C. Ransom, one of the African Methodist Episcopal Church's most radical church leaders, in the following terms:
"My first vision of the need of social services came to me as my wife
and I almost daily, went through the alleys and climbed the dark
stairways of the wretched tenements, or walked out, on the planks to
the shanty boats where our people lived on the river."[11] Blacks moving into these new areas faced job discrimination as labor unions
fought to keep them out, and employers provided only the most
menial positions. In addition, their rents were high, and housing
opportunities were restricted to the most depressed areas of inner
cities, where green spaces were limited, recreational opportunities

minimal, and health concerns widespread. Black migrants quickly realized they could not outrun discrimination and hostility. Novelist Richard Wright, in the book *Native Son*, provides a haunting depiction of this situation. Living during the last phase of the Great Migration, Wright's main character Bigger Thomas describes a life many migrants could claim: "A guy gets tired of being told what he can do and can't do. You get a little job here and a little job there. You shine shoes, sweep streets; anything. . . . You don't make enough to live on. You don't know when you going to get fired. Pretty soon you get so you can't hope for nothing. You just keep moving all the time, doing what other folks say. You ain't a man no more. You just work day in and day out so the world can roll on and other people can live."[12]

Despite such difficulties, blacks continued to migrate because even the dilemmas of life in these new areas of the country proved less troubling than the hardships facing blacks in rural areas of the South. While far from perfect, migration presented the ability to select a lesser of evils and differing degrees of inconvenience. Southerners who recognized the socioeconomic consequences of the Great Migration tried to dissuade blacks from leaving by pointing to the cold winters, dangers of city living, and what they argued was the cold attitude of northerners toward blacks. The historical moment was different, but the argument was the same as that during slavery: southerners know the black better than anyone else and are best equipped to deal with their particular needs.

Although socioeconomic and political conditions were relatively poor for most blacks, whites assumed blacks were taking over American society. Conversation revolved around the horror of bestial blacks destroying the fabric of American life. As Joel Williamson notes in his book *The Crucible of Race:* "The southern race problem of the nineteenth century became the national race problem of the twentieth, in part precisely because of the abandonment by the North of the Negro in the South."[13] Blacks, as historian John Hope Franklin reflects, "were viewed as aliens whose ignorance, poverty, and racial inferiority were incompatible with logical and orderly processes of government."[14] Arthur F. Raper records a popular sentiment when saying: "Hence asserts the popular white mind: 'Negroes are unclean by nature; they stink.' They are unclean morally, also, according to the usual insistence; this, too cannot be helped, for they have within themselves no basis for morality."[15] Blacks were understood as creatures of substance, but a substance that was dangerous, menacing, and in need of strong control.

Segregation and discrimination sanctioned by law was used to return blacks to their former status. For example, voting districts were divided in ways to weaken the black vote; fees were required in order to vote; complicated ballots were designed to confuse black voters; and blacks were disqualified from voting because of alleged and usually ridiculous crimes. Whites in power also tried to tie blacks to the land as sharecroppers, who were cheated out of wages and forced to accumulate debt that could never be paid off. According to ex-slave Laura Smalley, blacks were encouraged to take on debt; and whites "[would] let you go jus' as far in debt as you wan' to go you know. An' then see, uh, uh, they, they know your crop wasn' gonna, gonna clear it you know, an' then, then so next year you'd have to stay an' work out your debt. If you didn', you know, they'd take all your horses, cows an' everything away from you."[16] When philosophical-social rationales gave unsatisfactory results in the courts and when economic arrangements failed to properly restrain black ambition, extralegal means of maintaining blacks' status as objects were utilized. These extralegal means, usually unchallenged by courts and law enforcement officials, were quite brutal.[17] While this violence took a variety of forms, we will concentrate on its most graphic presentation: lynchings.

The Good Ol' Days:
Social Order and Popular Punishment

The etymology of the term *lynching* is a bit complicated. Sources indicate that the practice of "regulating" can be traced to North Carolina as early as 1765, when colonists used extralegal means to deal with dishonest authorities. Those who participated in this "raw" justice were simply referred to as the "Mob" until roughly 1768, when the name "regulators" was adopted and the following oath instituted: "We the subscribers do voluntarily agree to form ourselves into an association, to assemble ourselves for conference for regulating public grievances and abuses of power."[18] According to some accounts, the practice of lynching used by regulators gains its name from a meeting held at Lynch's Creek in South Carolina for the purpose of addressing issues of theft poorly dealt with by legal means available to those not living in Charleston. The *South Carolina Gazette* notes the existence of this group of regulators in a letter printed on September 2, 1768: "I wish you would inform me what is generally thought in town of the regulators, who now reign uncontrolled in all the remote parts of the Province. In June, they held a Congress . . . where a vast number of people assembled; several of the principal settlers . . . men of property, among them. . . . When these returned, they requested the most respectable people in these parts to meet on a certain day; they did so, and, upon the report made to them, they unanimously adopted the Plan of Regulation." Their goal entailed more than the regulation of "public grievances" associated with the North Carolina group; they sought to "purge, by methods of their own, the country of all idle persons, all that have not a visible way of getting an honest living, all that are suspected or known to be guilty of malpractices" and to establish lines of authority independent of those in Charleston.[19] Whether in established areas or new western territories, bands of regulators or rangers developed by request from the community or through self-appointment with a clear agenda: "[To] ferret out and punish criminals, to drive out 'suspicious characters,' and to exercise a general supervision over the interests of the settlements in which they lived."[20]

A connection between regulation and "lynch law" is difficult to establish. One possibility, however, concerns a Charles Lynch, a farmer and politician in the late 1770s. In Virginia, where Lynch lived, horse theft was extremely attractive during the Revolutionary War because of the money the armies were willing to pay and because legal recourse was less than adequate. As the story goes, in response to such crimes, Charles Lynch and his neighbors agreed to form an organization of citizens with the punishment of criminals as its task. Those accused of crimes were brought to Lynch's home and tried by members of the group, who then pronounced the person not guilty or administered suitable punishment, which usually entailed "thirty-nine lashes on the bare back." Political criminals—those who did not support the colonists' efforts for independence—were given these lashes and also "hanged up by the thumbs" until they yelled "liberty forever!"[21] Although community justice was frowned upon by authorities, it was imitated in other areas and, by 1818, the practice of community punishment was referred to as "Lynch's Law." First used as a means of quick justice—particularly in areas where more formal authorities were missing, inadequate, or corrupt— lynchings did not involve hanging or burning. Rather, they entailed whipping, as used in the case of Charles Lynch. In other cases, criminals were tarred and feathered or forced to separate from the community as a means of "reform." It was a painful but not deadly way of correcting behavior. Because available resources beyond traveler accounts are limited, it is difficult to give precise figures on the number of lynchings that took place during these early years. Yet, based on existing records, only rarely were blacks victims during the 1700s. They were not a prime target before the emancipation proclamation and the Civil War because most could be controlled through the slave system's forms of punishment or, if free, by the threat of being placed in slavery. On occasions when blacks were lynched, charges used to justify the punishment revolved around insurrection; in such cases, hanging was not uncommon.[22] Perhaps the first record of extralegal punishment of a black dates to 1740 with the execution of slaves involved in a South Carolina insurrection.

Blacks and the Practice of Lynching

During the Civil War, southern efforts to maintain control over the population took the shape of brutal attacks on slaves suspected of favoring—or at worst, aiding—the northerners' campaign.[23] Later, suppression of southern socioeconomic and political culture would end, and the delicate fabric of white superiority damaged during

Reconstruction would be restored.[24] After the Civil War, black bodies
had more questionable economic value; thus, it became more acceptable to protect social order through violence in the form of lynching.
In this regard, the social death of slavery was superseded by the threat
of lynching as the essence of status as object. It was also after Reconstruction—when blacks became prime targets—that lynching began
to harbinger death and also became "an integral part of southern culture," as primary to the popular southern imagination as the idea of
black inferiority.[25] As David Lyons describes this tension: "Whites
seemed to swing from seeing blacks as childlike, innocuous, loyal
pleasure-seeking plantation darkies, to another perspective from
which they were viewed as sexually aggressive, vicious and prone to
rape and violent revolt."[26] Some suggest alleged assault on white
women, murder, economic success, codes of honor, and cultural sensibilities as reasons for the lynching of blacks.[27] Recorded accounts
lend credence to such conclusions, particularly with regard to issues of
economic progress and culturally contrived codes of interaction. For
example, twenty-year-old Richard Coleman was lynched in Kentucky
for assaulting and killing a white woman. According to a *New York
World* account on December 6, 1899, he was

> burned at the stake at noon . . . in the presence of thousands of
> men and hundreds of women and children. Tortures almost
> unbelievable were inflicted upon the wretched negro. In all
> the vast crowd that witnessed the agonies of the man, not one
> hand was raised in humanity's behalf, nor a single voice heard
> in the interest of mercy. Instead, when some new torture was
> inflicted upon the shrieking, burning boy, the crowd cheered
> and cheered, the shrill voices of women and the piping tones of
> children sounding high above the roar of men. . . . The place of
> execution had been selected weeks ago, in accordance with all
> the other arranged details of the programme mapped out by
> the leaders of the mob. The prisoner was dragged to the sapling
> and strapped against the tree, facing the husband of the vic-
> tim. Large quantities of dry brush and larger bits of wood were
> piled around him, and oil was poured on the mass while he was

praying loudly for speedy death. . . . Some one with a knife slashed at the prisoner's chest. By a sort of cruel concurrence of action on the part of the mob not a single shot was fired. The purpose seemed to be to give the wretched the greatest possible amount and duration of torture.[28]

In another account, it is quite evident that motivation for the lynching revolved around the victim's financial success. When, on March 9, 1892, three black men who owned and managed the People's Grocery in Memphis were lynched, the lynchers were recorded as saying "the Negroes are getting too independent, we must teach them a lesson."[29] Furthermore, blacks offending the cultural sensibilities of whites, which could involve something as trivial as not yielding the sidewalk or bumping into a white person, might meet with severe punishment. Accordingly, on March 31, 1916, Jeff Brown was lynched because he "was walking down the street near the car tracks and saw a moving freight going in the direction in which he wanted to go. He started on the run to board the moving train. On the sidewalk was the daughter of a white farmer. Brown accidentally brushed against her and she screamed. A gang quickly formed and ran after him, jerking him off the moving train. He was beaten into insensibility and then hung to a tree."[30] Lynchers did not always feel the need to charge victims with crimes. On numerous occasions, there was no apparent reason for the lynching, no "crime" committed, no social norm discarded. The mere fact that the victims were black was enough, and gender distinctions were not considered. Hence, Cordella Stevenson, whose son was thought to have destroyed a white farmer's barn, was found "hanging from a tree, without any clothing, dead. She had been hung . . . after a mob had visited her cabin, taken her from her husband and lynched her after they had maltreated her."[31]

After the Civil War, lynching not only became associated with death but in the popular imagination also was linked to the Ku Klux Klan, the white-clad "knights" who supplanted the regulators and rangers.[32] Although first developed in 1866 by a group of young men in Tennessee for the purpose of entertainment opportunities, the

Klan later mutated into lynchers of blacks, inspired by the changing relationship of the South to blacks and by the threat black ambition posed to the status quo.[33] The Klan represents a formal, organized response to black life, one that gripped popular imagination and became an icon of terror. However, as the lynchings mentioned so far suggest, it did not constitute the only means of mob violence. Spontaneously formed groups of citizens who felt an outrage had taken place—or who just needed to exercise dominance through violence—frequently selected for death blacks whose carriage, words, or deeds demonstrated assumptions of equality and humanity. A sense of urgency was present; many whites believed blacks threatened the entire order of life, rending in two the delicate fabric of human meaning and purpose. Civilization was threatened by exslaves and their descendants; order, which hung by a thread, could be rescued by a strong rope. Again, the popular southern imagination—but by no means limited to the South—believed blacks were beasts who would destroy society if left unchecked. This situation is aptly described by Stewart Tolnay and E. M. Beck: "Years of racist propaganda had, in the minds of many whites, lessened blacks to simplistic and often anomalistic, stereotypes. These debasing images further depersonalized and dehumanized the victim, reducing him or her to a hated object devoid of worth."[34] The pseudosciences inspired by social Darwinism provided so-called objective evidence of this popular perspective, tying race bias to the natural order of things, to the inevitability of human progress. Put another way, "to establish . . . an African barbarism on the ruins of Southern society was a conspiracy against human progress. It was the blackest crime in the nineteenth century" because "the beginning of Negro equality as a vital fact is the beginning of the end of this nation's life."[35]

On a more general note, health officials like Dr. William Lee Howard made a connection between the supposed rape of white women and the animal nature of blacks. In an article published in the journal *Medicine* in 1903, Lee said that "the attacks on defenseless white women are evidence of racial instincts that are about as amenable to ethical culture as is the inherent odor of the race."[36] In addition to being buttressed by negrophobic academics and

physicians, the dehumanizing of blacks was also supported by popular culture—literature, minstrel shows, songs, and the film industry,
which developed early in the twentieth century. In the realm of
literature, no one did more in the early twentieth century to spread
this diabolical image of blacks than Thomas Dixon, an ordained
Baptist minister and author of *The Leopard's Spots: A Romance of the
White Man's Burden—1865–1900* and *The Clansman: An Historical
Romance of the Ku Klux Klan.*[37] An apology for negrophobia, the former was written to chronicle the history and social conditions from
the end of the Civil War to the violent disenfranchisement of blacks.
General Lee's surrender meant Confederate forces and their supporters had to prepare themselves to face northern political ideology,
but they were not prepared for what Dixon describes as "Negro
dominion, or Negro deification, or Negro equality and amalgama-
tion, now being rammed down their throats."[38] The basic argument
is that southern civilization was put in profound jeopardy when
blacks were freed and given license to exercise their barbarity and
ignorance in all realms of organized society. Dixon provides a portrait of this chaos within the political realm in his description of a
state House of Representatives taken over by blacks: "The reek of
vile cigars and stale whiskey, mingled with the odor of perspiring
negroes, was overwhelming. . . . The space behind the seats of the
members was strewn with corks, broken glass, stale crusts, greasy
pieces of paper, and picked bones. The hall was packed with
negroes, smoking, chewing, jabbering, pushing, perspiring." The
business of these black politicians, according to Dixon, was to "dis-
arm the whites and equip with modern rifles a Negro militia of
80,000 men; to make the uniform of Confederate gray the garb of
convicts in South Carolina . . . to force whites and blacks to attend
the same schools and open the State University to negroes" and in a
move that struck at the heart of southern culture, to "permit the
intermarriage of whites and blacks; and to enforce social equality."[39]

The fear expressed by Thomas Dixon and shared by his audience
is simple: former slaves will lord over their former masters, thereby
creating existential and ontological chaos. From the pen of Dixon
comes a lament over Reconstruction's political empowerment of

blacks and the manner in which, in his words, "the intelligence, culture, wealth, social prestige, brains, conscience and the historic institutions of a great state had been thrust under the hoof of ignorance and vice."[40] As if that were not bad enough, these blacks who destroyed the southern way of life through their freedom were being managed and organized by white "scoundrels" who lacked the sensibilities and loyalties good whites should maintain. Such a combination could only result in destruction, an example of which Dixon provides when writing about a southern gentleman who encounters a "gang of Negroes led by a white scoundrel" and is "knocked down, bound and gagged and placed on a pile of dry fence rails. They set fire to the pile and left him to burn to death."[41] Blacks were presented in a way that raised the question: do they even look human? One gets a sense of this from Dixon's description of a South Carolinian black: "He had the short, heavy-set neck of the lower order of animals. His skin was coal black, his lips so thick they curled both ways up and down with crooked blood-marks across them. His nose was flat, and its enormous nostrils seemed in perpetual dilation. The sinister bead eyes, with brown splotches in their whites, were set wide apart and gleamed ape-like under his scant brows. His enormous cheek bones and jaw seemed to protrude beyond the ears and almost hide them."[42] The physical form spoke to an equally sinister psyche, and so it was assumed aesthetically that beastlike blacks were capable of barbaric acts.

This strong a threat to the order of life had to be met with strong resistance. Dixon's imagery spun a certain fiction about such resistance, one that rendered it in keeping with the tradition of freedom fighters or revolutionaries. Turning again to Dixon's *The Leopard's Spots*, one finds this explanation for organized repression: "This Invisible Empire of White Robed Anglo-Saxon Knights [the Ku Klux Klan] was simply the old answer of organized manhood to organized crime. Its purpose was to bring order out of chaos, protect the weak and defenseless, the widows and orphans of brave men who had died for their country, to drive from power the thieves who were robbing the people, redeem the commonwealth from infamy, and reestablish civilization."[43] In *The Clansman*, Dixon continues this ahistorical romance of the Klan, remarking that "in the darkest hour of the life of the South, when her wounded people lay helpless amid rags and ashes under the beak and talon of the Vulture, suddenly from the mists of the mountains appeared a white cloud the size of a man's hand. It grew until its mantle of mystery enfolded the stricken earth and sky. An 'Invisible Empire' had risen from the field of Death and challenged the Visible to mortal combat."[44] Dixon argues that the goal of the Klan is not to prevent blacks from having rights, in fact, as a character named Gaston remarks, "We grant the Negro the right to life, liberty and the pursuit of happiness if he can be happy without exercising kingship over the Anglo-Saxon race or dragging us down to his level. But if he cannot find happiness except in lording it over a superior race, let him look for another world in which to rule."[45] This, of course, was a disingenuous proclamation at best, a statement that demonstrates a clear inability to think in terms of equality as anything more than a dangerous perversion of the established order.

It would have been difficult to ignore blacks because of, to use Michel Foucault's terminology, the "political investment" of the body, by which its economic use is highlighted and controlled. But the only way to control the body and its economic usefulness is to render it docile. In other words, "the body becomes a useful force only if it is both a productive body and a subjected body."[46] Blacks had identity, but it was a truncated identity that did not significantly vary from the ambiguity of being forged during the period of slavery. Difference, substantive difference, certainly existed between the period of slavery and the postslavery context. Nonetheless, both are defined by a form of subordination and violent suppression meant to maintain a certain racial order. Hence, the period of Reconstruction through the mid–twentieth century provided a change in the status of blacks. Slavery entailed blacks' having no will, no purpose, outside that determined by owners. The Civil War fostered a paradigm shift in that whites were forced to think about blacks in terms of rights and liberties, although these remained circumscribed and were discussed primarily in terms of the ability to commit crimes and be punished accordingly. In short, blacks had to learn to be happy with the identity—as objects of history—given them during the period of slavery; those who failed to find this contentment or who gave the illusion of defiance could easily face the lynch mob, a form of discipline and punishment perfected on black bodies, both male and female.[47] In the words of Frantz Fanon: "The white man is sealed in his whiteness, the black man in his blackness."[48]

These new rights and liberties functioned not to protect blacks but to justify punishment of blacks who breached the socioeconomic order of inequality. In this context, what is the real significance and meaning of being "self-possessed"? Saidiya Hartman's insight into this dislocation of identity is sharp and worth noting here: "While the inferiority of blacks was no longer the legal standard, the various strategies of state racism produced a subjugated and subordinated class within the body politic, albeit in a neutral or egalitarian guise. Notwithstanding the negatory power of the Thirteenth Amendment, racial slavery was transformed rather than annulled."[49] However, the shift was substantial enough to hold blacks accountable in ways meant to justify the abuse and violence they encountered; that is, blacks were recognized as human to the extent their bodies could be punished for offenses to codes of honor and civility. For example, like many newspapers, the *Rocky Mountain Telegram* assumed blacks were guilty of all charges and argued that blacks were actually to be blamed for lynchings because they were not attempting to stem the tide of crime being committed by their own. The paper stated: "We hold the Negro to blame for the repeated unfavorable publicity he receives. . . . No people can endure criminal assaults of the nature we constantly have called to our attention. Three cases of the nature to which we refer, have been brought forcibly to our attention within the last two weeks. One of them is so terribly obnoxious that we have a feeling of nausea whenever we consider it. . . . We have looked in vain for Negro leaders . . . to make even the slightest gesture of protest. The responsibility rests with the Negro."[50]

Rope, Violence, and Social Control

We can never be certain of the exact mixture of motivations leading to brutal killings. Yet it seems clear, and in keeping with the central concern of this book, that lynchings were a means of conveying a particular message regarding black bodies and black being: "By conducting the lynching in a circus-like atmosphere, by subjecting the victim to torture and mutilation, and by prominently displaying the corpse, preferably near the black community" lynchers, Tolnay and Beck argue, "could convey a clear message to the general black population."[51] The lynched black—or "strange fruit," to use singer Billie Holiday's terminology—has maintained its power as a fear-provoking image. Even today, such images neatly presented in books raise questions, as Hilton Als notes with haunting accuracy: "If you are even half-way colored and male in America, the dead heads hanging from the trees in these pictures, and the dead eyes or grins surrounding them, it's not too hard to imagine how this is your life too, as it were. You can feel it every time you cross the street to avoid worrying a white woman to death or false accusations of rape, or every time your car breaks down anywhere in America, and you see signs about Jesus, and white people everywhere and your heart begins to race."[52] However one conceives of lynching's place within the context of a changing U.S. society—whether as wanton expression of rage and violence or quasilegal efforts to punish criminals—it is certain that mob violence became a major mechanism of American life and a way of fixing black identity. This is not to say that whites ceased to be a target; to the contrary, whites continued to be lynched but less frequently. For example, between 1918 and 1927, 38 whites were lynched; but this number pales in comparison to the more than 400 blacks, including 11 women (a few of whom were pregnant) lynched during the same period. Between 1882 and 1968, only seven years failed to include the lynching of at least one black. A total of almost 3,500 blacks were lynched during that eighty-six-year period. Overall, at least one black was lynched yearly somewhere in the United States until 1952.[53]

It is interesting to note that by the time torture of black bodies as public spectacle increased in importance, Michel Foucault argues, the "body as the major target of penal repression [had] disappeared" in Europe.[54] Turning here again to Foucault's work, despite such contextual differences as legal versus extralegal modes, adds texture to our understanding of the psychology of terror at work in the process of lynching. Whereas the economy of death changes, according to Foucault, there was a time when executions were marked by a prolonging of torture and a ravishing of the body. Torture gives way to the prison system as punishment through loss of wealth or rights. This is a new technique for attacking the body, one less bloody and less visible but still somewhat effective. In the context of North America, however, violence against blacks could not transition smoothly because it was not premised upon a recognition of humanity, the type of shared ontological ground held among even Europeans of different classes and backgrounds. True, the desire to remove wealth and rights from blacks existed, but it remained popular thinking that blacks were beasts who deserved such rights as much as horses and other creatures. Blacks never had full exercise of the rights supposedly implicit in their freedom. How, then, could punishment be centered on the restriction of such rights? Punishment had to remain fixated on the body, not on the denial of abstract rights and privileges. Unlike the European prison system, with respect to blacks in the late nineteenth and twentieth centuries, destruction of the physical self was not a by-product of punishment. Rather, it was the purpose of punishment.

This being said, our concern here is not with the rationale for removing torture as a part of punishment but, rather, the initial purpose and meaning of the torture. Horror promoted by prolonged torture was meant to extend the punishment, to make the increasing pain more vivid and more traumatic than the thought of actual death. In fact, death is sought by the victim as a way of ending the dread. In the context of lynching, one gets a sense of this from stories in which blacks plead for a speedy execution as the only form of mercy they think the crowd might provide. For example, one victim, Dan Davis, turned to his lynchers and said, "I wish some of you gentlemen would be Christian enough to cut my throat."[55] And the cries for mercy of another victim, Jim McIlherron, "could be heard in the town, but after torturing the negro several minutes one of the masked men poured coal oil on his feet and applied a match to the pyre. As the flames rose, enveloping the black's body he begged that he be shot."[56]

Such stories are important for two primary reasons. First, Foucault acknowledges that even the emergence of the prison system does not destroy a fixation on the body—its "forces, their utility and their docility, their distribution and their submission"—as the target of punishment. Hence, the preoccupation with the black body in both slavery and freedom makes sense. Second, for those who raise questions concerning the decline in lynchings in the 1950s and argue an end to torture and terror as a tool of white supremacy, an extension of Foucault's analysis of the prison system is useful. As lynchings decreased in the late twentieth century, the use of such legal means of discipline as prison sentences gained ground. But even this points to a type of terror of the body, the continuing need to destroy black flesh. While transferring the context to the United States, pay attention to Foucault's argument: "But we can surely accept the general proposition that, in our societies, the systems of punishment are to be situated in a certain 'political economy' of the body: even if they do not make use of violent or bloody punishment, even when they use 'lenient' methods involving confinement or correction, it is always the body that is at issue."[57] Through the terror and torture of either lynching or the prison system as described by Foucault, the body is targeted and the victim is torn, literally or figuratively, into mementos—objects in which and through which the meaning of white supremacy is played out.

Destruction of Flesh and the Containment of Chaos

It is interesting to note that the mutilation of black bodies meant to elevate the threat of black chaos produced mementos or souvenirs that in fact made black bodies (and what they represent) transcendent. Or, in other words, through the making of mementos, despised social contaminants (that is, black bodies) were transfigured into powerful symbols. The power of lynching imagery and mutilation is not limited to its impact on the existential and ontological concerns of blacks. Lynchings are riddled with tensions, including the attraction/repulsion that represents the treatment of the victim's body. There is, then, an internal flaw in the process by which that "thing" most threatening is not destroyed but reinforced and given life through prolonged memory, thereby gaining a power that is not neatly bound. In an ironic twist, the former objects of history become shapers of history. Lynching of blacks represented an attempt to stymie progress, the changing nature of U.S. citizenship and labor, but on the other hand it represented a push to address modernization in terms of economic and political developments within the context of southern culture.

In free blacks, whites of all classes found a common enemy that at least momentarily provided a sense of unity—whites against the black menace. There were problems with the logic of lynching as the safeguard of society, but a passion for dominance, not reason, was the fodder for mob violence. Behind the rhetoric of honor, economic hardship, political instability, and social standards was an old, deep-running assumption that blacks were insignificant objects, things to be used. As a resident of Florida remarked: "The people of the South don't think any more of killing the black fellows than you would think of killing a flea . . . and if I was to live 1,000 years that would be my opinion and every other Southern man."[58] The power here is not confined to what happens with the actual victim; rather, it contains the ability of the act—lynching or imprisonment—to produce an economy of life options, a fixed identity as not quite human.

Lynching in the context of our discussion thus far is understood as a major ritual of reference during the late nineteenth century through the mid–twentieth century. It is a means of maintaining the "truth" of a particular system and the relationship of those within that system, of maintaining, in the words of Charles Long, the "second creation" of the black—the formation of the negro—as *the only creation*.[59] Slave auctions as a ritual of reference sought to destroy black identity through an assault on psychological well-being first.

But when lynchings came into vogue, the physical bodies of blacks became less important because they no longer provided free labor; thus, the assault on identity is directed at the body first and secondarily to the psyche through the display of mutilated bodies as a graphic warning, an image of terror, to others. Although both auctions and lynchings seek a total objectification of blacks through manipulation of black corporeality and a mutation of black consciousness, what differs between the two is the order of attack. In this context, lynchings, like earlier slave auctions, served as a festive drama or regularized celebration, a mechanism of terror, a "feast of blood, or ritualized killing in communal acts of human sacrifice," so to speak, by which whites sought to maintain their control over blacks and keep them as instruments of whites' pleasure and purpose.[60] The motivation for this ritual of reference is extensive: it was a fight, from the perspective of its perpetrators, against chaos—drawing together psychosocial, political, economic, and cultural concerns and ideologies and played out and reinforced through the manipulation and symbolic consumption of black bodies.[61] As a result of the Civil War and Reconstruction, blacks were challenging by their very existence outside the mores of the "old South" a cherished way of life. Lynchings were meant to correct this challenge to the cosmos by enforcing the long-held anthropology of blacks as subhuman things. One needed to view this ritual only once, as Lucy Miller of Daytona Beach, Florida, notes, in order to receive the clear message "so that there would not be any effort on the part of blacks to get out of their place."[62]

Lynching as Ritual of Reference

Blacks, through the forced shedding of blood, were the central element in a perverse form of atonement, a recognition of Reconstruction as evil and sinful and the required offering to restore proper order and relations. With this act accomplished, the world once again held meaning; the absurdity of black "freedom" was addressed and rendered moot because it was determined and fixed within the context of white need and desire. Giving primary attention to the psychological violence entailed, Frantz Fanon speaks to this overdetermination. He writes: "I am being dissected under white eyes, the only real eyes. I am fixed. Having adjusted their microtomies, they objectively cut away slices of my reality."[63] Blacks were a danger because, using the language of Victor Turner, they existed in a liminal space—not slave, not free. This "in-between" position marked them as "nonbeing" beings. As such, they could not be easily placed within existing social structures—what was their relationship to former white masters and overseers?—and this lack of fit threatened the entire system, a system that had already been weakened by the Civil War and its political ramifications. While the length of the ritual or some of its details might shift depending on the alleged crime and the temperament of the lynchers, certain elements surfaced continually: the crime was reported; the "seekers of justice" gathered, the victim was located, a ritual site was selected and the victim transported to it, the victim was lynched, and word of the lynching was spread to members of the black community as a warning.

According to popular imagination, punishment for murder and the protection of white women, "the divinity that claimed and received the chief worship of man," were the chief justifications for lynching. Yet those able to cut through the pretense were willing to admit that blacks were often lynched simply because they were black.[64] Actual guilt was of little importance because the torment and pain were all the proof required. As Foucault notes: "Every death agony expresses a certain truth. . . . The body has produced and reproduced the truth of the crime."[65] Nonetheless, the price for restoring order was paid in human flesh. Orlando Patterson's words on the rationale for human sacrifice are applicable here. He writes: "Societal transitions, moments when the entire community or nation is at risk, are, of course, the most serious, demanding the greatest sacrifices. There is a veritable convergence of liminal, or dangerous, transitional states: that of each and every individual whose life is at risk; that of the entire community, whose whole way of life is in peril; and that of time and history itself, which has been halted in the chaos of meaning as people try to come to terms with what has happened to them, to their community, to their culture, and to their history. It is during such moments of extreme, total transition that the most extreme form of sacrifice—human sacrifice—is called for."[66]

In some cases, the ritual nature of the lynching is played out in strong terms by the securing of body parts—the residue of what was commonly called a "barbecue"—such as ears and fingers, as souvenirs. According to an account of the Sam Hose lynching in 1899, some 2,000 people watched as Hose was burned to death. But, "before the torch was applied to the pyre, the Negro was deprived of his ears, fingers and other portions of his body with surprising fortitude. Before the body was cool, it was cut to pieces, the bones were crushed into small bits and even the tree upon which the wretch met his fate was torn up and disposed of as souvenirs. The Negro's heart was cut in several pieces, as was also his liver. Those unable to obtain the ghastly relics directly, paid more fortunate possessors extravagant sums for them."[67] Ritual remains were often displayed prominently in businesses, and in some cases they were turned into jewelry worn with pride, like a family heirloom or powerful charm. Also common were photos taken with the body, or what remained of it, as if to "signify" on the threat of blacks' presence and to pronounce white control over the enemy within. While the ceremony of public executions during this period (such as confession before execution and prayer in some cases) provided some of lynching's ritual elements, there was also a desire to instill a sense of terror through prolonged misery. To some degree, variance in the spectacle's intensity stems from the lynch mobs' psychosocial and economic motivation. It was not really a matter of justice for these mobs. If this had been the case, charges would have been more thoroughly investigated and court-sanctioned means of punishment utilized; as one lynching observer noted, "one Negro swinging from a tree will serve as well as another to terrorize the community."[68]

Lynchings were about the status quo, the highly visible and symbolic maintenance of a certain socioeconomic and cultural ethos that took place with little fear of reprisal by blacks. Torturing of black bodies produced at least a momentary sense of balance, which in turn was displayed by participating crowds as joy and power, and this method of control was practiced and passed on. As one child was heard to say after a lynching, "I have seen a man hanged, now I wish I could see one burned."[69] The more misery inflicted, the more complete was the ritual. Here I appeal again to Foucault for a description because accounts of lynchings in the United States mirror his depiction of torture in eighteenth-century Europe. Within both contexts, "the very excess of the violence employed is one of the elements of its glory: the fact that the guilty man should moan and cry out under the blows is not a shameful side effect, it is the very ceremonial of justice being expressed in all its force. Hence no doubt those tortures that take place even after death" demonstrate that "justice pursues the body beyond all possible pain."[70] In a related sense, as many accounts of lynchings suggest, it was also important to mutilate the body, to render it unrecognizable as human because in so doing the lynch mob's assumption that the black was a nonhuman being was given visible, albeit imposed, confirmation. If there were another meaning to this mutilation, would it be so difficult to find accounts of whites receiving the same treatment?

Because maintaining the status of blacks as things was all consuming for some whites, lynching became not only a means of psychosocial, economic, and political control but also a form of recreation and entertainment, complete with a concern for aesthetic considerations. Photos of the event satisfied, in a sense, the need to maintain the black's status as object and also allowed for a type of voyeuristic enjoyment of the event, a perpetual consumption of the black victim's being—in other words, the rehearsal of the black as an extension of white will. A chilling example is found on a postcard of a lynching received by a New York minister: "This is the way we do them down here. The last lynching has not been put on card yet. Will put you on our regular mailing list. Expect one a month on average."[71] Body parts and photos took on the fluidity and unpredictability of cultural memory; they symbolized long after the event the fixed identity of blacks while securing the dominance of whites through the containment of chaos that threatened communal history. This re-creation of blacks gives black bodies a materiality that could not be completely destroyed, not even through lynching and mutilation. Members of lynch mobs found themselves drawn to the very thing they despised.

Although ex-slaves and their descendants posed a threat to the social order that had to be put down through the destruction of black bodies, preservation of the social order also required the presence of blacks, albeit as placated creatures reminiscent of slaves of old. Again, black bodies as mementos became empowered objects communicating a tension between fear and desire, between horror and fascination, experienced by whites in regard to black bodies. Mutilation—including castration—became synonymous with objectification in that it made a clear and brutal distinction between blacks and whites.[72] As one southerner put it, "We southern people don't care to equal ourselves with animals."[73]

Even those who refused to accept the theory of blacks as beasts maintained a philosophy of perpetual dependence by which blacks were understood as childlike beings incapable of full participation in the life of the nation. Either way, as beasts or incompetents, blacks lacked full humanity and remained fodder for whites' historical constructions. Signs were often placed on ravaged corpses, either advertising products or warning blacks of the fate awaiting those who threatened the order of things and beings. When not presented in the form of lynching and the creation of mementos, tension was displayed in the minstrel shows, through which whites assumed the identity of blacks and expressed it in stereotypical ways—enjoying the freedom from the constraints of whiteness while also reinforcing the distinction between white and black. Minstrel shows—blackface performances—allowed whites to visually devour blacks while at the same time distancing themselves from blacks. It is, in a sense, a mutilation of black being with the same psychological effects as lynching.

A loose interpretation of anthropologist Mary Douglas's work sheds some light on the real and symbolic importance of the black body when arguing that the body represents the social world or social body. At one point, Douglas argues that the ritual sacrifice of an ox, for example, is "being used as a diagram of a social situation" but that the sacrifice of a person shifts, without necessity, the psychological perspective back to that of the individual, expressing "personal and private concerns."[74] While this might seem to refute the point made in this chapter concerning the social ramifications of lynching and slave auctions, careful inspection proves otherwise. The black body is considered no better, of no more significance, than the ox. Therefore, the ritual of reference has both personal and social implications. Both the ox and the black body function as scapegoats. Recall the words of the Floridian mentioned earlier: "The people of the South don't think any more of killing the black fellows than you would think of killing a flea."[75] Through control of black bodies, as with the sacrifice of animals in other cultures, lynchers and their audiences maintain control over their social world. The mutilated black body supports a comforting social order and its racially defined values and sense of honor.

For their perpetrators, lynchings were premised upon religious sensibilities, such as a somewhat unacknowledged reference to the biblical notion of the scapegoating of "misfits" as the horrific and dangerous carrier of social dis-ease.[76] In addition, the alleged crimes committed by blacks that sparked lynching were addressed using a warped reading of the Hebrew Bible's guidelines on crime, such as "an eye for an eye." In short, lynchers—many of whom were not only church members but church leaders—felt their actions had religious justification and that the process of lynching contained the ethos of church ritual and the religious re-creation of cosmic order. In short, maintenance of the social order was undertaken as a religious quest, the securing of the created order as God intended it. For whites, this ritual of reference promoted an illusionary sense of welfare and well-being; for blacks, it created a sense of terror or dread with significant ramifications.[77]

PART TWO

WAGING WAR

4

HOUSES OF PRAYER
IN A HOSTILE LAND

Responses of Black Religion to Terror

❖❖❖

As discussed in chapters 2 and 3, for slaves and their descendants, rituals of reference such as auctions and lynchings fostered a form of terror or dread by reinforcing and celebrating blacks' status as objects. This chapter will address the religious implications of rituals of reference. Concisely stated, the sense of terror or dread promoted by these rituals gave rise to the historical manifestation of religiosity. By this I do not mean rhetorical appeals to the sacred commonly found on the lips of those in pain and despair. Rather, promoting a sense of religion as human construction, I argue that this dread sparks the development of practices, doctrines, and institutional structures earmarked for historical liberation from terror.

I make no effort here to provide histories of black religious experience, or religious traditions, in a strict sense. Rather, in this chapter and the next, I outline a basic assertion: rituals of reference reinforce a fixed identity as object; recognition of this status fosters a form of dread or terror; and religion manifested in black life is a response to or wrestling against this terror, understood in terms of liberation.[1]

Richard Wright speaks to this origin of historically manifested religion when describing the development of Bigger Thomas, the protagonist of the novel *Native Son*. He writes: "There seems to hover somewhere in that dark part of all our lives, in some more than in others, an objectless, timeless, spaceless element of primal fear and dread, stemming, perhaps, from our birth (depending upon whether one's outlook upon personality is Freudian or non-Freudian!), a fear and dread which exercises an impelling influence upon our lives all out of proportion to its obscurity. And, accompanying this first fear, is, for the want of a better name, a reflex urge toward ecstasy, complete submission, and trust. The springs of religion are here."[2]

Blacks and Religion

I focus here on three aspects of religion as historically manifested response to the terror of dehumanization: (1) religion developed as institutional reality wrestling for liberation expressed in socioeconomic and political terms; (2) aesthetic and ritual dimensions of religion as liberation in spiritual terms; and (3) religious thought as liberation in theological terms. And while my approach does not exhaust the possibilities, I must limit my discussion to only a few religious traditions; for the sake of argument, I focus on the tradition of the Black Church in this chapter.

Let me explain my use of the term *tradition* in reference to the Black Church (and to the Nation of Islam in chapter 5). I agree with cultural critic Paul Gilroy, who argues that the idea of tradition is often used in ways that connote static and reified forms.[3] Gilroy's concern is with the manner in which culture is produced and defined in the diaspora—as a dialectical exchange between Africa, Europe, and America—and its epistemological, existential, and psychological ramifications. Through a rather loose and liberal application of Gilroy's critique of tradition as an explanatory category used to address developments in the African diaspora, I suggest that religious traditions are not static but are ever evolving in light of changing temporal conditions as well as the push for transformation or improvement generated by their own internal creativity and ingenuity. It is with regard to this second function—transformation vis-à-vis internal creativity and ingenuity—that black religious forms are more than reactive in nature.[4] Black religion is more than just a move against white actions; because they entail an evolving tension between reaction and creativity, black religious forms are not simply dependent on and reflective of white life. In fact, the survival of various forms of black religion, and the development of others, is premised upon a tradition's ability to adapt and adjust to the changing nature of attack on black humanity. For example, the development of black spiritual churches or black pentecostal churches speaks to the failure of such denominations as the African Methodist Episcopal Church and the National Baptist Convention, U.S.A., Inc., to address the needs of blacks within particular contexts.[5]

The Art of Christianization

Efforts to evangelize enslaved Africans were spotty at best.[6] At various times, Christian communities, such as the Anglicans, felt a need to take the gospel of Christ to the "dark" race, but severe limits on the number of available missionaries and resistance from slave owners meant limited results. Slave owners were reluctant to give sustained attention to the spiritual needs of blacks because they believed such attention would ultimately produce rebellions and a general weakening of important social arrangements. When preachers were allowed to work on plantations, slaves usually received formal instruction that involved an effort to reinforce their status as objects theologically by giving it a quasi-biblical grounding: Africans as the descendants of Canaan are cursed to serve whites.[7] According to one former slave, Richard Carruthers, many blacks, dissatisfied with status quo worship opportunities, "used to have a prayin' ground down in the hollow and sometime we come out of the field, between 11 and 12 at night, scorchin' and burnin' up with nothin' to eat, and we wants to ask the good Lawd to have mercy. He puts grease in a snuff pan or bottle and make a lamp. We takes a pine torch, too, and goes down in the hollow to pray. Some gits so joyous they starts to holler loud and we has to stop up they mouth."[8]

We cannot discuss these secret meetings with great certainty, but it is safe to say that slaves worked through bits of the Christian faith during these meetings and developed a response to their existential condition. As former slave Alice Sewell remarks: "We used to slip off in de woods in de old slave days on Sunday evening way down in de swamps to sing and pray to our own liking. We prayed for dis day of freedom. We come from four and five miles away to pray together to God dat if we don't live to see it, do please let our chillun live to see a better day and be free, so dat dey can give honest and fair service to de Lord and all mankind everywhere."[9] Furthermore, in the words of Walter F. Pitts Jr., who wrote on the development of the Baptist faith within these gatherings, "bits of Christian doctrine and ritual that slaves had gathered from the camp meetings and tales of Christian practices that seeped down to the slave masses became the new legends and traditions of the hush harbors."[10] By violating regulations against unsupervised gatherings, those participating in hush-arbor meetings addressed the terror of slave status through an exercise of will.

Slaves made every effort to maintain the secrecy of these meetings because they knew, as slave owners made clear, that unmonitored gatherings of blacks would be punished. Whites feared that such gatherings were sociopolitical incubators of rebellion and protest. In other words, unmonitored gatherings would result in blacks using religious doctrine to challenge the social order. There was good reason for such concerns; for example, the spirituals, which are assumed to have developed in hush-arbor gatherings, attest to a questioning of black inferiority and dehumanization. Developed to reflect the life circumstances of blacks, filtered through the Christian faith, songs such as the following provide a different outlook on the nature of black existence. They question chattel status using biblical terminology, expressed through a proclamation of the slave's rights to a full range of life options and opportunities:

You got a right, I got a right, We all got a right, to the tree of life.
Yes, tree of life. De very time I thought I was los'
De dungeon shuck an' de chain fell off.
You may hinder me here, But you cannot dere,
'Cause God in de heav'n gwinter answer prayer.[11]

Through these songs, slaves focused on their relationship with God, a type of relationship only possible between God and God's human creation. Messages in these songs were coded so that whites who might hear them sung outside hush-arbor gatherings would think of the tunes as referring only to an otherworldly spirituality, which posed no threat to the social system. For slaves, however, the message was much more subversive; it spoke to the importance of black lives in the sight of God. And if God would value blacks in this way, they must be more than the "things" and "objects" described by whites. Recognition of their full citizenship before God also brought into question the validity of the slave system irrespective of theological justifications offered by slaveholders and their ministers. A popular form of this critique involved a retelling of the story of the Children of Israel held in bondage in Egypt. As historian Albert Raboteau notes: "As they reflected upon the evil that had befallen them and their parents, they increasingly turned to the language, symbols, and world view of the Christian Holy Book. There they found a theology of history that helped them to make sense out of their enslavement. One story in particular caught their attention and fascinated them with its implications and potential applications to their own situation. That story was the story of the Exodus."[12] White America played the role of Pharaoh, who unjustly held God's people, and so those gathered sang:

When Israel was in Egypt's land;
Let my people go,
Oppressed so hard they could not stand,
Let my people go.[13]

This was a doubly potent story because the movement to the New World by Europeans such as the Pilgrims was premised on a similar understanding of themselves as the unjustly persecuted chosen people of God. They believed themselves a special group composed of those destined to develop the kingdom of God in a land set aside for them. Slaves, in singing these songs, critiqued the slave system by reworking the manifest destiny doctrine, dear to so many colonists.

Blacks and Independent Religious Institutions

Hush-arbor meetings and more docile church gatherings monitored by whites eventually gave way to established—that is, visible—religious organizations orchestrated by blacks. According to available records, black Baptist churches began to develop in the South as early as the 1750s, and black Methodist denominations were established in the North as of the early 1800s. In fact, by the 1860s, more than 100 black Baptist churches existed, and black Methodists had formed two denominations with great representation throughout the North. The names given to these two denominations speak to an appreciation for African heritage and the Christian tradition—the African Methodist Episcopal Church and the African Methodist Episcopal Zion Church. Furthermore, the emancipation of the slaves allowed northern black churches to move south and organize and allowed Baptist churches already in the South to evangelize more energetically. Thus, the number of both black Baptists and black Methodists grew tremendously. Many ex-slaves joined these black-run churches because they allowed for a visible affirmation of their independence and personhood: humans make choices, select their social arrangements, and act upon their beliefs.

This feeling for independence of thought and movement is significant because, to quote Benjamin Mays and Joseph Nicholson, "with races and individuals, there must be an opportunity for the development of initiative and self-direction if real character is to be developed, and if hidden potentialities are to be brought to the fore.

Certainly the Negro church has been the training school that has given the masses of the race opportunity to develop." This institutional independence is the Black Church's "genius."[14] Independence and the ability to determine one's affiliations would result in the proliferation of denominations and conventions as black Christians developed religious communities that addressed their particular needs and concerns. As of 2000, more than 60 percent of black Americans labeled themselves "committed born again Christians."[15] And while the vast majority of black Christians, roughly 80 percent, currently are found within seven denominations—the African Methodist Episcopal Church; the African Methodist Episcopal Zion Church; the Christian Methodist Episcopal Church; the National Baptist Convention, U.S.A., Inc.; the National Baptist Convention of America; the Progressive National Baptist Convention; and the Church of God in Christ—there are actually hundreds of smaller institutions meeting the needs of black Christians. The importance of Christianity as represented by these various churches is not to be ignored.

Implicit in the formation of independent black religious bodies was a recognition of the distortions to the Christian faith offered by religious supporters of the slave system and, after the Civil War, by supporters of Jim Crow regulations. In response, black churches critiqued hypocrisy and argued for an equality before God for blacks and whites. By means of a revised theological anthropology, the Black Church fought the "social death" suffered by blacks with rebirth into new relationship with Christ. The autobiography of Frederick Douglass, a former slave and abolitionist, shows this distinction between oppressive religion and liberating Christianity. In the appendix to his book, Douglass clarifies his position on religion:

> What I have said respecting and against religion, I mean strictly to apply to the slaveholding religion of this land, and with no possible reference to Christianity proper; for, between the Christianity of this land, and the Christianity of Christ, I recognize the widest possible difference—so wide, that to receive the

one as good, pure, and holy, is of necessity to reject the other as bad, corrupt, and wicked. . . . Indeed, I can see no reason, but the most deceitful one, for calling the religion of this land Christianity. I look upon it as the climax of all misnomers, the boldest of all frauds, and the grossest of all libels. Never was there a clearer case of "stealing the livery of the court of heaven to serve the devil in." I am filled with unutterable loathing when I contemplate the religious pomp and show, together with the horrible inconsistencies, which every where surround me. We have men-stealers for ministers, women-whippers for missionaries, and cradle-plunderers for church members. The man who wields the blood-clotted cowskin during the week fills the pulpit on Sunday, and claims to be a minister of the meek and lowly Jesus.[16]

As Douglass's biting critique suggests, blacks must be responsible for their own development because not even religiously inclined whites can be trusted to look beyond their own interests. What Douglass voices is an implied recognition of the need for independent black Christian organizations and also the activism and social programs orchestrated by these black churches.

Religion, Socioeconomic Transformation, and Political Liberation

During its more than 250 years of existence, the Black Church, when at its best, has developed forms of praxis geared toward addressing the terror and dread of objectification through the nurturing of sociopolitically and economically vital and vibrant Americans, who exercise all the rights and responsibilities endemic to full citizenship. Many volumes have outlined the Black Church's liberative activism, a mode of engagement that started early with the development of mutual aid societies to provide financial assistance to blacks. From these initial activities through social gospel activism to more recent modes of community engagement, black churches have grown to provide schooling, jobs, recreational and social outlets, and political influence.[17] While one might think this praxis is limited to the larger, better endowed churches, recent sociological studies point to work done by churches of varying sizes and means.[18] According to these studies, most churches maintain some type of outreach emphasis and thereby address the pressing needs of their particular communities. Of course, the number of outreach programs sponsored is proportionate to the size (and, one can assume, resource base) of the congregation: the larger the church, the more outreach programs sponsored.[19]

All things considered, however, much of what has transpired in this country with respect to civil rights and social betterment has been envisioned and orchestrated by black churches, by their pastors and members. Whether individual members would label themselves activists or not is difficult to say, but what is more certain is the manner in which black churches, again when at their best, have engaged the pressing issues of the day, often in cooperation with other agencies, including the National Association for the Advancement of Colored People (NAACP) and such government agencies as the Department of Housing and Urban Development. From the debate over slavery to the civil rights movement, black churches and their ministers, when maintaining a this-worldly perspective, have shaped the way political figures and the general public view race relations. This commitment to the welfare of humanity is premised on an embrace of Christian principles and their impact on daily life.

Even when many churches became, to use Gayraud Wilmore's term, "deradicalized" during the late nineteenth century and first half of the twentieth century, the otherworldly orientation did not lose sight of dehumanization as evil. Yet, while some churches approached transformation through sociopolitical and economic activism, churches holding to an otherworldly perspective addressed it more passively through a preoccupation with the spiritual condition of the black community. For the latter, the underlying rationale is simple: spiritual growth entails a closeness to God that must imply the full humanity of the practitioner. An otherworldly versus a this-worldly orientation should not be pushed too strongly because what occurs is not a complete displacement of one for the other. Rather, it is a matter of both orientations being present in tension, but with one being given priority over the other at a particular historical moment. The difference, then, involves liberation through spiritual means over against liberation through forms of societal engagement. As ethicist Peter Paris notes with great insight:

> The black churches have always had a profound concern for the bitter and painful realities of black existence in America as well as an abiding hope in a bright and radiant future (eschaton) free from any form of racial injustice. The latter, hope, designates the locus of ultimate value where all people are in harmony with the transcendent, holy, and supreme God of the Judeo-Christian faith. Traditionally, the black churches have interpreted human life, including all of its suffering and pain, in accordance with that ultimate goal in which they have never lost faith. The convergence of that sacred principle with their efforts for improved temporal conditions reveals the integral relationship of religion and politics in the black churches."[20]

Liberation from the vantage point of the Black Church revolves around a transformation of existing relationships, both physical and spiritual.[21]

Two noteworthy exceptions to this thinking exist: violent rebellions and the Back-to-Africa Movement of the nineteenth and early twentieth centuries.[22] With respect to the former, Nat Turner's revolt is probably the best-known example. Shortly after the revolt was put down, an effort was made to paint Turner as a deprived and dangerous beast, "a fanatical black man who dreams of going to bed with white women."[23] However, a more accurate depiction suggests that Turner, a Baptist minister and slave in Virginia, believed himself to have a special purpose, or calling, from God that obligated him to work toward the freeing of enslaved blacks. Drawing on scriptural references, Turner argued that biblical calls for justice easily translated into a divine hatred for slavery. After receiving what Turner considered a sign from God to act out against slavery, he and the group he organized over two years set out. Historian Gayraud Wilmore describes the ensuing events this way: "Before midnight [August 22, 1831], with only a hatchet and a broadax, they set out for the home of the man who at the time was Nat's own master, John Travis. At the Travis house they slaughtered everyone—Travis, his wife, and five others. They took what guns and ammunition they could find, and, dressing their lines like infantrymen, they marched off to perform the bloodiest slave insurrection in American history. By Tuesday morning, August 23, at least seventy slaves had killed fifty-seven whites in a twenty-mile area of the Boykins district of Southampton County."[24] Whereas slave rebellions like Turner's might appear extreme to some, in one sense they point to a demand for full inclusion in the life of the United States. And, in an ironic twist, these rebels, like the colonists during the Revolution, acknowledged that the establishment of full citizenship with all its rights must often come through the shedding of blood.

This was also the attitude of many blacks during the Civil War because it was theologically presented as a just war through which redemption would occur, if leaders were obedient to the leadings of God. A 1862 speech by Daniel Alexander Payne, a bishop in the African Methodist Episcopal Church, speaks to this teleological understanding of American history: "Now, to manage this war, so as to bring permanent good to all concerned, requires more than human wisdom—more than human power. To legislate so as to make the masses see and feel that the laws are just, wise, beneficial, demands more than human learning or skill in government. To determine the sense and just application of these laws as Judges—to execute them faithfully and impartially as a Chief Magistrate, O how much of the spirit of God is needful! How much in the President! How much in his Cabinet!"[25] However, oppressive socioeconomic and political arrangements after the war resulted in some becoming disillusioned with the United States. Within the Black Church, this cynicism fueled a minority perspective known as the Back-to-Africa

Movement, a form of black nationalism wed to a philosophy of human progress. Ministers and laity who held this perspective often took their cue from Episcopal priest and early advocate of emigration Alexander Crummell. Regarding the need for permanent relocation, Crummell said in 1865: "If you send a missionary to Africa, you send, indeed, a good, holy, faithful minister; but he is but an individual; he may, or he may not, plant Christianity in the field. The probability is that he will not; for the greatest of saints can only represent a partial Christianity. Hence the likelihood, the almost certainty is, that his work will have to be followed up by others. When, therefore, you send a single individual, as a missionary, you do not necessarily send Christianity to Africa; albeit you send a devoted Christian. On the other hand, when you send out a company of Christian emigrants, you send a church."[26]

According to Henry McNeal Turner, who was introduced to this movement by Crummell, only through a return to Africa could blacks hope for a better life. Turner was firm in this position, arguing that the plight of blacks made this a logical move: "For the would-be emigrants . . . the decline in their farm income, the background of increasing racial tension and violence, and the general conclusion that the United States was a white man's country combined to make them 'ready to emigrant.'"[27] Some blacks, influenced by the work of Turner, Crummell, and others, believed God set them aside and prepared them to bring the gospel to Africans. Recognition of this special purpose, through a theodicy of redemptive suffering, must include more than spotty missionary work; it must also entail a form of black nationalism generating the development of a new country. Only in Africa would blacks gain the self-esteem and fulfill the socioeconomic and religious potential given them by God. For advocates of this position, the United States was meant by God to be only a training ground, not a permanent home. This perspective was commonly justified theologically by arguing that God allowed the enslavement of Africans in order to fit them with the Christian faith and an understanding of democratic principles. Once this information was secured, blacks were to leave for Africa. They saw this as the fulfillment of Scripture—"and Ethiopia shall stretch forth her hands unto God"—that spoke to Africa's regaining God's favor and thereby its former glory.[28]

Although widely discussed, in practice this agenda was limited to a small group dominated by southern blacks whose life in rural areas suggested no escape from poverty and racism except emigration. Talk of unmatched economic opportunity in Africa did not translate into actual gain; however, it did allow for the expansion of black churches into other parts of the world. One example is the Liberian Exodus Joint Stock Steamship Company, developed in 1877. According to historian Lawrence S. Little: "Stockholders raised enough to buy a ship, the *Azor*, characterized by [Martin] Delany as the 'African Mayflower.' In 1878, several families and individuals including AME missionary Simon F. Flegler emigrated to West Africa. Although lack of money and preparedness doomed the colonizers and forced investors to sell the ship, the venture provided missionaries the opportunity to establish the church in West Africa."[29]

The Back-to-Africa agenda would lose its appeal during the early twentieth century because of hardships such as those faced by the crew of the *Azor*, lack of finances, and the death of its major spokesperson, Henry McNeal Turner, in 1915. It would surface again, with no greater success, through Marcus Garvey and his Universal Negro Improvement Association, which was brought to the United States in 1916. Garvey's work represented the largest mass movement of black Americans in the history of the United States. However, it lacked the formal links to the Black Church represented by earlier efforts. Furthermore, its impact was foiled by criminal charges against Garvey that resulted in a five-year prison sentence at the Atlanta Federal Penitentiary. The charges, which involved misuse of the postal system by selling what was deemed problematic stock in the Black Star Line, were questionable at best. In response to a campaign to overturn the conviction, President Calvin Coolidge pardoned Garvey and deported him to Jamaica in 1927.

Religion, Conduct,
and Aesthetics as Liberation

In addition to programs and platforms meant to alter social surroundings and political realities, liberation was also understood to
require self-imposed restraint on behavior. In other words, it was
argued by black churches and their ministers that the proper place of
blacks in society as respected citizens could be developed more fully
as blacks proved themselves moral and ethical beings. One captures
this sense of proper practice—how black Christians ought to
behave—through attention to the Black Church's religious social
ethic. While the role of terror should not be underplayed, it is also
important to present the manner in which blacks, through religion,
reshaped their environment by a liberative understanding of their
own agency, practiced by a creative ethic of liberation. The ethic
generating this outlook and activity was played out on the collective
level, although in imperfect and often inconsistent ways, as the sexism, homophobia, and heterosexism of most black churches demonstrate.[30] Although applied imperfectly, this ethic of liberation was
meant to forge what might be referred to as responsible selves, able
to exercise agency in ways that transform existing sociopolitical structures. Such agency forces moral accountability in a way that is
appropriate only for those who are subjects of history, not objects of
property.[31]

Turning once again to Peter Paris, we find an apt statement of this
transformative agenda. Paris writes: "Constrained in every dimension of their common life by the dehumanizing conditions of white
racism, blacks made their churches agencies for teaching the race
how to respond to racial hostility in creative and constructive ways."[32]
This is not to say that whites ever really maintained full control over
blacks, that whites had "pure will" and blacks were completely without will; this relationship of whites to blacks during the period of
slavery and beyond was not total and complete.[33] Whites maintaining the ideology of white supremacy wanted—or, rather, needed—
this to be the case, and they developed rituals for living out this

desire. But blacks always fought the situation, to wrestle against dehumanization. The best example of this ethic in the twentieth century is the civil rights movement, through which black Christians, in cooperation with others, brought the gospel of Christ and its ethical implications to bear on the socioeconomic and political life of the United States. The movement's primary spokesperson, Martin Luther King Jr., in his "Letter from a Birmingham Jail," said the following concerning the Christian's requirement to work for justice and the full humanity of the oppressed:

> There was a time when the Church was very powerful—in the time when the early Christians rejoiced at being deemed worthy to suffer for what they believed. In those days the church was not merely a thermometer that recorded the ideas and principles of popular opinion; it was a thermostat that transformed the mores of society. . . . Things are different now. So often the contemporary Church is a weak, ineffectual voice with an uncertain sound. So often it is an arch-defender of the status quo. Far from being disturbed by the presence of the Church, the power structure of the average community is consoled by the Church's silent—and often even vocal—sanction of things as they are. But the judgment of God is upon the Church as never before. If today's Church does not recapture the sacrificial spirit of the early Church, it will lose its authenticity, forfeit the loyalty of millions, and be dismissed as an irrelevant social club with no meaning for the twentieth century.[34]

Besides this corporate agenda, black churches also promoted a personal application of this ethic that was often displayed through appeals to temperance and moderation. It was assumed that conservative conduct would force whites to recognize blacks as worthy of full citizenship and inclusion in the social life of the country. As sociologist Cheryl Townsend Gilkes remarks, this exemplary conduct was rewarded through the bestowing of titles that not only denoted importance within the church setting but kept whites from naming

blacks in belittling ways. What Townsend Gilkes uncovers concerning pentecostal or sanctified churches applies to some degree within
the collective Black Church. Reflecting on the racism of the times,
Townsend Gilkes says: "At the time when white Americans were calling black people a nation of 'thieves, liars, and prostitutes,' Sanctified
Church members were calling each other 'Saints.'" Moreover, when
this title was not used, "even cornerstones and signs listing church
officers give only first initials and surnames. . . . In church publications, elders, church mothers, and all others are also identified in
this way. All this was (and still is) intended to prevent white racists
from calling black Saints by their first names, a white practice used
as a strategy to depersonalize and to devalue black people."[35] This
practice also includes the use of such titles as "brother," "sister,"
"mother," "elder," "evangelist," and so on.

In addition to prohibitions on personal activity and the use of
titles, of particular interest is the manner in which the public presentation of black bodies reflected comportment and thereby was
understood as an extension of moral and ethical conduct. As Shane
and Graham White put it: "The human body may serve as a site for
the inscription of historical processes. In freedom, as in slavery, the
black body could become a surface on which the struggle between
black and white was often cruelly etched, and on which the record
of that struggle may be read."[36] As discussed in chapter 2, during the
period of slavery, blacks were dressed beyond the bare essentials only
when their bodies were paraded across the auction block; this was a
way of enhancing their value for slaveholders, hence serving to
extend social control over blacks. In response, slaves used whatever
means available to them, particularly the use of celebratory dress for
special events such as church services, to counter popular depictions
of black bodies and to soften the impact of chattel status on the carriage of the black body. This use of expressive or material culture was
vital because for enslaved blacks dress had both visual and symbolic
value, drawing attention to their individuality and to their participation in community.[37] In short, whether purchased, given by whites,
or produced by slaves, clothing represented, if even momentarily, a

more liberated existence, because civilization was measured and social order guarded in part through dress.

If this was the case in religious services organized and controlled by whites, for the benefit of whites, it was even more important within the context of independent black religious gatherings. Hence, in the Black Church, clothing was not a sign of one's value for others as their objects; rather, it was a sign of one's value for one-self, one's community, and one's God. Put another way, clothing did not symbolize why whites were in power; rather, it debunked long-accepted rationales for white superiority. It was a sign of personhood and self-worth. By means of dress or appearance—a black aesthetic of liberation, the donning of certain clothing with accompanying ideals and attitudes—black Christians give expression to their humanity, to a liberated identity, through the compromise of oppressive social boundaries and their supporting ideologies of white superiority.

Through the presentation of the body, black Christians speak to their value and beauty. Clothing has always served as aesthetic enforcement of the social order, and blacks, through the careful selection of their attire, subverted this order through a manipulation of expressive culture. By decorating the body in this manner, blacks forced their visibility and reshaped social space, the social environment. In this sense, the aesthetics of personal appearance as highlighted in the Black Church seeks to locate blacks and to simultaneously change the dynamics—the norms—of this setting. Dress presents both spiritual and secular beliefs and desires, agency and control within both realms.[38] A prime example of this is the uniform worn by women who are spiritual leaders. Across denominations, these women are easily recognizable by their plain gray, white, or black dresses and matching hats. The process of claiming a new social being did not simply entail such conservative attire; it also involved creative and elaborate clothing meant to call attention, as if to say "Look at me!"—beautiful clothing for a beautiful person. It is a reclaiming of the body and a displaying of it accessorized over against white proscriptions of blacks as objects themselves. Or, as

Charlene Graves notes with respect to elaborate hats, "when a
COGIC [the Church of God in Christ] woman walks in with a hat
[on], she walks in with an attitude."[39] These hats, as an allusion to the
meanings of head gear during slavery, are a matter of status, of social
importance, part of a larger aesthetic of style that reinforces the ethic
of liberation. According to Audrey Easter, a member of the Church
of God in Christ, "hats were a sign of status for black women. Once
you got up on your feet and started working, you bought some hats.
To be ladylike, you also bought gloves and shoes with a matching
pocketbook."[40]

Spiritual Practices, Ecstatic Behavior,
and Liberation

Tied to the proper presentation of black bodies in social settings is a
concern for the proper inner health of blacks and their connection
with divinity; this, in fact, is yet another presentation of the body as a
denouncement of the terror of dehumanization.[41] While salvation is
probably the most basic form of spiritual struggle against dehumanization and fixed identity, other activities and practices after this
event deserve mention. For example, many churches across denom-
inational lines promote fasting as a way of cleansing the body and
increasing the individual's sensitivity to the Divine. It is considered
an effective mode of spiritual renewal because it restricts behavior by
focusing attention away from carnality and the social functioning of
sensuality, something that was often cited as bestial by whites and
used to justify oppression. In this regard, it is possible that exercises
such as fasting feed, so to speak, the liberative agenda of the Church
in subtle ways by controlling the physical body. Individual control is
used to signify or twist social control. Hence, it retards over the short
term the social system's ability to exercise traditional power relationships with respect to the spiritually centered black body. Fasting is
not a rejection of this struggle for status; rather, it can be a recognition of the depth of struggle, of the possession of a soul. Black Chris-

tians engaged in spiritual cleansing are, in a sense, taking back their souls with style.[42]

This liberative agenda has been played out in the very worship of black Christians.[43] The Black Church as a manifestation of religion responds to terror by seeking to establish blacks as agents of will; Christian gatherings orchestrated by churches served as a ritual of "exorcism" in that they fostered a break with status as will-less objects and encouraged new forms of relationship and interaction premised upon black intentionality. The black body as ugly and important only as a tool of labor was signified during church gatherings, and it was transformed into a ritual device through which the glory of God and the beauty of human movement were celebrated. One gets a sense of this early in the development of the Black Church in the form of ring shouts, a rhythmic movement of the body that must have resembled the sway and jerk of bodies associated with trances and ecstatic behavior in many traditional African religions. An interesting account of the ring shout follows:

> A true "shout" takes place on Sundays or on "praise" nights through the week, and either in the praise-house or in some cabin in which a regular religious meeting has been held. Very likely more than half the population of the plantation is gathered together. . . . But the benches are pushed back to the wall when the formal meeting is over. . . . All stand up in the middle of the floor, and when the "sperichil" [spiritual] is struck up, begin first walking and by-and-by shuffling around, one after the other, in a ring. The foot is hardly taken from the floor, and the progression is mainly due to a jerking, hitching motion, which agitates the entire shouter, and soon brings out streams of perspiration. Sometimes they dance silently, sometimes as they shuffle they sing the chorus of the spiritual, and sometimes the song itself is also sung by the dancers. But most frequently a band, composed of some of the best singers and tired shouters, stand at the side of the room to "base" the others, singing the body of the song and clapping their hands together

> on their knees. Song and dance alike are extremely energetic,
> and often, when a shout lasts into the middle of the night, the
> monotonous thud, thud of the feet prevents sleep within half a
> mile of the praise house.[44]

Although despised by many church leaders because the practice
reminded them of the culture of slavery and perhaps the stereotypical depictions of Africa, ring shouts demonstrated the beauty and
value of black bodies, which could do more than plow fields, in that
bodies could bring people into proper relationship with God and
could channel God's spirit. Such bodies had to be of profound value
and worth. Through the ring shout, black bodies were redeemed in
ways that fought against continuing efforts to terrorize them. And a
ritualized preparation for spiritual renewal and visitation continues
within black churches, both pentecostal churches and others influenced by what is commonly referred to as the neopentecostal or
charismatic movement.

When spiritual awareness is increased by means of fasting or other
rituals, the individual is open to more intimate connection with the
Divine in the form of shouting and possession.[45] With the development of Pentecostalism in the late nineteenth century, and particularly the founding of the largest black pentecostal denomination in
the country in 1897, the Church of God in Christ, spirit possession—which church folk refer to as being filled with the Holy Spirit
or baptized in the Spirit—became an increasingly important mode
of redress against rituals of reference and their existential and ontological consequences. The story of Bishop Charles H. Mason,
founder of the Church of God in Christ, demonstrates this transformative process. In reflecting on the travail leading to his baptism in
the Spirit, Bishop Mason links the ministry of Christ as struggle
against evil with his own need for the Holy Spirit and the ability to
look beyond human dealings in an effort to perfect himself: "That
night the Lord spoke to me, that Jesus saw all of this world's wrongs
but did not attempt to set it right until God overshadowed Him with
the Holy Ghost. And I said, 'I am no better than my Lord, and if I

want Him to baptize me I will have to let the people's rights and wrongs all alone, and look to Him and not to the people.'"[46] Blacks were not will-less objects, subhuman things, because God manifested God's power, beauty, and purpose through them.

This relationship with God was evidenced by speaking in tongues (glossolalia)—in a language unknown to the person prior to the moment of possession—as well as dancing in the Spirit.[47] The terror of fixed identity is attacked through the body's role as an instrument of God's presence in the world. Beyond addressing negative depictions of blacks, baptism in the Spirit also provided a subtle critique of sexism within black churches in that the Spirit descended on women and men, without prejudice. In one particular case:

> The organ drops out entirely and the voices . . . come together again and again. The organ returns with more power yet, and the congregation erupts into applause. Two women at the front of the church jump into the aisles and whirl in praise of the Lord. "Bless him, bless him, bless him, bless him!" the congregation shouts. "Praise him, praise him, praise him," they chant over and again. Fifteen or twenty people are in the aisles, some whirling, some leaping in place, some running up and down before the altar. All hands in the church are clapping in heightened double time. A number of people have come from the aisles to assist those manifesting the spirit. Sometimes three or four people will surround a person in the spirit, gently supporting him or her, and rocking in rhythm to the driving hand claps and the swelling, soaring organ.[48]

As the music plays, people sing, shout, and dance the "holy dance." The Holy Spirit fills believers and often provides messages, at times in special languages interpreted by others, that respond to the pressing issues faced by blacks living in a hostile land.[49] Truth is no longer defined by the ability of a group to enforce its will, its desires, its recollection of things. Now, through increased spiritual vitality, the truth about blacks, about existence, is tied only to the power of God to manifest in the flesh of believers. The rules and tortures associated with dehumanization are momentarily mitigated by the Holy Spirit's presence and establishment of *communitas*—a space in which external dilemmas are held at bay and harmony is the rule.[50]

Theological Rhetoric as Liberation

Efforts to address terror thus far have been articulated and celebrated in the theological discourse for which the Black Church is known. The linking of sociopolitical and economic concerns found in the writings of many early church leaders foreshadows what would emerge in the twentieth century as the "black" social gospel.[51] Initially concerned with bringing the gospel of Christ to bear on issues of class and poverty, black religious leaders—such as Reverdy C. Ransom of the African Methodist Episcopal Church and Adam Clayton Powell Jr. of the National Baptist Convention, U.S.A., Inc.—used this social Christianity to address issues of racism and racial uplift. This commitment to the social gospel gave way during the civil rights struggle of the 1950s and 1960s to a more radical, black power–influenced form of theological discourse, developed by ministers and professional theologians to address the changing nature of the Church's commitment to the welfare of black Americans.[52] It is with this theological shift that liberation is most forcefully presented as the metaphor for the Black Church's work.

Beginning with editorials published in the *New York Times* by the National Conference of Black Churchmen in the late 1960s, black theology has made an effort to address black Americans' need for liberation within the context of the Christian gospel.[53] During the black consciousness movement of the late 1960s and early 1970s, black theology's impact was unprecedented.[54] It was the most powerful depiction of black power's liberation agenda because it gave this sociopolitical platform a divinely black face. As the spoken word artist Gil Scott-Heron proclaimed earlier this century, the revolution will not be televised—that is to say, it will not feed into a status quo format.[55] But, if black theology is correct, one can add to Gil Scott-Heron's sentiment an additional assertion: the revolution may not be televised, but it will be in color . . . so to speak.

While some objected to its failure to denounce violence as a legitimate means of protest, black clergy and professional scholars who advocated black theology—such figures as J. Deotis Roberts, James Cone, and Gayraud Wilmore—maintained God's participation in the struggle against injustice, arguing that reconciliation without liberation (or justice) was impossible. Furthermore, they insisted that only the oppressed had the capacity to determine the proper mode of resistance because, as Cone notes, "no one can tell us what liberation is and how we ought to struggle for it, as if liberation can be found in words. Liberation is a process to be located and understood only in an oppressed community struggling for freedom."[56] Black theologians working on this project argued that black experience had to be the starting point for practicing theology and for the systematic dismantling of oppression.[57] It, theology, was a second-order discourse used to explore and explain the practices of black people and to promote increased resistance to oppression through the destruction of mechanisms of power and perverted authority.

Gaining inspiration from Martin Luther King Jr., Malcolm X, and an informal theological discourse as old as black Christianity, black theology envisioned itself the voice of the oppressed and the theological wing of the black Christian tradition. It was a shift in theological perspective, tied to the history, culture, experience, needs, and religious tradition of blacks. Perhaps the most radical dimension of this new theology was the ontological blackness of God advocated by James Cone.[58] Drawing on an early tradition present in Henry McNeal Turner's 1895 proclamation "God is a Negro!" Cone, in his early texts published in 1969 and 1970, argued that God is so identified with the oppressed—best represented in the United States by blacks—that God is ontologically black. That is to say, according to Cone, "blackness is the primary mode of God's presence" within the context of historical encounters and relationships.[59] Such a doctrine of God forces a revisiting of Christology as well. Historical manifestation of this ontologically black God is found in the god-human Christ. According to Cone:

> Where is "the opening" that Christ provides? Where does he lead his people? Where indeed, if not in the ghetto. He meets the blacks where they are and becomes one of them. We see him there with his black face and big black hands lounging on a streetcorner. "Oh, but surely Christ is above race." But society is not raceless, anymore than when God became a despised Jew. White liberal preference for a raceless Christ serves only to make official and orthodox the centuries-old portrayal of Christ as white. The "raceless" American Christ has a light skin, wavy brown hair, and sometimes—wonder of wonders—blue eyes. For whites to find him with big lips and kinky hair is as offensive as it was for the Pharisees to find him partying with tax-collectors. But whether whites want to hear it or not, Christ is black, baby, with all of the features which are so detestable to white society. To suggest that Christ has taken on a black skin is not theological emotionalism. If the Church is a continuation of the Incarnation, and if the Church and Christ are where the oppressed are, then Christ and his Church must identify totally with the oppressed to the extent that they too suffer for the same reasons persons are enslaved. In America, blacks are oppressed because of their blackness. It would seem, then, that emancipation could only be realized by Christ and his Church becoming black.[60]

Black theology forged an ontological link between black people and the Divine that was expressed in the physical realm of blackness. What better way to forge liberation out of a context of terror and dehumanization than to demand an understanding of liberation and justice as part of divine personality and character manifested in the faces of oppressed blacks? In popular parlance, "black is beautiful!" This position, however, is qualified as Cone acknowledges: "The focus on blackness does not mean that only blacks suffer as victims in a racist society, but that blackness is an ontological symbol and a visible reality which best describes what oppression means in America. . . . Blackness, then, stands for all victims of oppression who realize that their humanity is inseparable from man's liberation from whiteness."[61] Cone asserts that true Christians must identify also with the oppressed (blacks) so strongly that they too become ontologically black. Clearly, this position did not mean that whites must become physiologically black, or that skin color—and I stress this—is the only measure of blackness. In Cone's words: "To be black means that your heart, your soul, your mind, and your body are where the dispossessed are. . . . Therefore, being reconciled to God does not mean that one's skin is physically black. It essentially depends on the color of your heart, soul, and mind."[62]

The ontological shift demanded here means that earlier notions of chosen status, of selection as the special people of God, are reformulated in black theology and articulated in the language of black power. With time, this notion of black power was refined through the use of Marxist social theory, by which black theology's critique of oppression and vision of liberation grew to include issues of class.[63] Yet those involved in the struggle for liberation were reminded that social theory must inform but not replace action. Regarding this point, Cone writes: "We may hear about Marx, Fanon, and Gutiérrez in white seminaries, but we must not mistake revolutionary rhetoric for actual praxis in the community of victims. Rhetoric is learned in the classrooms by reading Marx's *Das Kapital* and Fanon's *Wretched of the Earth*. But if we are to take Marx seriously when he says, 'it is not consciousness that determines life but life that determines consciousness,' then we must conclude that a true revolutionary consciousness is formed only in the social context of victims. Only as we join the poor in their struggle can we encounter the divine Spirit of liberation disclosed in their fight for justice."[64]

Although radical in nature, the theological shift suggested by Cone's proclamation of ontological blackness was not radical enough from the perspective of black women in academe. Beginning in 1979, black women doing theology and ethics insisted that black theology and black churches can only be true to their mission if they take seriously the experiences of black women. That is to say, liberation must include not only an end to racism and classism but also an end to sexism. This work, from various disciplinary perspectives, is meant, according to ethicist Katie Cannon, to buttress the voice of women in the practice of theology and in the life of the Church by giving due attention to "less conventional" and "more intimate and private aspects of Black life," thereby speaking in powerful ways to the "real-lived texture of Black life and the oral-aural cultural values implicitly passed on and received from one generation to the next."[65] Drawing on Alice Walker's term *womanism*, a new mode of theological reflection—womanist theology—developed and took seriously the history and cultural reality of black women as major resources for church activity and thought. In addition to forcing a response to sexism within the black community and the larger society, womanist scholars have also increased sensitivity to the issues of environmental racism and homophobia and to health crises such as HIV/AIDS within black communities, arguing that these evils also dehumanize.

What occurs through black and womanist theologies is a paradigm shift by which whiteness is no longer the primary symbol of humanity and connection with divinity. These forms of theological discourse are opposed by some blacks and whites within academe, but the greatest challenge stems from the changing sociopolitical and economic status of blacks. Is it possible to maintain this position of radical black consciousness and black epistemology during the more recent period of black middle-class growth and relative contentment? Some recent scholarship has questioned the usefulness of these theological moves in that they denote a restricted epistemology of blackness and thereby limit the possible ways of expressing or being black. Victor Anderson has been one of the most vocal opponents of ontological blackness. In his book *Beyond Ontological Blackness: An Essay in Black Religious and Cultural Criticism*, Anderson asserts that ontological blackness as a concept is too narrow, causing friction between it and "contemporary postmodern black life."[66] The result is an artificial limit on what constitutes proper black behavior and attitudes. To counter such harmful restrictions, Anderson proposes the concept of "grotesquery" as the inspiration for black thought. He is not talking in terms of black identity as a comical distortion, nor does he mean black identity as repulsive or absurd. Rather, this new principle, he argues, is helpful because it connotes a fuller range of life options and sensibilities— all expressions, actions, attitudes, and behavior—interwoven and creatively expressed. Through this philosophical shift, black religious thought is able to address issues of survival and the larger goal of cultural fulfillment, which is Anderson's version of liberation. That is to say, by placing "blackness" alongside other indicators of identity, blacks are free to define themselves in multiple ways while maintaining community involvement and recognition.

Theological positions have shifted to some degree over the course of the past thirty to forty years, in keeping with the changing tone and texture of black community. Yet the idea of ontological blackness continues to mark the work of professionals in black religious studies. Granted, this theological assumption has been modified to include more of the diversity of black Americans, but as a foundational category it has maintained its importance. This position is clearly persistent and is passionately debated by opponents and supporters, but, as we shall see in chapter 5, it pales in comparison to the claims made by the Nation of Islam.

5

COVERT PRACTICES

Further Responses of Black Religion
to Terror

◇◇◇◇

Drawing on the institutional developments, practices, and theology of the Black Church, chapter 4 demonstrated how this mode of religious expression fosters a creativity and ingenuity through which a vision of liberation is developed and used to (1) arrest efforts to dehumanize blacks and (2) construct modes of activism that seek to free blacks, to forge new roles by which they become full citizens with all the accompanying rights and responsibilities.

Moving away from the Black Church, this chapter provides another look at religion as response to terror by addressing covert practices in the Nation of Islam. The term *covert* as used here is not a negative assessment of this tradition's importance or relevance. Rather, it is used only to denote the sheltered, protected, and secretive nature of the tradition—sheltered in that the Nation of Islam's teachings and practices were initially and explicitly geared toward a limited community in order to safeguard that community until it was prepared to fulfill its destiny, and secretive in that the teachings and symbols were, and to some extent remain, shrouded in mystery, discernible only to those familiar with a form of divine mathematics, so

to speak.[1] This chapter focuses on three aspects of the Nation's assertion of liberation: (1) religion as institutional reality wrestling against
socioeconomic and political dependence; (2) aesthetic and ritual
dimensions of religion as liberation; and (3) ethics and religious
thought as liberation.

Blacks and Their Proper Religion

Master Fard, or Master Fard Muhammad, first appeared in "Paradise
Valley," a black section of Detroit, in 1930, selling goods and preaching a doctrine highlighting the distortions of history and culture
under which blacks live in the United States. He linked his religious
doctrine to a general need for blacks to conduct themselves in
proper ways, to save money, to work hard, to eat properly, to respect
authority, and to deal honestly with people. According to one of his
early converts: "He told us that the silks he carried were the same
kind that our people used in their home country and that he had
come from there. So, we all asked him to tell us about our own country. . . . So, we all wanted him to tell us more about ourselves and
about our home country and about how we could be free from
rheumatism, aches and pains."[2] Little was known about Master Fard,
although legends and theories abound, and when plied with questions, his response was cryptic: "My name is W. D. Fard, and I come
from the Holy City of Mecca. More about myself I will not tell you
yet, for the time is not yet come. I am your brother. You have not yet
seen me in my royal robes."[3] It was only with time that Master Fard
Muhammad began to reveal to some followers that he was in fact the
one prophesied about, the Messiah. His mission was expressed with
clarity, and blacks needed to only convert to his teachings, to Islam,
and they would prosper. Within a short period of time, meeting in
various homes became impractical and a rented hall was secured to
accommodate the alleged 8,000 followers.

Among the new arrivals to the Nation of Islam's meetings was Elijah Poole, who had moved from Georgia in search of greater economic opportunities.[4] Initially drawn to the black nationalism of

Marcus Garvey and church ministry, Poole was impressed by Master Fard's mystical and millenarian message of black worth and ultimate triumph over evil.[5] In 1931, with his economic health in question, Poole received word from Master Fard that he should preach Islam under his authority and with his permission. Once Master Fard disappeared in 1934, Elijah Poole, by then known as Elijah Muhammad, gained control of the organization and continued teaching the doctrine given him by Master Fard Muhammad. This was a rough transition, one requiring him to leave Detroit for a time, during which he lived in Chicago and Washington, D.C., and also served a prison sentence on charges of sedition. Regardless of setbacks, by 1946 he had spread the teachings of the Nation, gained converts, and made Chicago the organizational headquarters. In an effort to theologically justify or explain his authority over the Nation, the cosmological framework was altered, whereby Master Fard became understood as Allah incarnate—the Supreme Ruler of the Universe—and the Honorable Elijah Muhammad became the last prophet of Allah, sent to enlighten the lost-found nation of blacks within the wilderness of North America. In his words:

> I'm here as a brother, a friend to you, and one of the first from the resurrection. I am the very first. I am the first of those who submitted to the Will of Whom praise is due forever. I am the first. I am he of whom it is written that was dead and now alive. I am he. I am he of whom it is prophesied as the Messenger of God in the last day who is with God in the resurrection of the dead. I am he. Let your ignorant enemy of the righteous and the truth deceive you against these truths, if you want to take such a one for your guide and for your interpreter. You will suffer the torment and hell of this life. The rejection of the Almighty God, today, and His Messenger will get you nothing but hell in this life, not after you are dead, but while you live.[6]

Through the Honorable Elijah Muhammad's teachings and structural developments, the Nation of Islam grew to encompass temples across the country. No one knows for certain the Nation's exact membership, but accounts suggest more than fifty temples and a membership of somewhere between 10,000 and 500,000 before 1965.

Those who became part of the Nation did so by rejecting black identity as constructed through white power; the rejection of slave names like Jones, Williams, or Pinn was a symbol of this move. The name change is important because it speaks to a deeper meaning, a foundational shift in mind-set and historical orientation. According to Malcolm X, speaking in 1960: "Now then, if you ask a man his nationality and he says he is German, that means he comes from a nation called Germany. If he says his nationality is French, that means he came from a nation called France. The term he uses to identify himself connects him with a nation, a language, a culture and a flag. Now if he says his nationality is 'Negro' he has told you nothing—except possibly that he is not good enough to be 'American' . . . where is 'Negroland'? I'll tell you: it's in the mind of the white man!"[7] Until proper names were provided, most members of the Nation of Islam used the symbol "X." So James Williams became James X and so on. More than just an affirmed rejection of white supremacy, the "X" also signified the unknown. In taking this new name, black Muslims acknowledge the fragile, fractured nature of cultural and historical memory. This is not an embrace of despair and cultural amnesia; rather, it is the embrace of mystery in anticipation of the fulfillment of the black race's destiny.

Even those who did not join the Nation were exposed to its teachings through easy access to the papers and pamphlets sold on street corners throughout black communities. Failure to convert some blacks was not taken by the Nation as personal failure. The choice not to convert was understood as the complete acceptance of dehumanization by the reluctant. As Herbett Hazziez, a member of the Nation, notes, some "Negroes are not ready to pursue a decent and moral life. They are not ready for civilized life. They don't feel responsible and they enjoy their irresponsibility. They think white. They desire to be white; made to hate black. Islam teaches us to be ourselves; to love ourselves, our brothers and sisters; to act for ourselves; stop being liars, being afraid; stop being the laughing stock of the world; to become men among men, women among women; stop beings boys and girls all our lives."[8] In fact, according to the Nation's teachings, rejection of the Messenger and embrace of the Christian faith are ways in which blacks participate in their existential and ontological demise, their mental slavery. It is a misguided effort to love and work with white people who continuously treat them as objects, as subhuman things. That is to say, the relationship between blacks and whites is one of socioeconomic and political masochism:

> For 400 years, we have served you with our labor, sweat and blood, the lash of your whip, your killings, lynching and burning of our innocent Black flesh, without even a hearing in a court of justice, nor even our murderers being punished. Although we are marched before your enemies, and there we pour out our lives for the freedom of your lives, children and your country, we return home to meet an even worse enemy. We are hated and kicked out in certain places like an "unwanted dog" who has caught the game but was not given a taste of it (only that which the hunter could not and should not eat himself). The god, being too ignorant to recognize the injustice done to him by his master, will jump to his feet again at the call of his master to offer his life for his master's life. This we have and still are doing for you.[9]

Religion and Socioeconomic Development as Liberation

This embrace of masochistic tendencies and its overtones of utter dependence had to be changed, and so the Nation's activities revolved around self-sufficiency and nationalist identity fostered through (1) socioeconomic opportunities and (2) a new theological anthropology, with accompanying modes of conduct. In one of the few cases in the teachings of the Nation of Islam in which whites are to be emulated, the Messenger encouraged black Muslims to watch the economic success of whites and to model their willingness to work hard and support their own. Out of this philosophy grew business ventures, including a farm, restaurants, bakeries, and publishing enterprises owned by the Nation. With respect to income, black Muslims were also encouraged to save money and avoid unnecessary expenditures that simply embrace the worst aspects of American consumerism. This was vital if a sense of self-sufficiency was to be fostered as part of the black Muslim's responsibilities.

Regarding the accompanying moral and ethical standards, Malcolm X, in 1960, offered an apology giving particular attention to the radical shift in character of the Messenger's teachings: "When a man becomes a follower of Mr. Muhammad, no matter how bad his morals or habits were [before], he immediately takes upon himself a pronounced change which everyone admits. . . . He has taken men who were thieves, who broke the law—men who were in prison— and reformed them so that no more do they steal, no more do they commit crimes against the government. I should like to think that this government would thank Mr. Muhammad for doing what it has failed to do toward rehabilitating men who have been classed as hardened criminals."[10] Even if Malcolm X's statement is an overgeneralization and placing issues of orthodoxy aside, there is a sense in which the Nation's theological rhetoric provided a release from some of the tension and pressure a hostile societal environment generates. For many who experienced life as otherwise absurd, Mr. Muhammad's teachings provided relief, a rationale or cosmological blueprint wrapped in eschatological urgency that stimulated the imagination and satisfied a natural desire for restitution.

While the Honorable Elijah Muhammad believed the United States should support the agenda of the Nation for a set number of years, in exchange for centuries of free labor from "so-called Negroes," this did not entail governmental control.[11] Instead, the Nation's objective was to create a "nation within a nation" or, in other words, to establish an independent black territory carved out of several existing states. Money secured from the government would be used to finance for roughly twenty-five years the initial development of such a place.[12] In preparation for participation in this new nation, black Muslims were encouraged to avoid overt signs of support for the United States (by refusing to recite the pledge of allegiance; involvement in the political system (by refusing to vote); and participation in the military (by refusing to register for the draft). Yet attached to this nationalist ideology and political detachment is a concern with the federal government's perception of the Nation; members of the Nation through their conduct seek to prove themselves good citizens, respectful of the laws (but only "just" laws), until Allah brings judgment.[13] The Nation seeks a disconnect with the larger society on some level. Nonetheless, this does not entail, as should be clear at this point, ethical and moral indifference. Members of the Nation of Islam are required to adhere to a strict code of life, observed in interaction among members as well as between members and the larger society. Some of this code is aesthetic in nature. For example, based on the Honorable Elijah Muhammad's own conservative dress—dark suits and bow ties—men within the Nation of Islam are to dress modestly, and women are to do likewise, covering their bodies to avoid perceptions of moral laxity. Children must also be dressed with modesty and in conservative colors. Furthermore, black Muslims are encouraged to adopt a mild manner and to avoid aggression unless attacked. Concerning this, the Honorable Elijah Muhammad states that within the Nation, "a brother would not attack another brother. Planting of pimps at our meeting would not help provoke trouble. This tactic of our enemies is bound to fail. Both the beliefs of Islam, the laws, and the punishment which would be imposed on a follower are enough to check outbreaks of violence. Islam is peace, and it teaches against violence."[14]

Health and Aesthetics as Liberation

The Nation of Islam believes itself guided by four principles: peace, freedom, justice, and equality.[15] Through proper attire and carriage, it seeks the respect and admiration of the larger black community and recognition from whites of the seriousness of its mission. In addition, the Nation teaches its members to maintain physical health through proper exercise and diet to counter the physical ramifications of racial discrimination on health and overall welfare. The goal is to promote a better quality of life through obedience to divine regulations on food consumption as an important component of the practices associated with their true nature. Put another way, the Nation argues that some foods promote destruction of character because those who consume them also consume the habits and characteristics of the food: "Allah taught me that this grafted animal was made for medical purposes—not for a food for the people—and that this animal destroys the beautiful appearance of its eaters. It takes away the shyness of those who eat this brazen flesh. Nature did not give the hog anything like shyness. Take a look at [whites'] immoral dress and actions; their worship of filthy songs and dances that an uncivilized animal . . . cannot even imitate."[16] Each member is made aware of foods not to eat, including pork, collard greens, black-eyed peas, corn bread, rabbit, possum, squirrel, and catfish. The Messenger taught that these foods do not promote health and should be replaced by one meal per day in the evening consisting of such items as trout, bass, salmon, beef, lamb, tomatoes, carrots, okra, eggplant, string beans, and cauliflower. Through strict food selection, particularly when combined with periodic fasting, black Muslims believe they avoid many of the health dangers, such as high blood pressure, that plague black Americans.[17] To eat forbidden foods destroys the total being, and so Mr. Muhammad pleads: "Please, for our health's sake, stop eating it; for our beauty's sake, stop eating it; for our obedience to God and His laws against this flesh, stop eating it; for a longer life, stop eating it and for the sake of modesty, please stop eating it."[18]

Whites encouraged blacks to eat these foods as an additional symbolizing of the dehumanized status of blacks, and the Nation seeks to counter this. Mr. Muhammad warned those who would listen that "beauty appearance [*sic*] is destroyed in us—not just our facial appearance, but the most beautiful appearance about us, our characteristics (the way we act and practice our way of life). We achieve one of the greatest beauties when we achieve the spiritual beauty and characteristics through practicing them. We achieve the spiritual beauty through practicing or carrying into practice the spiritual laws. We know that we have been made ugly by our enemies' rearing of our parents. We know that many of our people throughout the earth have been made ugly by not practicing culture that would beautify them."[19] Furthermore, other problems such as poor self-image, all related to the objectification of blacks, are avoided through a rejection of alcohol, gambling, and illicit drugs. Modes of entertainment promoted by the white world are rejected and replaced by activities organized by the various temples, including plays, documentary films dealing with Islamic issues and concerns, and museum visits.

Ethical Conduct as Liberation

In addition to proper economic habits, modest attire for both men and women, proper diet, and exercise, black Muslims must study the Nation's teachings and develop proper relations with other black Muslims. Mr. Muhammad summarizes this code of life through ten points:

1. Keep up prayer;
2. Spend of what Allah (God) has given him in the cause of Truth (Islam);
3. Speak the truth regardless of circumstances;
4. Keep himself (or herself) clean, internally and externally, at all times;
5. Love his brother (or sister) believer as himself (or herself);
6. Be kind and do good to all;
7. Kill no one whom Allah has not ordered to be killed;
8. Set at liberty the captured believer;
9. Worship no God but Allah;
10. Fear no one but Allah.[20]

This code of conduct promises righteousness—the individual's consciousness resurrected and the community fortified—in that it stymies criticism of black self-sufficiency. Drawn from the theological teachings of the Messenger, the code is often summed up in five principles that maintain only a small connection to the pillars of Islam as practiced by "orthodox" Muslims: (1) belief in Allah, (2) belief in the prophet of God, (3) belief in the scriptures, (4) belief in the resurrection, and (5) belief in the final day of judgment.[21] These basic themes are present in the prayer ordinarily recited as part of the Sunday service:

> In the Name of Allah, the Beneficent, the Merciful. All Praise is due to Allah, the Lord of the Worlds' Master of the Day of Judgement. I bear witness that there is none to be worshipped, but Allah, and that Muhammad is His Servant and Last Messenger. O! Allah, Bless Muhammad here in the Wilderness of North America, and bless the followers of Muhammad too, as Thou didst bless Abraham, and the followers of Abraham. O! Allah, make Muhammad successful, and the followers of Muhammad successful, here in the Wilderness of North America, as Thou didst make Abraham successful, and the followers of Abraham. For surely Thou art Praised and Magnified in our midst. Amen.[22]

Because information available outside the Nation of Islam is distorted and processed by whites to maintain white supremacy and to hide the true nature of black Americans, it becomes vital for the Nation to provide the elements of truth leading to freedom. The "Supreme Wisdom" offered by the Honorable Elijah Muhammad counters the enslavement and dehumanization that mark the interaction between whites and blacks.[23] There are three major areas covered by this Wisdom: (1) knowledge of the black community's history and destiny, (2) knowledge of the white community's nature and purpose, and (3) knowledge of Islam as the proper religion for blacks.[24]

Countering the status of blacks as objects of history, Master Fard's teachings as outlined by the Honorable Elijah Muhammad were clear: blacks were not only formed in the image of God, but they are divine creatures meant to dominate the world. Blacks do not represent evil personified; rather, they are good, and whites represent evil. Indeed, whites are considered the very personification of evil intent and demonic desire. According to the teachings, how else can one explain the relatively unchecked destruction perpetuated by whites? Answering this question properly is a component of self-understanding. The Nation of Islam fights the terror of dehumanization through a new theological assertion of black consciousness pointing to the damaging nature of white formulations of black identity, while asserting the ontological superiority of blacks. One gets a sense of this paradigm shift in the words of a member of the Nation: "Elijah Muhammad told the people what they needed to hear at the time. They needed somebody to make them feel good about themselves. Somebody to tell them yes, they were good. Whereby the white man had treated us so bad and made us out to be the bad ones. Well, the Honorable Elijah Muhammad came along and did the reverse."[25] The original people in this way become the supreme subjects of history who will eventually regain control over the universe. White hegemony will be destroyed through final judgment, the earth will be purged by fire, and the original people will rule the new world.

Whereas the Black Church's approach to liberation involves an effort to better integrate blacks into the fabric of American life, the Nation of Islam rejects what it perceives as integration into a damned society. Why seek full membership in a society that is destined for destruction, partnered with those incapable of right living? Civil rights and citizenship are not the ultimate goals for the Nation of Islam. Complete independence is. Furthermore, the Nation of Islam conceives of liberation as the movement of Allah over which they have no control because Allah's actions are part of the current cycle of history, the preordained development of world events. Muslims must simply be true to the teachings of Allah as presented by the

Honorable Elijah Muhammad and, by acquiring proper under-standing of the black race, prepare themselves for their prophesied greatness.

The Honorable Elijah Muhammad directly linked this agenda to the struggle against rituals of reference when saying: "You are beaten, raped, lynched, burned . . . and denied justice by the gov-ernment [which is] defended with [your] blood. . . . White lynchers and rapers of our people are judged innocent. . . . You continue like sheep among wolves to go on suffering. . . . The government makes it clear to you that it is no defense for us against injustice. . . . The only alternative left is to unite as one on the side of Allah."[26] Contin-uing this line of reasoning, life in the United States fosters a sense of dependence on and fear of whites that is, according to Mr. Muham-mad, "the cause of their [blacks'] suffering and will be the cause of their [blacks'] destruction in hell, with the devils whom they love and fear."[27]

While the Black Church asserted equality of blacks and whites as the basis of its theology and practice, the early Nation of Islam pro-posed a reversal of order in which whites became inferior, barely human, and constructed for the pure purpose of committing evil acts. It was, as Albert Raboteau insightfully notes, a signification, of Amer-ican epistemology and eschatology in that "black Muslims turned American exceptionalism on its head. America was special all right; America was Satan!"[28] The Nation argued that the current condition of blacks stems from the reign of terror Allah allowed. Whereas Orlando Patterson's work mentioned in earlier chapters affords an understanding of black subjugation as social death, the Nation of Islam refers to this experience as a form of ontological forgetfulness or a pacification of consciousness. Brought to North America in chains, blacks were brainwashed and robbed of their identity. In place of healthy self-consciousness (self-understanding), slaves were force-fed the Christian faith, by which their condition was justified.[29] Some blacks, the worst type of black, not only embraced this faith but served as spokespersons for it and by so doing gave full participation to the demise of their community. Why, the Nation rhetorically asks, would black people accept the religion and identity put forth by their slave masters? Can the outlook on life promoted by the holders of power do anything but reinforce their dominance? Addressing these questions through a theodicy of instruction, the Honorable Elijah Muhammad informed followers that whites were allowed to rule for a set number of years to punish blacks for rejecting Islam and to prepare blacks for their return to glory. In a way that confirms the Nation as a religious response to the terror described in these chapters, the Nation associates this divinely sanctioned evil with slave trafficking in the New World. That is to say, "the countdown for the era of evil started in 1555, when the devil John Hawkins arrived at the shore of Africa piloting the slave ship Jesus. He kidnapped members of the twelfth tribe, headed by Imam Shabazz—scripturally known as Abraham— and brought them as chattel to a life of slavery in the wilderness of North America."[30]

Theology of Special-ness as Liberation

This enslavement was not, as whites asserted, the natural consequence of black inferiority and white superiority; rather, it was the result of disobedience on the part of blacks who rejected the religion of Islam. But this was a temporary situation, a period of pain and hardship allowed by Allah in order to strengthen and train blacks for their destined greatness. Blacks, according to the teachings of the Nation, maintained their special-ness, their closeness to Allah, even during their period of punishment, their time in the "wilderness of North America" as the "lost" nation. It is, however, more than simply a manifest destiny argument through which humans are selected by God. The teachings of the Messenger indicate that blacks are in fact divine, of the same substance as Allah. C. Eric Lincoln, one of the first scholars to write on the Nation, explains the divine nature of blacks as follows: "A strong Platonic idealism permeates the Black Muslim concept of Allah: Pure Black is equivalent to Absolute Perfection. Again and again the thesis is sounded that black is the primogenitor of all that exists. All colors are but shades of black; white is but the absence of color; hence the whites are incomplete and imperfect. All things that are, are made by humanity; and only black humanity is truly wise and creative."[31] Whereas black Christians claim the favor of a spirit-God who came in human flesh through Jesus Christ, members of the Nation of Islam rejected the idea of a spirit-God and argued that God, Allah, is the Supreme Black Man, who, contrary to what Christianity teaches, only exists in flesh. Only a God who is flesh could be concerned with flesh. Yet the Christian faith developed by whites some 6,000 years ago perverts the truth and teaches a reliance on a detached, spiritualized world. In essence, "the teachings of Christianity have put God out of Man into nothing (spirit). Can you imagine God without form but yet interested in our affairs who are the human beings? What glory would an immaterial God get out of a material world?"[32] The Nation's answer: there is no glory for an immaterial God in a material world; no deep connection is possible between the two.

Placing a different spin on the concept of ex nihilo creation—creation from nothing, or the belief that all that exists must have always existed—the Nation seeks to replace a Christian understanding of life's genesis (and its system of color symbolism) with a concern for the central importance of materiality cast in terms of blackness. In short, blackness is not the absence of something, a mode of privation; rather, it is the color of the creative impulse. Yet even this shift in perspective maintains a degree of mystery, a recognition of limits to our understanding. And so, trillions of years ago, out of the stagnant universe emerged a single atom. From this small bit of matter developed flesh and intellect, which became self-conscious and took the name Allah. When questioned about this account of Allah's self-creation, Elijah Muhammad replied: "Take your magnifying glass and start looking at these little atoms out here in front of you. You see that they are egg-shaped and they are oblong. You crack them open and you will find everything in them that you find out here. Then were there some of them [atoms] out here? Well who created them? I want you to accept the Black God. You say, 'There is no beginning or ending.' I admit that. But we do know that they had to have some kind of beginning. But how it happened, we don't know. That's why we say that His beginning we don't know anything about."[33]

This first person, Allah, a black person, continued the process of creation by developing other beings in his image. These first humans, supreme beings, created the heavenly bodies and earth (or Asia, as it was first called). Because they are supreme beings, of the same substance as the creator, all people of color participate in divinity through a power to create situations and transform them; yet Allah is supreme among all divine beings. In more precise terms: "24 scientists write our history. 23 do the writing and it is then brought to the 24th and He acts as Judge to determine what will come to pass and what won't. This 24th one is called Allah, the Supreme Being. Notice He is called the Supreme "Being," this is because He is human like you and I. The difference is that He is the Wisest Human."[34] Allah is the standard in that he is all-wise and all-powerful. In short, Allah and black people are of the same substance but with differing degrees of power and knowledge.

Moving into his own time period, the Honorable Elijah Muhammad argued that blacks in America are ontologically and biologically connected to the original people, the "Asian Black Nation," the tribe of Shabazz, one of the thirteen original tribes of humans created by Allah. The tribe of Shabazz lived in Egypt and Mecca and remained in that area of the earth even after one of the wise scientists caused an explosion that divided the planet into two pieces—the earth and the moon. Although it did not cause spiritual demise, the explosion served as a marker for the changing religious values of the original people, many of whom lost sight of Islam as their proper religion and began to develop other practices. As punishment for this religious rebellion, some were forced to leave Mecca and migrate to what we now refer to as North America. This, however, did not change the nature of the original people, "the first and the last, and maker and owner of the universe; from [it] come all—brown, yellow, red and white."[35]

Theological Anthropology on Its Head

The mention of whites in the previous quotation is significant because it introduces a fundamental distinction between the original people and whites: the former were *created* by Allah, and the latter were *made* through a less glorious process. Unlike blacks, who date back to the beginning of the universe, the history of whites dates back not even 7,000 years.[36] According to the Nation's theological anthropology and mythology, whites were created by Yakub (or Yacub), a scientist who rebelled against Allah. This, however, was rebellion in a limited sense because it was ordained by Allah and recorded in the history of the world. That is to say, as part of the most recent cycle of history, some 6,645 years ago, Allah allowed the development of a race—the white race—that would test the original people and would serve as their punishment for straying away from the true teachings of Allah.

Born near Mecca, Yakub grew up when most people were satisfied with their religion and way of life. But Yakub's preaching, based on a perversion of the Islamic faith, was geared toward the roughly 30 percent of the population that expressed dissatisfaction and whose desire for wealth could be easily manipulated. Great discontent resulted from his activities, with Yakub and his followers eventually being forced to migrate to the biblical Isle of Patmos.[37] Once in this new location, Yakub continued his work, lacing his preaching with a hatred for those still in Mecca. He promised, in keeping with his destiny, to have revenge on them. To achieve this end, he would create an aggressive race of people who would use violence, and what the Nation of Islam refers to as "trickology," to enslave the original people. Genetic manipulation through the grafting of recessive genes was the process used to create this new race.[38] Yakub recognized that the original people's genetic structure—the "germ" of blacks—contained both a black element and a brown element. He was eventually able to create whites by grafting the brown element of the genetic structure until it produced white people. But this came with consequences; white bodies were fragile, their health poor, and their nature destructive. In short, by altering their color, he also compromised their humanity. It was possible to create an evil race of people from a righteous people, according to the Nation, because, in Mr. Muhammad's words:

> We had that germ left in us from the creation of us. [This is] a germ that was not purified—one that we have in us today—whereas, it could be channeled into a wicked germ. Another people—a white people—could be made from us today, as we stand now. Regardless to how righteous we may be, we still contain the germ of unrighteousness. That is why we can do unrighteousness, because the germ is still there. So, the great scientist by the name of Yakub, went after it. He brought it out of us and gave the germ a form—a body, and then taught that form his wisdom. . . . He, Mr. Yakub—the mighty scientist and maker of the white race or white man—was no fool by any means, just because He made an enemy for us. This made us still great to know that in us was the germ of a whole race of people.[39]

The Nation's framework is much easier to utilize when the physical coloring of "original" people and "whites" is bold. However, what of people who cannot be easily placed in one of these categories because their physical features are not stereotypically connected with one or the other? According to Mr. Muhammad:

> Now the world must know how to distinguish the real devils from the non-devils, for there are thousands of our peoples throughout the world who can hardly be distinguished, by color, from the real devil. There are certain climates which seem to change the white race into a "red" or "brown" color. And where they mix freely with our own kind, their skin and eyes show a difference in color. Their eyes are brown and grayish blue. By carefully watching their behavior, you can easily distinguish them from our people (dark, brown, yellow or red). The characteristics of their children are easily distinguished

from the original children, regardless of how near in color they may be. The devil children, whenever they are around and among original children, like to show off, and love to make mockery of the original children. They teach them evil; talk filth; sing filthy songs; filthy dancing; and games; and will not leave the original children without starting a fight.[40]

Once the process was completed, the white race made its way back to Mecca and caused social chaos, for which it was eventually exiled to Europe—an area of wilderness. According to the myth, whites, once in Europe, began to regress culturally until they ate, walked, and behaved like animals. One sees here a reversal of fortunes in that whites are associated with inferiority and blacks are associated with superior sociocultural skills and abilities. Blacks, in other words, are presented in this mythology as subjects of history and whites as objects of history, formed to serve the destiny of blacks. Whites are mere tools or objects within a drama being played out. History, within this myth, is clearly teleological in nature, and whites are simply fodder for the unfolding of its purpose. In a passage related to this point and phrased in terms of divine initiative, Mr. Muhammad speaks to the distinction between blacks created by Allah and whites made by Yakub: "One God is the God of the Universe. Everything that is of life and everything that is of metal or everything that is matter in the Universe came from Him. He created it! The Holy Qur'an says to the white race: show Us what you have created? What part of the Universe have you created? None, none, no part! Well, then, if you didn't create all of this that you are living off, why not serve Allah then? He said, 'I can't serve Him. You made Him; You made Him Black, and You made me of clay. And I just can't bow to that. I wasn't made like that. You didn't make me to serve Black. You made me to serve my white self and made Black serve me until the day that they are raised up into the knowledge of me. That will be the end of me then.'"[41]

Because of the history written by the wise scientists and the ultimate purpose of whites, the white race could not be left in its

regressed state.[42] So Allah sent Moses to restore it to a proper level of
civility. Jesus, whom the Nation argues was a Muslim, was sent at a
later time to bring them into an understanding of Islam. Because of
their nature, whites did not accept the teachings offered but continued their destructive practices also outlined in Scripture (Genesis
1:26, 28): "Let us make man in our image, after our likeness: Let
them have dominion over the fish of the sea; and over the fowl of the
air; and over the cattle, and over all the earth; and over every creep-
ing thing that creepeth upon the earth. And God said unto them: 'Be
fruitful and multiply; and replenish the earth, and *subdue it*'" (italics
added). This final phrase, "replenish the earth, and subdue it," is key
in that it speaks to destruction and domination, the hallmarks of
white civilization and its spread across the globe. According to the
Honorable Elijah Muhammad: "The world that the Caucasian race
built (the present world) is full of evil and bloodshed and one in
which there is no peace for the black nation—the real owners of the
earth." Furthermore, "the Revelation of the Bible under the title of
John, teaches us that the old dragon beast (referring to the white civilization) deceived the whole world, and they have done just that.
Allah has taught me they deceived 90 per cent of the total population of the planet earth."[43]

What this theological anthropology promotes is a response to the
terror of dehumanization that is not fear driven. Rather, black Muslims are taught that "fear is the worst enemy that we (the so-called
Negroes) have, but entire submission to Allah and His Messenger
will remove this fear."[44] Once blacks recognize their true purpose
and embrace the Islamic faith as outlined by Master Fard and taught
by the Honorable Elijah Muhammad, they will have the knowledge
of self necessary to restore order.[45] As Claude Andrew Clegg III notes,
this existential and ontological reawakening brings final judgment,
during which "the Black nation would construct a new world upon
the smoldering ashes of the dead civilization of the Caucasians. A
new people, numbering a bit more than the 144,000 prophesied in
Revelation, would build a new government 'based upon truth, freedom, justice, and equality,' which would live forever under the guid-

ance of Allah. Sickness, fear, grief, and the vices of the old world would be eliminated."[46]

This does not mean a resurrection or life beyond the grave; rather, judgment and the restoration of blacks amounts to a new consciousness and the rule of the earth by subsequent generations. How will the earth be made ready for the righteous rule of blacks? A combination of natural disasters and the white world's tools of destruction accomplish the task. According to the Nation, Allah "has warned us of how He would (one day) destroy the world with bombs, poison gas, and finally fire that would consume and destroy everything of the present world." But in addition to this, a fantastic use of technology, something we would associate with the best of scientific, fictional imagination and scriptural imagery, completes the work. That is to say, "Allah (has) pointed out to us a dreadful looking plane in the sky that is made like a wheel. It is a half-mile by a half-mile square; it is a human-built planet. . . . It was built [by Master Fard Muhammad] for the purpose of destroying the present world. Allah has also hinted at plaguing the world with rain, snow, hail and earthquakes." Once destruction of the old world is complete and the new world is forged, the reign of terror, the dehumanization of blacks, will be completely overcome and blacks "will become the most beautiful, the most wise, the most powerful and the most progressive people that ever lived."[47]

Louis Farrakhan and the Nation's Agenda

The Honorable Elijah Muhammad's death in 1975 left a leadership void that was filled by his son, Wallace Deen Muhammad, who ultimately rethought the Nation's doctrine and practices.[48] He argued that his father's teachings were allegorical and useful for a time. However, this usefulness passed and the cosmological structure once offered to faithful followers had to be rethought and reformulated. This was to be accomplished first through a recognition that Master Fard was not Allah but a minister living in California. The aims of the organization had to be brought in line with the recognized pillars of Islamic faith and other elements of "orthodox" practice. In addition, the physical space of the mosque was changed to more closely resemble traditional mosques, not churches with pews and a pulpit. Some embraced the changes that placed the American Muslim Mission, formerly the Nation of Islam, in line with the larger Islamic world, while others believed these changes a dangerous move.[49] Numerous splinter groups developed during this period, the most important of which was Minister Louis Farrakhan's reconstitution of the Nation of Islam in 1978, based on the following vision:

> On September 17, 1985, Minister Farrakhan . . . received a vision in which his divine power was further reinforced. In the vision Farrakhan walked up a mountain to an Aztec temple together with some companions. When he got to the top of the mountain, a UFO appeared . . . and a voice called Farrakhan to come closer. . . . He obeyed, and as he walked closer, a beam of light, resembling the sunlight piercing through a window, came out of the wheel. Farrakhan was told to relax and was brought up into the plane on this beam of light. . . . After docking, the door opened and Farrakhan was escorted by the pilot to a door and admitted into a room, which was totally empty except for a speaker in the ceiling. From that speaker Farrakhan heard the well-known voice of the Honorable Elijah Muhammad, which confirmed his being alive. Farrakhan was authorized to lead his God-fearing people through the latter days.[50]

A reformulation of the cosmological structure followed from this vision: Master Fard is Allah incarnate, the Honorable Elijah Muhammad is a Christ-figure, and Minister Farrakhan becomes the Messenger. As part of this reformulation, much of the Nation's doctrine loses its literal relevance and becomes understandable in terms of its metaphorical and symbolic importance. It points toward a truth. For example, theological anthropology concerning whites has more recently entailed a critique not of white people but of white supremacy as demonic. Whites are no longer condemned as "blond hair, blue-eyed devils." Instead, deeds stemming from white supremacist ideology are targets for contempt. What we have, then, under the new Nation of Islam is the maintenance of the spirit of the Messenger's teachings, but with a heightened sensitivity to the allegorical dimension of the more controversial assertions. This shift is a theologically significant development, and in soft tones it spoke to an increasing interest in conversation with the larger Islamic world. The insular nature of the perceived mission is ruptured based on what came to be understood as "the connection between the Prophet Muhammad and Elijah Muhammad insofar as the former's life was the model for the latter's actions. In addition, the importance of the Qur'an as the basis of knowledge for both orthodox Muslims and the Nation was highlighted. In terms of ritual, this shift was premised on the Messenger's gradual embrace of more orthodox worship activities and patterns, and by the development, under the leadership of Louis Farrakhan, of a Qur'anic study program."[51]

While a black nation remained viable, the Nation of Islam's involvement in politics, including members running for office, as well as the sociopolitical and economic platform laid out in Farrakhan's book A Torchlight for America connotes a mainstream take on national developments. This is the case because it highlights problems within the American system that many outside the Nation of Islam would recognize as valid points of discussion, based on a system of ethics and morality, of corporate accountability, not uncommon in dominant political discourse. For example, Minister Farrakhan defines the fundamental problem facing contemporary America this way: "The whole society is modeled after division and that old mind set of haves and have-nots; of the lord and the servant; the slave master and the slave; and the male and the female. These mind sets are reflected in the doctrines of white supremacy and black inferiority, and are perpetuated by the root problems of greed and pervasive immorality."[52] What is more American than a rhetorical appeal to self-help and self-determination, blended with a small pinch of liberalism? Is not this the tone of Farrakhan's directive as culled from Mr. Muhammad's economic plan of responsibility, sacrifice, and unity? Farrakhan continues: "Without the will to make sacrifices the country will go down. The rich have to be imbued with that spiritual and moral desire to sacrifice more of their profits to help America survive. . . . They [politicians] take money from the taxpayer, and from the elderly who have paid their dues to the society, to cover the federal debt, thus spending the country's future."[53] This statement points to Farrakhan's socioeconomic platform as couched in religious language, an appeal to increased spirituality that is popular in many quarters of the United States. Hence, "greed represents a moral problem. It's a spiritual disease. The country needs a spiritual awakening and a spiritual change that will lead to moral consciousness. Even some of the spiritual teachers must be freed from this spiritual disease."[54]

Farrakhan applies the same hermeneutic of moral vision to education, arguing that the system needs to be recalibrated to enliven as essential the "proper cultivation of the gifts and talents of the individual through the acquisition of knowledge." This cultivation of abilities is connected to knowledge of self as a primary tool of manifest destiny. That is, "true education cultivates the person—mind, body and spirit—by bringing us closer to fulfilling our purpose for being, which is to reflect Allah (God)."[55] Spiritual awakening as outlined by Farrakhan would promote overall well-being—reduction in physical disease and general poor health—because, in keeping with Mr. Muhammad's teachings, "most of our sickness can be traced to our rebellion against Divine Law," and responding properly to God's will means an increase in quality and length of life.[56] What Farrakhan's book does is to articulate more explicitly the middle-class values present in the Honorable Elijah Muhammad's teachings. Minister Farrakhan must be well aware of Elijah Muhammad's proclamation: "If only the American so-called Negroes had knowledge of the time in which we now live, they would accept Islam at once; for it is just the *acceptance of Islam which will bring the so-called Negroes the things they desire; good homes, money, and friend-*

ship in all walks of life."[57] The traditional signs and symbols of success in the United States, such as economic security and a stable
home, are encouraged by the Nation of Islam, but with a twist: much
of what is occurring in the United States is part of the 25,000-year
cycle and can be resolved only through execution of the divine
will—in other words, judgment. What is destroying the United States
and moving it swiftly toward destruction? In Farrakhan's words: "Sexism is sinking the country. Classism is sinking the country. Racism is
sinking the country. White supremacy is sinking the country. Black
inferiority and a slave mentality are sinking the country."[58] White
superiority is a regressive behavior, and black inferiority is the
residue of terror that must be rejected. Hence, the benefits and
responsibilities of democracy are embraced but are viewed through
a hermeneutic of suspicion that keeps black Muslims mindful of the
need to reject the ideological trappings of white supremacy and to
remember the destiny of the black race.

While Farrakhan's rhetoric and often cryptic statements continue
to elicit strong reactions from some quarters, Farrakhan believes the
demand for divine justice necessitates the continuation of the
Nation's platform because recognition of the Messengers' teachings,
and the faithful execution of his platform, will facilitate healthier
relations between blacks and whites. Interaction between the two
will then be premised upon changed hearts and minds. But who
changes? The Honorable Elijah Muhammad's teachings contain an
underlying theme of the white race's intrinsic flaw, the inevitability
of their destructive activities. Yet Minister Louis Farrakhan seems to
suggest a softening of this perspective: can whites be "saved"? There
is hope for whites who acknowledge the Messenger's teachings, just
as there is damnation for blacks who reject the message. According
to Minister Farrakhan, such a turnabout can mean regeneration and
redemption. Although possible, it remains unlikely that whites will
destroy the structures and ideologies—the basis of white
supremacy—that promote the dehumanization of blacks and the
privileges of whiteness.[59] To borrow the language of Reinhold
Niebuhr, such a change is an impossible possibility.

In this and the previous chapter, I have implied a certain theory of religion—religion as a historical wrestling with dehumanization, articulated through institutional developments, ritual innovations, and theological formulations. Now it is necessary to discuss the methodology—the mode of study—dictated by both my description and my theory of religion. Chapter 6 addresses this through attention to a basic and straightforward question: how does one study religion as historical struggle against dehumanization and fixed identity?

6

"I'LL MAKE ME A WORLD"

Black Religion as Historical Context

We now move away from description of black religion and raise a more abstract consideration: how does one study black religion so conceived? Responses to this question in the form of black religious studies are relatively recent, beginning during the early twentieth century and achieving substantial levels of production and direct attention in academe through such figures as sociologists W. E. B. DuBois, Benjamin E. Mays, and E. Franklin Frazier; historian Carter Woodson; and theologian Howard Thurman. While much of my thought on black religion is undeniably indebted to these figures as well as to the writings of more recent scholars, I discern difficulties in their approaches that I seek to correct in the method briefly outlined in this chapter.[1]

Fragile Cultural Memory and the Study of Religion

Because the understanding of religion generated in chapters 4 and 5 renders it a reality embedded in cultural developments—not a form of prelanguage and privileged experience—I start with a cautionary note on the problematic nature of cultural resources.[2]

The study of black religion is dependent upon the historical and cultural traces of religious institutions, thought, and activity. It requires a trail or range of clues maintained in and expressed through the community's collective memory. Yet, while recognizing the inevitability of this arrangement, we must also acknowledge its limitations. Put plainly, I must emphasize the fragile nature of the historical and cultural "memory" upon which our study is based. First, double-talk and signification have been vital in the preservation of black life on a variety of levels, making possible a viable form of resistance or counteridentity. But signification has a downside: blacks have, in some cases, forgotten the "rules" to these games and have misplaced vital cultural information. Aspects of cultural memory—our connective tissue—have been lost, and the stories and historical movements that have informed and shaped religious developments are incomplete. In addition, much of what has been collected concerning black culture and cultural memory has gone through several translations before reaching its final form. For example, many Work Projects Administration (WPA) workers—who were paid by the government during the Great Depression of the 1930s and who collected very good information in the form of ex-slave narratives—were dealing with generations who had forgotten (for many reasons) the nuances accompanying the cultural artifacts they shared.[3] Furthermore, even when such information had been maintained, would ex-slaves and their descendants really share all the details and inner workings of their lives with strangers holding tablets and recorders simply because the request for information was politely articulated? And finally, the context of the WPA workers, their own experiences and perceptions of the southern black world they entered, was unavoidably involved in their translation and interpretation of the cultural artifacts presented to them.

Ports of memory retention and retelling are clogged and therefore unstable. Pierre Nora, although referencing France, speaks to this situation when acknowledging that "memory has been torn—but torn in such a way as to pose the problem of the embodiment of memory in certain sites where a sense of historical continuity persists."[4] Under such strain, the culture of the oppressed in order to survive often becomes "condemned to secrecy" and stored away in protected corners.[5] In part, this is a discussion of black collective memory in "contact" with oppressive forces, and of the development of tools for liberation in light of this predicament. It is a challenge, in the words of Susan Willis, to "work through the complicated relationship between white and black cultures as these have been articulated in mass form and structured by the politics of domination, exploitation, and at times, subversion."

Why is this the case? Because, turning again to Willis, "in any society defined by social inequality, culture is a terrain of struggle."[6] The situation is methodologically grim but not hopeless because, while it is not a replica of the cultural products and the contextual arrangement they point to, collective cultural memory is never completely lost. Our contact with these materials involves a type of "bringing together" of cultural artifacts that we seek to translate and interpret as best we can, realizing that these artifacts never completely reveal the inner life of blacks. Novelist Toni Morrison speaks to this in a way that is relevant for black religious studies. She writes: "Memory weighed heavily in what I write, in how I begin and in what I find to be significant. Zora Neale Hurston said, 'like the dead-seeming cold rocks, I have memories within that came out of the material that went to make me.' These 'memories within' are the subsoil of my work. But memories and recollections won't give me total access to the unwritten interior life of these people."[7] Based on the force of this recognition, a kind of intellectual realism and modesty must be exercised when piecing together bits of memory. "Nothing is more fully agreed than the certainty that memory fails," writes Karen Fields. Memory fails because it leaves blanks, areas of historical and cultural uncertainty. But this is only part of the failure; memory also fails because it fills "blanks mistakenly." In doing so, "memory collaborates with forces separate from actual past events, forces such as an individual's wishes, a group's suggestions, a moment's connotations, an environment's clues, an emotion's demands, a self's evolution, a mind's manufacture of order, and yes, even a researcher's objectives."[8]

We often fail to heed such warnings. Instead, we fill gaps that allow for the construction of a scholarly program that seems consistent, refined, perhaps even undeniable. Although scholarly study is important, it appears to be in part based upon a misuse of cultural resources because it fails to hold in tension cultural memory, which is at best ruptured and always fragile. The cultural memory of blacks is too often taken at face value. And while not intentionally deceptive, such an assumption of structural integrity does not allow for the most "accurate" portrayal available to us. This is worth restating: at this point, with the artifacts we know about, the most "accurate" portrayal is not the one that covers up shortcomings and holes; rather, it is the presentation that includes as part of its findings a recognition of gaps. That is to say, we must become comfortable with "slippage" in our stories, in our understanding of black life; we must recognize that our sources do not reveal everything we want to know. Perhaps in failing to provide us with complete understanding, cultural memory urges us, in subtle ways, to look more carefully and in diverse places for pieces of a community's collective story. The study of black religion as conceived in this chapter is useful because it facilitates, and in fact requires, the challenging of assumed cultural history and findings. In short, if cultural meaning is fragile, or as Nora comments, "torn," we must look at all modes of expression, all materials, for what they say, because the winds of human struggle may have forever hidden some materials while they may have also blown and scattered other pieces of torn cultural memory into little-noticed spaces.

Method, Part One:
Archaeology as Metaphor and Practice

Mindful of this cautionary note, how might one go about uncovering modes of presentation beyond the more obvious institutional structures, through which religion as liberation quest emerges? Once these modes are uncovered, how does one interpret and understand them?

In response to the fragile nature of the cultural memory shaping our ability to study religion, I suggest an approach first defined by archaeology as a metaphor for a flexible fashion of exploration marked by a comfort with uncertainty and a recognition that one must dig deep and in varying places to secure information, or what I label "artifacts." Elements of cultural production, or artifacts, are remnants of human activity and creativity, whether current or past, "open" to history. They are no longer "owned" by their creators and are located in countless places, both obvious and hidden. Guided by this metaphor, it becomes much more necessary for the study of religion to include attention to a continually unfolding array of cultural products. And while I think this metaphor provides the sensibilities necessary for the exploration of troublesome materials shaping cultural memory, I also believe archaeology as a discipline allows for useful presentation of how religious developments are embedded in material culture. That is to say, material culture points beyond itself to more fundamental modes of meaning and expression.

I am not suggesting that my approach—religious studies as archaeology—is a foolproof mode of investigation. Instead, it provides important sensitivities and valuable materials. Archaeology might help us understand how material culture speaks to the construction of liberation in historical terms, within an oppressive environment, through physical structures and physical space. For example, archaeology exposes architectural developments and does so in a way that opens to investigation how these structures speak to issues of identity formation, because they are in fact an articulation of purpose.[9] Leland Ferguson sees in the "clay-walled houses" and log cabins built by slaves in South Carolina important stories of life forged in a new land, a life that entailed a response to their environment but one that also maintained elements of their African past. Through these structures, he argues, we learn a great deal about antebellum life for blacks. Ferguson also reflects on slave homes in Virginia. He notes that researchers have, with great regularity, uncovered in these homes "root cellars." One archaeologist, William Kelso, came across these cellars so often that he identified them "as a distinguishing feature of Virginia slave quarters."[10] While commonly believed to have been a storage area for food, or perhaps just the hole left when clay was taken to build the hearth, it is also possible that these cellars housed organized activities. For example, Kelso found ceramics and other items that speak to the possibility of cultural activities taking place that slaves did not want whites to observe.[11]

For those in religious studies, these findings should spark curiosity with regard to the secret meetings mentioned in chapter 4. We typically think about these meetings as taking place in wooded areas or well-guarded portions of the main living quarters. But perhaps these cellars were an alternate site for worship, for the development of spirituals, for the forging of what would become the Black Church and other religious traditions. It seems reasonable to believe that the work of these social scientists—when devoted to an understanding of the complex relations and interactions within black communities as opposed to simply the recovery of "Africanisms"—will "unearth" information related to the quest for liberation. The possibility alone, whether it ultimately provides hard evidence or not, should make archaeology of methodological significance for black religious studies. Archaeology can be a means of assessing the process and forms through which blacks seek to shape their world and create a space of more liberative interactions and intentions.[12] It is a process of uncovering, done in such a way as to maintain a creative tension between historical accounts and the undefined past and in the process help us sort through contending interpretations and perspectives.[13] The development of a stronger base in cultural artifacts is possible because nothing is dismissed out of hand; all findings are important because they say something about the creativity and agency of blacks in their struggle for a liberated existence. The emphasis on cultural production's link to issues of humanization over against objectification remains clear in the words of Theresa Singleton, who comments as follows concerning the utility of archaeological inquiry: "To ignore the consequences of forced migration, enslavement, legalized discrimination, and racism, misses the very essence of how African

Americans created their world and responded to that of the dominant culture. African Americans did not simply adopt a world . . . nor was their world insular to those of other communities. The challenge for archaeological research is to pry open places where the material world can inform the analysis of these complexities."[14]

Black religious studies relies heavily on what Singleton refers to as "contemporary and remembered practices stretching back into the nineteenth century."[15] The form of archaeology suggested here understands the manner in which cultural memory—the "contemporary and remembered practices"—is developed and forgotten, or is remembered only in bits and pieces. As a result, this approach is suspicious of resource certainty and its accompanying arrogance, preferring instead to investigate everything available: written historical records, autobiographical accounts, works of fiction, music, clothing, architectural information, folk art, folktales, folklore, fieldwork related to various sites, and so on. It is possible that archaeological findings and analysis may result in richer resources and greater comfort with nonwritten "textual" materials.[16] By extension, such explorations could provide useful information on the "material manifestations that integrate . . . identity"; through archaeology, blacks are observed in the process of meaning-making, the struggle against overdetermination.[17]

Method, Part Two:
Archaeology and the Hermeneutic of Style

Any approach to the study of black religion that does not operate according to bad faith must clearly state the norm that guides it. This method's norm is liberation, which involves a moral indictment against restricted modes of "being" and a vision for new life possibilities expressed through a full range of responsibilities and opportunities. The study of religion presented up to this point is premised upon an assumption that religion is concerned with this understanding of liberation, the development of a full range of life options expressed with all the privileges made available through the proper exercise of democratic sensibilities. Furthermore, if liberation is, as theologian James Cone argues, "a process to be located and understood only in an oppressed community struggling for freedom," it should involve more than structures and doctrine.[18] It also should involve a certain style or rhythm by which the process of struggle for new ontological and existential status unfolds through black bodies because of the strong connection between oppression and the manipulation of the body. I am proposing that attention to cultural artifacts brought to the surface of our investigation speaks to a certain style of being that seeks, through cultural creativity, to counter the process of dehumanization. I believe sensitivity to this style is vital for a proper interpretation of black religion and its cultural markers.

Take spirit possession during charismatic church services as an example. The movement of bodies so possessed says something about a renewed humanity, a surrender of the body to a more "authentic" power, a kinetic realization of our connection to what is best about the universe. Furthermore, the proud, erect posture of members of the Nation of Islam, who through the presentation of their bodies reject dehumanization, is another example of style as I understand it. With these examples in mind, we can begin to discern the many ways in which religion's push for liberation means, to borrow a phrase from Hazel Carby, blacks "experiencing their bodies in new ways."[19] Again, this has to do with style or aesthetics.

At this point, the challenge is to think through the proper process for finding the ways in which liberation is embedded in artifacts and to gain some sense of the meaning of these artifacts—what they say and the claims they make. This requires a hermeneutic particularly geared toward such an investigation, one in tune with the norm of liberation and the importance of style. And while I am not prepared to offer a full discussion of such a hermeneutic—that involves a much larger project and more study of the tradition on my part—I would like to sketch some of its possible features.

Many argue that archaeology by nature should entail this type of interpretative work. Nevertheless, as archaeologists themselves note, it is difficult to draw links between a group's material culture (or arti-facts) and its style of being, because the actual meaning of artifacts can be difficult to assess.[20] This admission does not harm the useful-ness of archaeology for my project. However, it does mean that archaeology alone cannot constitute the method. I know this diffi-culty of intent—the purpose behind cultural production—can only be lessened and not removed. And so I suggest an explicit hermeneu-tic that makes connections between artifacts and lived communities while being sensitive to the surges and recessions of cultural memory. Concerning this hermeneutic, I maintain the perspective I have expressed elsewhere: "Its guiding criterion is the presentation of black life with its full complexity, untainted by static tradition . . . a hard and concrete orientation in which the 'raw natural facts' [in this case, cultural artifacts] are of tremendous importance, irrespective of their ramifications."[21] This approach to interpretation urges an investiga-tion of resources that highlights a sensitivity to black life experience as it occurs through movement, display, and ornamentation—that is, the "flow" of struggle for more life.

Modes of interpretation, such as a hermeneutic of suspicion, used by many in black religious studies—including black theology, ethics, biblical studies, and history—are limited in that they point out the bad faith of the status quo but offer little more than this awareness of oppression. I suggest a hermeneutic of style, with style understood as the ebb and flow of the black creative impulse and the values and sensibilities that direct the historical movement of black bodies and interests. This hermeneutic is an attempt to understand the content of black cultural expression and history as devices of transformation. But it also involves investigation and understanding of the underly-ing rhythm or aesthetic quality as an important component of strug-gle for liberation. It is a concern with both "things and the perception of things" as they relate to black struggle for a humanized existence.[22]

By this attention to style or aesthetics, I hope to highlight the importance of the arts because, in a way, through art blacks find themselves as they are and as they wish to be.[23] "Art work" according to Nicholas Davey, "allows us to see entities in the world which we would not otherwise see" and, "although as human beings we will never know our ultimate destination, art, by illuminating and mapping the complexities of our experience, lights up our present course and offers some guidance as to where we might steer towards."[24] But how does the struggle for liberation encode itself in cultural production? How do the arts—understood as "aesthetic experience"— enliven and empower, and how do we present this process?[25]

Hermeneutic of Style and the Body

These questions lay out a challenge, a call for examples. I suggest that a good starting point for responding might be the most central element of struggle and creativity, that element upon which all thrust toward liberation depends—the body. Starting with the physical body is justified in that the body represents the major site of contestation, the space in which and upon which terror is manifest.[26] As my colleague at Macalester College, Paula Cooey, has argued: "As concept, 'religion' depends for its realization or substantiation upon structuring or mapping actual bodies, as well as mapping human identities as subjects represented by human bodies."[27] Cooey's point concerning human identities is taken up in chapter 7, but the first assertion in this quotation is important for our current discussion: religion is a "mapping," so to speak, "of actual bodies." Slave auctions and lynchings both focused on the body, and efforts to counter rituals of reference must redeem, so to speak, the body. Power relationships arranged and affirmed through rituals of reference place restraints on flesh, restraints and limits that define fixed identity. To counter this, black religion as discussed in the previous two chapters amounts to a reconstruction of bodies by situating them differently, presenting or visualizing blacks to themselves and to whites in new, and liberated, ways.[28]

Black bodies have a history and are a product of history.[29] By this, I intimate an understanding of the body as constructed (as metaphor or symbol) and as lived, as being a physiological and biochemical reality set in historical experiences.[30] For some, this physiological form is problematic because it changes over time, therefore changing the way it is experienced. But for blacks, some things do not change. Therefore, the signs of age do not lessen many ways in which society seeks to essentialize the black form as symbolization of ontological and existential restrictions. In addition, some might argue that the body is not a unique mode of expression in black communities. All humans share this physiology. Yet this shared human physiology is not enough to negate the value of the movement of black bodies for an understanding of black religious experience because, as Mary Douglas argues, this shared physical form does not produce universal symbols.[31] Furthermore, the social system (complete with norms, language, and socioeconomic and political structures and substructures) determines patterns for the presentation and function of these bodies represented in religious experience as opposition and struggle. The social body and physical body act on each other, the former attempting to define the possibilities of meaning and movement for the latter. They exchange meanings through a dialectic process of pressures and restrictions.[32] In short, the social system seeks to determine the ways in which the physical body is perceived and used. With this in mind, black religion, or black religious expression, entails an effort to move beyond this exchange, beyond the pressures and restrictions of the social system. Whereas Douglas notes a type of concordance between the social and the bodily expression of control, I argue for dissonance between the social body and black bodies, a discord that sparks and fuels religion as historical liberation because the former operates through a process of bad faith, on corrupt intentions.

As the blues poetically express, the relationship of control between the social system and the physical body is antagonistic. It is a fight by individual persons and communities for a reconfiguration of the system that seeks to disembody, to use Douglas's term, interactions in ways that for blacks revolve around invisibility or being as less than fully human. Or, in general terms, it is the black body fighting hard times:

Hard times here everywhere you go.
Times is harder than ever been before.
Well the people are driftin' from door to door.
Can't find no heaven, I don't care where they go.[33]

For blacks, social control and bodily control (or liberation) are oppositional and adversely related. The loss of control over black bodies (on a variety of levels) was a necessary component of the social system, and structures were put in place to guarantee this loss of control, as a type of irrelevance that deforms blacks. I believe this process is what Ralph Ellison had in mind when describing the purpose of his novel *The Invisible Man*:

> So my task was one of revealing the human universals hidden within the plight of one who was both black and American, and not only as a means of conveying my personal vision of possibility, but as a way of dealing with the sheer rhetorical challenge involved in communicating across our barriers of race and religion, class, color and region—barriers which consist of the many strategies of division that were designed, and still function, to prevent what would otherwise have been a more or less natural recognition of the reality of black and white fraternity. . . . Most of all, I would have to approach racial stereotypes as a given fact of the social process and proceed, while gambling with the reader's capacity for fictional truth, to reveal the human complexity which stereotypes are intended to conceal.[34]

Ellison also points to this problem of control and relevance in the haunting words that start the novel: "I am an invisible man. No, I am not a spook like those who haunted Edgar Allan Poe; nor am I one of your Hollywood-movie ectoplasms. I am a man of substance, of flesh and bone, fiber and liquids—and I might even be said to possess a mind. I am invisible, understand, simply because people refuse to see me. Like the bodiless heads you see sometimes in circus sideshows, it is as though I have been surrounded by mirrors of hard, distorting glass. When they approach me they see only my surroundings, themselves, or figments of their imagination—indeed, everything and anything except me."[35]

Recognition of social control over black bodies, the ability of the larger society to reshape and make blacks as they see fit also informs the struggles outlined in a sermon given in Toni Morrison's novel *Beloved*: "Here, she said, in this here place, we flesh; flesh that weeps, laughs, flesh that dances on bare feet in grass. Love it. Love it hard. Yonder they do not love your flesh. They despise it. . . . Love your hands! Love them. Raise them up and kiss them. Touch others with them, pat them together, stroke them on your face 'cause they don't love that either. You got to love it, you! . . . This is flesh I'm talking about here. Flesh that needs to be loved."[36] Years after the setting for Morrison's book, Richard Wright struggles against a similar denial of black worth in such novels as *Black Boy* and *Native Son*.[37] In the latter, Wright points to this pattern of existential and ontological neglect when describing the birth of the character Bigger Thomas:

> As my mind extended in this general and abstract manner, it was fed with even more vivid and concrete examples of the lives of Bigger Thomas. The urban environment of Chicago, affording a more stimulating life, made the Negro Bigger Thomases react more violently than even in the South. More than ever I began to see and understand the environmental factors which made for this extreme conduct. It was not that Chicago segregated Negroes more than the South, but that Chicago had more to offer, that Chicago's physical aspect—noisy, crowded, filled with the sense of power and fulfillment—did so much more to dazzle the mind with a taunting sense of possible achievement that the segregation it did impose brought forth from Bigger a reaction.[38]

The connections between these two bodies—the social and the physical—also mean that freedom for black bodies must entail the restructuring of the social system. I am not suggesting that the two—the social system as body and the physical body—come apart. Rather, I suggest that the goal of religion is a transformation of both through the increased freedom of the latter. This is because the black body is not an image of society in the strict sense; rather, the dehumanization of the black body promoted by the social system is meant to maintain the system and reflect both its wishes and its fears. Structures, as we have seen, were put in place to guarantee this lack of control, and additional means are utilized to punish breaches. Attention to the body, for example, through the pseudosciences was used to support social arrangements, and the findings of supposedly objective studies provided the grounding for sociopolitical and cultural attacks on blacks, particularly blacks who threatened social stability. I am drawn here to the words of cultural critic Michele Wallace: "In the context of mass culture, the image of the black is larger than life. Historically, the body and the face of the black have posed no obstacle whatsoever to an unrelenting and generally contemptuous objectification."[39]

Display of Black Bodies:
Expressive and Decorative Culture

Black bodies, through their placement, movement, or flow, manifest certain codes that speak to the religious nature of black experience. One could easily relate this understanding of the body to Hortense Spiller's understanding of flesh as "that which holds, channels and conducts cultural meanings and inscriptions." According to Spiller, and I agree, enslavement (and, I would add, continuing dehumanization) seeks to strip the body of its flesh, but this is never completely accomplished. Rather, the flesh is transformed; it is hidden from view, covered by protective layers. That is to say, the cultural and historical memory that informs the institutional religion discussed in the previous two chapters is preserved in the physical body—its movement, its decoration, its posture and placement.[40] What results is a sense of how cultural artifacts on other terrains are concealed in the open. Sensitivity to artifacts hidden in plain view should spark new ways of examining and understanding black religion, ways that are more sensitive to the religious impulses emanating from the decorative and visual arts that mark black life.[41] Because of the pivotal role played by cultural production and images in the objectification of blacks, it is to be expected that the struggle against objectification—or the reclaiming of black bodies—should be visible within expressive and decorative culture.[42] The arts are important because, within black life, they have been more than a self-indulgent process devoid of larger content. That is to say, art, in the words of Houston Baker, is "a product and producer in an unceasing struggle for black liberation. To be 'art,' the product had to be expressivity or performance designed to free minds and bodies of a subjugated people."[43]

 · Beginning with expressive culture, even the importance of dressing for Sunday—still a common practice in historically black denominations—speaks to a deeper sense of religiosity. The social systems restricted black bodies; during and after slavery, blacks were expected to dress and carry themselves in ways that represented their status. Whites expected to look at them and—through blacks' body language, the style and quality of their dress, and their overall comportment—feel confident that blacks understood and accepted their lot in life.[44] But through church attire, blacks "were declaring, in effect, that there was more to life than work, and that a sense of dignity and self-worth could survive the depredations of an avowedly racist society. Work clothes—non-descript and uniform—tended to erase the black body; Sunday clothing enhanced and proclaimed it. . . . In this private world of African Americans' own making, meanings were conveyed not merely through dress but through a range of culturally distinctive bodily movements that characterized religious celebrations."[45]

Others expressed a rejection of oppressive and dehumanizing social ordering through an embrace of bodily movement. In other words, as Shane White and Graham White argue, using the period of slavery as an example, "by aestheticizing the black body, by putting its vitality, suppleness and sensuality defiantly and joyously on display," blacks expressed without words their determination to be more than potential physical labor, to present the beauty of their muscles that had nothing to do with lifting or hauling for the benefit of others.[46] When viewed through cultural production as a lens on the black body and its struggle against the social system, liberation entails a stylized movement against warped depictions of black identity, against limitation on participation in the life of society.

While dressing for church service speaks to this, so do the nineteenth-century parades and strolls by blacks in northern cities. On Sundays, blacks moved along the streets displaying their finery, good tastes, and achievements, exploring themselves through experiments with the body, decorating it and moving it in ways that fought against the societal tendencies of the day. That is, "at an individual level the result was a venture out onto the city streets by African Americans garbed in colorful and, what often seemed to whites, bizarre combinations of clothes—ensembles that reflected the existence of an African American aesthetic . . . and a prideful bearing of the blacks' bodies so adorned."[47] The same type of "rethinking" of black value and humanity is expressed through the Nation of Islam's restrictions on dress. One of the prime examples of this attention to the aesthetics of liberation is found in the splendid uniforms seen during the "Saviour Day" celebration each year. I attended one of these celebrations in the 1990s, in Atlanta. It was clear during the course of the program that the sense of self-worth and value embraced by members of the Nation of Islam was made visible through the careful attention to presentation of the body—impeccable white outfits on women and dark suits covering the military-like movements of the men who made up the "Fruit of Islam."

The importance of this style of presentation is in part affirmed through the white backlash, the manner in which style of presence was limited through Jim Crow regulations and extralegal punishments such as lynching. Such behavior on the part of whites was not simply a matter of socioeconomic and political maintenance. Rather, at its deeper levels, it was an effort to quench the religious yearnings of blacks, to break their consciousness and reduce it to a demeaning subhumanity.

Overdetermining blacks, whether during slavery or freedom, did not amount to a completely sealed process by which all liberative structures and realities were cut off. A creative thrust remained intact. For example, beyond clothing, enslaved Africans pushed toward a more liberated existence by rethinking their social and cultural context and often expressed this process in the decorative arts. Quilts and wall collages were texts full of images and patterns that spoke to a larger, more free perspective on life, which Gladys-Marie Fry describes as "diaries, creating permanent but unwritten records of events large and small, of pain and loss, of triumph and tragedy in their lives. And each piece of cloth became the focal point of a remembered past."[48] This is significant because the push for a more liberated form of individual and communal life, the substance of religion as historically manifested, is discernible not only in official records of religious institutions or other easily identifiable and analyzed materials and actions but also in the rather mundane materials of daily life. These tools of daily life have been overlooked by most in black religious studies—after all, what is the academic significance of a piece of cloth used to keep warm during the cold winter?—yet their value is noteworthy.[49] "Every great quilt whether it be a patchwork, applique, or strip quilt," according to Bill Arnett, "is a potential Rosetta stone. Quilts represent one of the most highly evolved systems of writing in the New World. Every combination of colors, every juxtaposition or intersection of line and form, every pattern, traditional or idiosyncratic, contain data that can be imparted in some form or another to anyone."[50] Clearly, the creative impulse represented in this art pointed to struggle against an essentialized identity as beasts of burden through the creation of a cultural space encoded in quilts and other everyday materials. In this sense, black cultural production represents an aesthetic of liberation.[51] The actual patterns and techniques point

to the style of this struggle for liberation and rehearse the collected
stories that summarize this religious experience.

Bodies Celebrated:
Visual Arts and Literature

Through decorative and expressive culture, black bodies were
rethought, reshaped, and placed in new spaces that reminded slaves
of a more liberated existence and spoke without words to the liberation struggle of their descendants. While a useful resource, very few
of these quilts have survived. This suggests a need for additional
clues to the struggle for liberation in other areas of cultural production, such as modern black art. In fact, quilts and wall collages that
decorated modest dwellings served as the inspiration for visual arts in
the twentieth century. Romare Bearden, for example, used the wall
collage style in his collage art. Moving from the social realism, the
mainstream thematics and style of his early work, Bearden embraced
the cultural context and sensibilities of his youth. This shift, which
he named "prevalence of ritual," is apparent, for example, in such
works as "Carolina Shout." Such pieces express the realities of his
North Carolina home as well as the continuation of this certain style
of ritual in places such as Harlem.[52]

Bearden's goal in these works was to place blacks in contexts of
individual and communal health and to destroy, as Ralph Ellison
notes, "the accepted world by way of revealing the unseen," to show
the depth of black humanity. Through his work, Bearden rescued
blacks and re-created them. By taking modest pieces of material and
arranging them, Bearden represented how blacks creatively manipu-
late and signify upon social resources in order to rethink themselves
and develop spaces of liberty.[53] In this way, Bearden maintained the
vitality of "dangerous memories," the stories of black personhood
and value. As Mary Schmidt Campbell puts it, "Bearden's own
phrase, the 'Prevalence of Ritual' underscored the continuity of a
culture's ceremonies, marking the traditions and values that connect
one generation to another."[54]

By paying attention to the ritual behaviors and practices generated by blacks, Bearden celebrated the communal and moral dimensions of black life that were denied by the larger society; he often
presented this in the symbol of the "Conjure Woman." Through this
figure, found in many of his collages, Bearden developed a conduit
of cultural and historical memory that linked blacks in America to a
power of creation, working in opposition to white supremacy's pro-
motion of a fixed black identity. Sharon F. Patton writes: "She [the
Conjure Woman] represents the African diaspora. She is an herbal-
ist, a diviner, a priestess who manipulates unseen, unfamiliar forces
that heal or destroy. Her mysterious personae and penetrating gaze
denote her traditional stature and power in society and her significance in the culture of African Americans."[55] Like the practice of
conjure represented by the Conjure Woman, Bearden claims a more
liberated existence for blacks through mundane but powerful
"objects that tell more than one story."[56]

Guy C. McElroy argues that black artists in the twentieth century
are responding to depictions of blacks that are distorted in that white
artists seek to support a sense of blacks as bizarre creators or freaks
capable of entertaining, serving, or threatening whites, but certainly
incapable of matching the human qualities, beauty, and talents of
whites.[57] For example, William Sidney Mount gave great attention to
the fine points of life in his paintings. In so doing, "black men and
women were characterized by physical appearance or stereotypical
behavior that emphasize their 'otherness' rather than by a full spectrum of emotional and intellectual activities. In many ways his contradictory attitudes toward the identity and proper place of
African-Americans exemplified the sentiments of his contempo-
raries in the face of growing racial tensions."[58] In other cases, white
artists directed their gaze on the black body and rendered it exotic.
As the "Ethiopian Form," a painting by Paul Outerbridge Jr., suggests, the black male body is desired for its depiction of masculinity,
a play on the "bestial" or "natural" quality of the black body that
serves to render women invisible while it essentializes the black
male in that he becomes valuable only to the degree he can be consumed.[59] Many whites, through voyeuristic means and more deadly

turns, attempted to live through blacks, to use black bodies to satisfy their desires and fantasies, regardless of how degrading or destructive.[60] In this sense, minstrel shows and other forms of voyeuristic exploitation amount to the demonic—life working against life through a process of imposed reification, of stereotypes and essentialized forms. Black artists countered this with images demonstrating a stronger sense of value and importance within the context of both individual activities and communal existence. This was the case in the visual arts through the work of such artists as Henry Tanner ("The Banjo Lesson," 1893) and Ellis Wilson ("Haitian Funeral Procession," 1950), but it was also, in a more general sense, the nature of all artistic expression.

This undoubtedly represented a visual statement of a struggle for meaning beyond the restrictive categories offered by white America. It is in twentieth-century literature—the Harlem Renaissance and Black Modernism, for example—that the United States is most convincingly reminded of the link between language and reality, or language as reality. Black writers begin, during this period, to describe life and identity with little respect for the parameters of good sense and good taste as defined by whites. They seek to develop complex and rebellious individual and communal understandings of "being." Alain Locke's anthology titled *The New Negro* points to this dimension of the arts. For example, Albert Barnes, a contributor to Locke's volume, writes: "The contributions of the American Negro to art are representative because they come from the hearts of the masses of people held together by like yearnings and stirred by the same causes. . . . It is a great art because it embodies the Negroes' individual traits and reflects their suffering, aspirations and joys during a long period of acute oppression and distress. . . . It has lived because it was an achievement, not an indulgence. It has been his happiness through that mere self-expression which is its own immediate and rich reward. Its power converted adverse material conditions into nutriment for his soul and it made a new world in which his soul has been free."[61]

Bodies in Motion:
The Ethics of Perpetual Rebellion

I cannot conclude without giving some attention to the system of ethics accompanying my understanding of black religion as struggle for liberation.[62] I suggest a reciprocal relationship between our creative impulses expressed in culture and the activities we consider appropriate and right: we are "moved" to behave in certain ways, to value certain interactions and to disregard others through the power of our creative impulse, our artistic expression in its various forms. Understanding cultural production teaches lessons concerning values, choices, and power that can move us ethically. So as not to give the impression that aesthetic experience is always considered positive, let me qualify my assertion by saying that, at the very least, interaction with cultural production forces a confrontation with ethics and moral sensibilities: what does a song, painting, novel, or style of dress say to us? What behavior does it inspire or dissuade?

Within what I call an ethics of perpetual rebellion is a continuing concern with liberation from dehumanization, but it is understood that struggle may not provide the desired results. However, in place of this outcome-driven system, my proposed ethical outlook locates success in the process. That is to say, we continue to work toward liberation and maintain this effort because we have the potential to effect change, measuring the value of our work not in the product but in the process of struggle itself. Liberation is the norm; perpetual rebellion is the process. Regarding this, I am in agreement with ethicist Sharon Welch. There is no foundation for moral action that guarantees that individuals and groups will act in "productive" and liberating ways, nor that they will ultimately achieve their objectives. Therefore, ethical activity is risky or dangerous because it requires operating without the certainty and security of a clearly articulated "product."[63] Ethics in this sense is a commitment to rebellion, a rejection of reified and truncated identities, an endless process of struggle for something more. It is symbolized to some extent by Sisyphus's task, one described by Albert Camus:

> At the very end of his long effort measured by skyless space and time without depth, the purpose is achieved. Then Sisyphus watches the stone rush down in a few moments toward that lower world whence he will have to push it up again toward the summit. He goes back down to the plain. . . . I leave Sisyphus at the foot of the mountain! One always finds one's burden again. But Sisyphus teaches the higher fidelity that negates the gods and raises rocks. He too concludes that all is well. This universe henceforth without a master seems to him neither sterile nor futile. Each atom of that stone, each mineral flake of that night filled mountain, in itself forms a world. The struggle itself toward the heights is enough to fill a man's heart.[64]

There is no certainty, no way of knowing our efforts will have long-term benefits or sustained merit. But this is not the point. In this system of ethics, the goal of social activism, or struggle, is concerned with fostering space, broadly defined, in which we can undertake the continual process of rethinking ourselves in light of community and within the context of the world. Through this process at its best, we chip away at the structures of dehumanization and in their place foster the formation of more liberative possibilities. In other words, we are, as Stuart Hall remarks, "always in negotiation, not with a single set of oppositions that place us always in the same relation to others, but with a series of different positionalities. Each has for us its point of profound subjective identification."[65]

I believe this understanding of religion as historical struggle for liberation and the ability to examine its development is vital. Yet I am convinced that black religion actually is two-dimensional in nature and that what has been described so far amounts to just the first dimension, the most obvious dimension. In the next chapter, I will make an argument for the second dimension of black religion as an underlying impulse that informs religious institutions, doctrines, and practices.

PART THREE

SEEKING TRIUMPH

7

CRAWLING BACKWARD

Toward a Theory
of Black Religion's Center

Without diminishing the importance of the approach discussed in chapter 6, I now argue in this chapter that an understanding of religion as historical manifestation of a struggle for liberation embedded in culture does not fully capture the nature and meaning of black religion.[1] Religious institutions, thoughts, and actions are an attempt to rupture or break history through the assertion and securing of a full range of rights and privileges.[2] In other words, the religious experience we study is historically situated and culturally bound, dealing with "the material world of outer nature" and "the human world of social life."[3] While this is important, there is a deeper and more central concern resting behind such historical expressions as the Black Church and the Nation of Islam. I label this central concern the *quest for complex subjectivity*, an underlying impulse that gains historical manifestation in the above institutional forms.

Dehumanization and Subjectivity

This quest means a desired movement from being corporeal object controlled by oppressive and essentializing forces to becoming a complex conveyer of cultural meaning, with a complex and creative identity. In the words of philosopher Robert Birt: "Every struggle for human liberation is invariably a struggle for a liberated identity. . . . It is the formation of a new kind of person with 'a new language and a new humanity,' that is the central thrust of any genuine struggle for human freedom."[4] This subjectivity is understood as complex in that it seeks to hold in tension many ontological possibilities, a way of existing in numerous spaces of identification as opposed to reified notions of identity that mark dehumanization. While some might question the true religious significance of this approach, I argue that it is distinguishable from other wrestlings with history by its comfort with tension and complexity. For example, U.S. progressive politics is concerned with identity and identity formation as they revolve around issues of democracy and citizenship. Liberal economic reform in the United States is concerned with identity within the realm of production or control over the means of production. The yearning for complex subjectivity described in this chapter differs in that it seeks to hold or bind together all of these various threads of identity development in a way that makes them essential components of a larger, tangled, and all-encompassing sense of being in more absolute terms.

In arguing for complex subjectivity as the center of black religion, I am aware of thinkers such as philosopher Lewis Gordon who argue that humans should not be understood as subject or object, or even as a combination of the two. Rather, humanity is best defined by "ambiguity," a complexity and multidimensionality. Gordon writes: "This ambiguity is an expression of the human being as a meaningful, multifaceted way of being that may involve contradictory interpretations, or at least equivocal ones. Such ambiguity stands not as a dilemma to be resolved, as in the case of an equivocal sentence, but as a way of living to be described." My sense of complex subjectivity is meant to maintain this multidimensional notion of being.[5] Furthermore, this quest is not achieved in one act or in one moment in which a new status is secured, nor does it depict a separate or distinctive element of reality. Rather, it involves an unfolding, a continuous yearning and pushing for more, an expanding range of life options and movements. It must be understood that this does not entail a turn toward strict individualism. This subjectivity means individual fulfillment within the context of concern and responsibility for others. Again drawing on Robert Birt: "To become human and develop a human identity is a process of invention (self-invention), of personal and collective action conditioned by social relations. . . . Thus, oppression may be seen as an existential violation, an ontological crime. Is this not what is meant when we describe oppression and exploitation as dehumanizing? But since this violation of the human being is social, the struggle to create an identity is also social."[6] In this sense, it is the struggle to obtain meaning through a process of "becoming." It is religious in that it addresses the search for *ultimate* meaning, and it is black because it is shaped by and within the context of black historical realities and cultural creations.[7]

Conversion Experience
and Complex Subjectivity

Conversion as a mode of religious experience can shed some light on the theory of religion proposed here. That is, conversion accounts say something important about the underlying motivation for religious experience and, in this way, point to the feeling or impulse that generates religion as historical wrestlings. My thesis is quite simple: conversion, made possible through elemental feeling for complex subjectivity, is based on a triadic structure of (1) confrontation by historical identity, often presented in terms of existential pain and some type of terror; (2) wrestling with the old consciousness and the possibility of regeneration, or in William James's language, a reconstitution of the soul; and (3) embrace of new consciousness and new modes of behavior affecting relationship with the community of believers—those who have had a similar response to elemental feeling—and the larger community.

Literary figures have expressed the nature of conversion in clear, crisp ways that merit our attention and serious consideration. A prime example is found in novelist James Baldwin's autobiographical text, *Go Tell It on the Mountain*. The book recounts the external challenges and inner struggles of being black in America, and of being a black sinner seeking the meaning of life within community. As its back cover argues, the book is the story of "a family in Harlem. . . . The father is an angry, eloquent storefront preacher, unable to conquer the lusts of his flesh, or truly communicate with his children; the mother, a woman of superb stoic courage in the face of the tragedies of life. The older son is a proud, bitter, doomed rebel; the younger, a sensitive boy [John] making the difficult passage to manhood, desperately searching for his own identity."[8] This wrestling, the struggle for meaning, ultimately takes John Grimes, a fictionalized Baldwin, to the front of a small pentecostal church and a mystical conversion experience. Near the end of the book, John is on the floor of this church, slain by the spirit of God and wrestling with the absurdity of existence as less than fully formed human. Faced with death as the symbol of this lack of meaning, John encounters a darkness and a haunting sound, one that ties his terror to a pain as old as the presence of blacks in America and exemplified by mutilated bodies.

> He began, for terror, to weep and moan—and this sound was swallowed up, and yet was magnified by the echoes that filled the darkness. This sound had filled John's life, so it now seemed, from the moment he had first drawn breath. . . . Yes, he had heard it all his life, but it was only now that his ears were opened to this sound that came from darkness, that could only come from darkness, that yet bore such sure witness to the glory of the light. And now in his moaning, and so far from his bleeding, his cracked-open heart. It was a sound of rage and weeping which filled the grave, rage and weeping from time set free, but

bound now in eternity; rage that had no language, weeping
with no voice—which yet spoke now, to John's startled soul, of
boundless melancholy, of the bitterest patience, and the
longest night; of the deepest water, the strongest chains, the
most cruel lash; of humility most wretched, the dungeon most
absolute, of love's bed defiled, and birth dishonored, and most
bloody, unspeakable, sudden death. Yes, the darkness hummed
with murder: the body in the water, the body in the fire, the
body on the tree. John looked down the line of these armies of
darkness, army upon army.[9]

There is an existential and ontological terror to this mystical conversion experience because John's fear results from a connection to
these tortured souls. And so, Baldwin writes:

Fear was upon him, a more deadly fear than he had ever
known, as he turned and turned in the darkness, as he moaned,
and stumbled, and crawled through darkness, finding no hand,
no voice, finding no door. Who are these? Who are they? They
were the despised and rejected, the wretched and the spat
upon, the earth's offscouring; and he was in their company, and
they would swallow up his soul. The stripes they had endured
would scar his back, their punishment would be his, their portion his, his their humiliation, anguish, chains, their dungeon
his, their death his.[10]

John faced in the storefront church the terror of what it means to
be created a negro, to be a modern experiment or, as W. E. B.
DuBois phrased it, a problem: "a strange experience,—peculiar even
for one who has never been anything else." John's conversion, his salvation, entailed a recognition of this history—"How does it feel to be
a problem?" to be an object of historical curiosity, an oddity—and a
wrestling with it that set him free to develop a more complex and liberated consciousness.[11] For John, the ability to undertake this
wrestling, to bring together the threads of his life, speaks to the

importance of Jesus, whom John saw, "for a moment only; and the darkness, for a moment only, was filled with a light he could not bear. Then, in a moment, he was set free."[12] There is a new consciousness here, a recognition of larger possibilities, that I believe is captured in the last few lines of the novel. John, having gone through conversion and having been encouraged to maintain his faith, represents the recognition of a new direction for life, a new sense of self, to which he says, "I'm ready, . . . I'm coming. I'm on my way."[13]

Baldwin provides one of many examples of the nature and meaning of conversion experience, one that encompasses the three components mentioned earlier. And while I find Baldwin's account intriguing and useful for my project, it is not enough. Attention must also be given to accounts less nuanced by the conventions of literary theory and practice. For this focus, I turn to recorded conversion accounts by earlier figures in the Black Church tradition, drawn from the Fisk University collection of conversions reported by former slaves and published under the title *God Struck Me Dead*.[14] Slaves marked their humanity through an aggressive embrace of activities that point to their bodies as sources of personal pleasure and social relevance extending beyond work for others. While this served as a strike against their status as tools of labor, it also pointed, from the perspective of converts, to areas of sinfulness—a problematic engagement of the world. Hence, in conversion accounts, a rejection of life's physical pleasures, such as dancing, drinking, shameful sexual activity, and so on, is standard. As former slave Charlie notes, he spent a great deal of his free time after escaping slavery engaging in such activities, only to face the conviction that this behavior was morally offensive to God. Feeling remorse, Charlie "went into the woods and said, 'Lord, have mercy on me. I have been a sinner all my days.'" The day after this recognition of sinfulness, he attended church, where "the brothers and sisters prayed around me. Then, like a flash, the power of God struck me. . . . I lay on the floor of the church. A voice said to me, 'You are no longer a sinner. Go and tell the world what I have done for you.'"[15] This encounter brought about a new consciousness and sense of self requiring more responsible behavior, a new way of being in the world that allowed him to have this conversation with his former owner:

> When we whip dogs, we do it just because we own them. It is not because they done anything to be whipped for, but we just do it because we can. That is why you whipped me. I used to serve you, work for you, almost nurse you, and if anything had happened to you I would have fought for you, for I am a man among men. What is in me, though, is not in you. I used to drive you to church and peep through the door to see you all worship, but you ain't right yet, Marster. I love you as though you never hit me a lick, for the God I serve is a God of love, and I can't go to his kingdom with hate in my heart. . . . Whenever a man has been killed dead and made alive in Christ Jesus, he no longer feels like he did when he was a servant of the devil. Sin kills dead but the spirit of God makes alive.[16]

Charlie's conversion experience represents confrontation with historical objectification and the forging of a new sense of self through a feeling of personhood running contrary to old ways of being. Past arrangements of servitude and abuse lose their ability to determine Charlie's value because God has made him "alive" and thereby open to new possibilities for individual fulfillment and relationships of equality.

While Charlie points to social license as the motivation for his conversion, another former slave points to his being sold away from his mother and the cruelty of his new owner as the context within which his religious experience takes place. Reflecting on the existential hardships encountered from the slave market to the fields, this former slave said:

> When selling time came we had to wash up and comb our hair so as to look as good as we could and demand a high price. Oh yes, we had to dress up and parade before the white folks until

they picked the ones they wanted. I was sold along with a gang of others to a trader, and he took us to Louisiana. There, I believe, I was sold to the meanest man that God ever put breath in. . . . At times we worked all night. We never got enough to eat. . . . We were always in the field and at work long before sunup. Away by and by the dinner cart would come. This was a little mule and cart they used for bringing meals to us when we had to go a long enough to eat and maybe take a drink of water. By the time the cart got back to the house, I would be feeling like I hadn't had a bite to eat. I started to praying and calling on God, and let what come that might. I somehow found time and a chance to slip to the bushes and ask God to have mercy on me and save my soul.[17]

The autobiography of this former slave does not go into detail concerning the conversion, but it becomes clear that—whether a terrific event or a subdued occasion—it caused a new vision of the world and a new sense of self and self-worth. Speaking of his preaching opportunities after his conversion, he notes this new consciousness when saying, "About this time I was beginning to feel myself much of a man. I was preaching the gospel and praising God every day."[18]

Although recorded at different times and on differing occasions, both accounts pay similar attention to a traumatic event as the precursor of the conversion experience. For Charlie, it involves the effort to escape socially and psychologically years of slavery's abuse through strong drink and questionable conduct. For the unnamed former slave, the traumatic experience involves being purchased by an extremely abusive person. For Julia A. J. Foote, who becomes the first woman ordained a deacon in the African Methodist Episcopal Zion Church, the trigger for conversion seems to entail witnessing the hanging of her schoolteacher and what she labels her own "undeserved whipping." The hanging marked her in that "the remembrance of this scene left such an impression upon my mind that I could not sleep for many a night. As soon as I fell into a doze, I could see my teacher's head tumbling about the room as fast as it could go; I would waken with a scream, and could not be quieted until some one came and staid with me."[19] The beating Foote received for a crime she did not commit only compounded the absurdity of the world. And unlike Camus's rebel who seeks rebellion over surrender to absurdity, Foote thought of suicide as the proper response: "That night I wished over and over again that I could be hung as John Van Paten had been. In the darkness and silence, Satan came to me and told me to go to the barn and hang myself. In the morning I was fully determined to do so."[20]

Foote did not follow through but was left with existential angst: how could she address her lack of agency in a brutal world? The initial response was to demonstrate will through what Foote referred to as sin. In other words: "The experience of the last year made me quite a hardened sinner. . . . The pomp and vanities of this world began to engross my attention as they never had before."[21] Yet such activity did not satisfy her desire for a meaningful existence, for a stronger sense of being. This, according to Foote's autobiography, only came through an encounter with religion. One Sunday as the minister preached, Foote had a conversion experience: "As the minister dwelt with great force and power on the first clause of the text, I beheld my lost condition as I never had done before. Something within me kept saying, 'Such a sinner as you are can never sing that new song.' No tongue can tell the agony I suffered. I fell to the floor, unconscious, and was carried home. . . . Every converted man and woman can imagine what my feelings were. I thought God was driving me on to hell. In great terror I cried: 'Lord, have mercy on me, a poor sinner!' The voice which had been crying in my ears ceased at once, and a ray of light flashed across my eyes, accompanied by a sound of far distant singing; the light grew brighter and brighter, and the singing more distinct, and soon I caught the words: 'This is the new song—redeemed, redeemed!'"[22]

Such a dramatic conversion was not without ramifications for conduct. Foote had a new sense of importance and meaning that required manifestation, despite periodic lapses into doubt concerning the reality of her new nature. Drawing on holiness doctrine and the strength of her calling, Foote exercised her ministry. And so she proclaimed: "Though I did not wish to pain any one, neither could I please any one only as I was led by the Holy Spirit. I saw, as never before, that the best men were liable to err, and that the only safe way was to fall on Christ, even though censure and reproach fell upon me for obeying his voice. Man's opinion weighed nothing with me, for my commission was from heaven, and my reward was with the Most High. I could not believe that it was a short-lived impulse or spasmodic influence that impelled me to preach."[23]

The examples of conversion I have provided from the Black Church all have existential situations of pain, suffering, or injustice as a central impetus for recognizing the inner need for change, the core impulse for more meaning. One also finds a similar trigger in the conversion accounts of members of the Nation of Islam.[24] You will recall from chapter 5 that the Nation developed during the height of the Great Migration, amid the socioeconomic disillusion-ment of migrants who found not opportunity and prosperity in big cities but discrimination, poor conditions, and poverty. It only makes sense, then, based on this context, that the Nation's growth resulted primarily from the inclusion of those angered by their existential condition. Unlike many accounts of Christian conversion, which contain episodes of a mystical variety, conversion within the Nation of Islam is much more a matter of reason played out. One gets a sense of this, for example, in that during the earlier years, potential converts were required to think through the Nation's teachings and, when ready, to draft a letter:

> Dear Savior Allah, Our Deliverer:
>
> I have attended the teachings of Islam, two or three times, as taught by one of your ministers, I believe in it. I bear witness that there is no God but Thee. And, that Muhammad is Thy Servant and Apostle. I desire to reclaim my Own. Please give me my Original name. My slave name is as follows.[25]

Only letters perfectly written, without error and in good style, were reviewed and given consideration. Once the letter was accepted, the person was admitted to membership, and as a sign of this conversion the last name—the slave name—was replaced by an "X."[26] This, as C. Eric Lincoln notes, is only "the most outward token of rebirth. Perhaps the deepest change promised—and delivered—is the release of energies that had been buried in the old personality."[27] It is through a new consciousness—knowledge of self in the language of the Nation—that the convert is able to reject old ways of being in the world. According to Minister Lucius X, "Islam dignifies the black man, and it gives him the desire to be clean, internally and externally, and to have for the first time a sense of dignity. It removes fear, makes one fearless."[28]

Conversion was premised on an internal yearning for more meaning, a stronger identity than was available elsewhere. From the perspective of converts, life in the United States involved a dehumanization with little hope for improvement. Trying to foster their own liberation from dehumanization only resulted in acts of frustration serving to reinforce a proscribed existence. According to another member of the Nation, blacks "needed somebody to make them feel good about themselves. Somebody to tell them yes, they were good. Whereby the white man had treated us so bad and made us out to be the bad ones."[29]

While this account of the circumstances leading to conversion is common, it is probably best known from and most vividly described in *The Autobiography of Malcolm X*.[30] Even before Malcolm's birth, his identity was shaped by white supremacy because, in his words, "when my mother was pregnant with me, she told me later, a party of hooded Ku Klux Klan riders galloped up to our home in Omaha, Nebraska, one night. . . . The Klansmen shouted threats and warnings at her that we had better get out of town because 'the good Christian white people' were not going to stand for my father's 'spreading trouble' among the 'good' Negroes of Omaha with the 'back to Africa' preaching of Marcus Garvey."[31] Confrontations between his family and dehumanizing forces would continue with the burning of his family's home, severe poverty, and the murder of his father. Having had these experiences, it is no wonder Malcolm would discuss his early years within the context of a nightmare. These events undoubtedly affected his sense of being and importance, suggesting that he, and all blacks by extension, are less than or inferior to whites and subject to their whims.

Even when liked by whites, as Malcolm was liked by the whites who took him in after his mother's hospitalization, such affection was premised on an epistemological blind spot because of which "it just never dawned upon them that I could understand, that I wasn't a pet, but a human being. They didn't give me credit for having the same sensitivity, intellect, and understanding that they would have been ready and willing to recognize in a white boy in my position."[32] Malcolm's perspective was more than a suspicion; his teacher, an adult he trusted, made Malcolm's status very clear when discussing career options with students. It was suggested that Malcolm give up lofty ideas and concentrate on a career working with his hands, a not-so-subtle reminder that blacks are tools of labor. Even from one who supposedly liked Malcolm the good student, the words were damaging: "Malcolm, one of life's first needs is for us to be realistic. Don't misunderstand me, now. We all here like you, you know that. But you've got to be realistic about being a nigger. A lawyer—that's no realistic goal for a nigger. You need to think about something you can be. You're good with your hands—making things. Everybody admires your carpentry shop work. Why don't you plan on carpentry?"[33] Malcolm knew what this meant. He had already reached a conclusion: "They didn't give me credit for having the same sensitivity, intellect, and understanding."[34] At this point, Malcolm "began to change—inside." He "was smarter than nearly all of those white kids. But apparently," Malcolm reflects, "I was still not intelligent enough, in their eyes, to becomes whatever I wanted to be."[35]

Moving through New York and Boston, Malcolm hustled and stole, using his street wisdom to survive. This eventually landed him in prison, with time to think. It is in this context, confined to a prison cell while serving a ten-year sentence, that Malcolm's conversion to the Nation of Islam begins. Malcolm was not a stranger to religion; his father was a minister, and his mother was involved with the Seventh Day Adventists when he was young. In addition, his brother Philbert, who belonged to a holiness church in Detroit, tried to enliven religious yearnings in Malcolm. Yet, while familiar with the beliefs and practices of Christianity, Malcolm found them less than appealing. It was not until Malcolm began studying history under the tutelage of another inmate and was contacted by his brother Reginald, a Muslim, that he slowly opened to the possibility of transformation. What study offered was sensitivity to historical context, and Reginald promoted religious reality in a way that spoke to a reshaping of Malcolm's immediate, physical surroundings: "Malcolm, don't eat any more pork, and don't smoke any more cigarettes. I'll show you how to get out of prison."[36] Not fully understanding why, Malcolm followed his brother's instructions, only to learn later that in so doing his "first pre-Islamic submission had been manifested."[37] Over the course of time, Reginald shared additional information with Malcolm, all revolving around "knowledge of self," all leading to a central question: Malcolm, who are you? There was no flash of light, no disembodied voice calling for repentance, Malcolm simply thought as well as analyzed the Nation's teachings in light of the terror faced during his life, his inner need for meaning, and a desire for a strong identity forged early in life.

In prison, Malcolm had no access to the historical manifestations of religion described in chapter 5—no mosque to attend, no access to proper attire by which to distinguish himself, limited use of the Nation's literature, and so on. However, what he had was a yearning for more—more meaning from life, a new consciousness not premised on inferiority. He had always had a feeling that his proscribed status in the world was not who he really was, and this is why he had fought existing social arrangements, albeit in unproductive ways. But when introduced to the Nation of Islam, Malcolm had an experience, a "setting right," so to speak, of which he remarked: "I was going through the hardest thing, also the greatest thing, for any human being to do; to accept that which is already within you, and around you."[38] The consequences were profound: "I," he wrote, "found Allah and the religion of Islam and it completely transformed my life."[39]

There are lessons to learn from these various conversion accounts. Malcolm's conversion as well as the others discussed earlier hint at an underlying motivation for experience of religion, what I started this chapter by calling the impulse toward complex subjectivity. In the remainder of this chapter, I move from examples or "tellings" of religious experience to a theoretical analysis of the nonmaterial reality undergirding this experience.[40]

Conversion and the Nature of Religion

Despite available resources suggesting a plethora of religious forms within black communities, much of what has passed as the study of black religion has been hopelessly biased toward Christian sensibilities and themes, if not the Black Church. Joseph Washington's proclamation made several decades ago still echoes in many contemporary discussions. He writes: "In the beginning was the black church, and the black church was with the black community, and the black church was the black community. The black church was in the beginning with the black people; all things were made through the black church, and without the black church was not anything made that was made. In the black church was life, and the life was the light of the black people. The black church still shines in the darkness, and the darkness has not overcome it."[41]

Based on this assumption, much of the work done under the banner of black religious studies has been apologetic, theoretically framed by a commitment to the Christian faith as the ground of black religious being. At times, black religious studies has made concessions to "non-Christian" realities, yet its conversation effectively excludes these realities as anything more than elements external to the true focus of black religious experience—the Christian faith. Recent work by archaeologists, for example, which affirms black religious diversity, should make it difficult to maintain this position with any integrity. In short, what we are learning about the religious life of enslaved Africans, combined with contemporary and overt appreciation for "non-Christian" forms of religious experience, serves as a challenge to narrow depictions of black religious experience and identity by suggesting a variety of ways in which blacks have reshaped existential circumstances and developed new ways of participating in the world.

What is more harrowing than the myopic depiction of black religion as synonymous with the Black Church tradition, from my perspective, is the manner in which black religion is often discussed as extracultural and involving a prelanguage reality that has privileged status and is therefore not open to hard questioning. One gets this perspective from those who argue against a functional definition of religion. Harold Trulear, for example, argues against the tendency in sociology to talk in terms of black religion as antiracism programming.[42] By so doing, he writes, "sociological theory has sentenced black religion in general and the black church in particular to appear in the sociological literature merely in terms of what they do, that is, how they function, without careful attention given to what they are—the nature and character of black religion itself."[43] There are epistemological implications to this. What is the basis of the Church's thought, and how do we come to know this focus? Trulear's concern seems in keeping with the danger Mircea Eliade saw in functionalist perspectives that are unauthentic vis-à-vis a failure to recognize the essence of religion as a transhistorical "Sacred."[44] Like some in the history of religions, Trulear pushes beyond historical considerations and frames black religion in terms of the *Mysterium Tremendum*, which, unlike the material stuff of religion, is not a product of human creativity's reworking of normal objects of experience. Black religion becomes reducible to something outside humanity, defined in terms of notions of transcendence and the transcendent. Peter Paris's *Social Teachings of the Black Church*, a landmark text of social ethics, points toward this perspective and provides a mild affirmation of the *Mysterium*

Tremendum paradigm through the central position given to the idea of the "Sacred" as radical "Other" in relationship to humanity.[45] Early in the text, Paris writes: "Nothing more important can be said of the black churches than that they represent the historical embodiment of a universally significant principle. That alone—an anthropological principle grounded in the biblical understanding of the nature of humanity and its relation to God—constitutes their uniqueness in American religious history."[46]

The real danger of this position is simple: it has an assumed degree of religious certainty that is troubling. And, in agreement with Cornel West, such certainty easily leads to dogmaticism that is counterproductive. It does not allow for doubt and fluidity of perspective and position—considering these dangerously close to nihilism. I believe this is the consequence of a tendency in black religious studies to think of the most important element of knowledge as grounded in faith, based in metaphysical and transcendent claims.[47] This approach does not provide a language for contingencies; metaphysical reality makes all things theologically certain, and human agency can only be taken so far. Such a dogmaticism premised on theological certainty retards human potential and limits the range of ways in which subjectivity can be expressed. I agree that religion, black religion in this case, must be understood in expansive terms that give it a depth beyond simplistic formulations. Yet even this deeper level is connected to human reality and open to investigation and interpretation. Experience remains key. Religious consciousness is tied to historical processes and thus to a wrestling with the past and present in the construction of a future hoped to be different in tone and texture. The rituals of reference stir a sense of dread, which is responded to, in one way, through religion. Religion, then, stems from the terror of losing oneself, of having one's very being stripped away. One becomes an object, an object of historical development meant for manipulation: "Look, a Negro!" Here the *Mysterium Tremendum*, if this terminology is used, relates to a suspicion of ontological nothingness—not an encounter with something great in a positive sense, but resistance to an ontological and existential slide into irrelevance. One does not feel oneself drawn to this "less than" as a matter of desire; the dread stems from the sense of helplessness to avoid it, to stop one's descent.

Black Religion as Quest
for Complex Subjectivity

Again, black religion at its core is the quest for complex subjectivity, a desire or feeling for more life meaning. In other words, black religion's basic structure entails a push or desire for "fullness." And this central concern for subjectivity that is black religion is not limited to a particular tradition. Therefore, this basic structure or primary impulse accounts for the black Christians' talk of connection to the image of God in ways that subvert racist or sexist depictions of blacks as inferior beings. It accounts both for the Nation of Islam's proclamation of the black person as "god" and for the recognition of the human's connection to divine powers found in traditions such as voodoo. In this way, complex subjectivity stands for a healthy self-concept that allows for—even requires—adherence to the privileges and responsibilities associated with those who shape history. It is, then, the creative struggle in history for increased agency, for a fullness of life. Religious experience hence entails a human response to a crisis of identity, and it is the crisis of identity that constitutes the dilemma of ultimacy and meaning. In some ways, this may be described as a form of mystical experience, a type of transforming experience that speaks to a deeper reality, guided perhaps by a form of esoteric knowledge. Nonetheless, I argue that even this depiction of black religion—often presented in terms of hidden symbols and obscure signs—ultimately points back to this yearning for complex subjectivity. And it is conditioned by culture and thereby related to history, although as the opponent of oppressive historical developments. Robert Birt, quoted earlier, speaks of consciousness and social realities in ways that shadow my understanding of religion. What I see as the inner impulse and its manifestations is similar to what Birt describes as consciousness and social realities as dependent realities. That is why, according to Birt, "there can be no social liberation without a liberating consciousness."[48]

Conceiving of religion in this way raises epistemological issues I would like to briefly address. What I outlined in chapters 4 and 5 entails a historically and culturally determined reality that is known through sociopolitical, economic, and cultural structures and practices. Yet this is only one dimension of black religion, and if this were the end, one might think black religion could not exist without the process of dehumanization. But there is a deeper, elemental impulse, an inner stirring, that informs and shapes religion as practice and historical structure. This impulse is known or understood in part through historical manifestation, but it is also presented as a "feeling" that informs or substantiates wrestling with history. This feeling, which underlies institutional and doctrinal manifestations of religion, is a creative impulse that would be present regardless of historical circumstances because the human makeup allows for continual transformation. Religion would persist regardless of historical circumstances, to borrow a statement from Eliade, because humans "thirst for being" and any number of things beyond white supremacy could provide context for the satisfying of this thirst and the celebration of consequential growth.[49]

Experiencing Religion

How should those involved in the study of black religion make sense of this quest and its ramifications? Void of interpretation, religious experiences such as conversion are little more than psychological moans and groans that, in biblical language, "cannot be uttered" with efficacious intonation. In this sense, to play on Wayne Proudfoot's argument, religious experience cannot be known unless it can be interpreted, and it cannot be interpreted unless there are real connections to a social context and practices that have formative consequences for the meaning of the experience.[50] Here is that troublesome word, *experience*. But what does it mean? What is experience? Better yet, what is religious experience or conversion experience? One might say that a religious experience is any encounter that the person involved considers religious. I think there is something to this in that the person's history and description of the encounter is important information for scholars of religion, but it can lack a necessary critical component if it handcuffs the scholar by requiring that the scholar's remarks be approved by the convert. While members of a given religious community should see themselves and their religious worldview expressed in any description of a conversion or religious practice, it is unnecessary and potentially damaging to limit critical analysis to comments members of that community find acceptable on an explanatory level.[51] Still others might argue that religious experience is that which cannot be reduced to natural occurrences or explanation because it entails an encounter with the sacred.[52] Taking a chance on being labeled reductionist, I have already rejected such a definition through my argument for religion as determined by social and cultural environments and developments.

While it is unlikely that I can suggest a definition for religious experience that will satisfy most, I would like to define religious experience, in the context of black America, as *the recognition of and response to the elemental feeling for complex subjectivity and the accompanying transformation of consciousness that allows for the historically manifest battle against the terror of fixed identity.* While this experience may not result in sustained sociopolitical and cultural transformation, it does involve a new life meaning that encourages continued struggle for a more liberated existence. This process is not limited to the individual but also entails community; new consciousness and struggle for liberation from fixed identity require connection to and work with like-minded people. Any serious attention to manifestations of religion clearly demonstrates that religious experience at its best is manifest in liberative practices and beliefs on the communal level. However, this elemental feeling and new consciousness can be interpreted and acted on in a variety of ways, some less progressive than others. In all cases, converts in community understand themselves to be working toward liberation, but the outcomes of this effort do not always manifest this attitude. For example, during the early years of the Black Church, both accommodationist and more radical approaches were espoused by those committed to the welfare of blacks, but with differing results. And it is only in recent years that black religious organizations have given any attention to the issue of homophobia. Clearly, the liberative potential of religion manifest in history exists under the shadow of interpretation. That is to say, the importance of various manifestations also says something concerning the interpreter and his or her sensibilities and agenda. What we have here is the dilemma between experiencing religion and explaining religion. Like Wayne Proudfoot and Ann Taves, I want to keep these two in creative tension.[53]

The argument made so far would suggest that history is not ignored in religious experience but, rather, is fought, wrestled in ways that promote new possibilities of being. Hence, turning once again to conversion experience, according to psychologist of religion Edward Wimberly, there is a basic structure attested to by slaves and postslavery blacks that "precipitated a radical turnaround in thinking and behavior which became nurtured and acted out in Christian community." Although discussed by Wimberly in terms of the Judeo-Christian tradition, the work of religious experience outlined is certainly relevant to other traditions present in black communities. Religious experience within any number of black traditions entails meaning that comes "as a result of reshaping the past according to present experiences."[54] Think back to chapter 5. This "radical turnabout" is certainly in keeping with the attitude of the Nation of Islam with respect to the productive life new converts undertake. But something must initiate or inspire this process; the catalyst for this religious experience is the impulse or feeling I spent the first portion of this chapter describing. I believe this impulse is present at least in soft tones in each person and that a particular arrangement of historical circumstances experienced in a particular way sensitizes some to this feeling in ways others do not encounter. While I want to clearly state that this religious experience can lead to involvement in a variety of traditions, some less well known and of questionable status within the study of religion and popular opinion (such as humanism), I want to hold in tension as a real possibility the "nonreligious" person. At this stage of my study, I propose that not every person can speak of a religious experience, a recognition of and response out of the inner impulse. People may be able to outline the inspired embrace of a particular political platform, economic system and philosophy, or cultural formation, and these may be said to constitute life-changing experiences. However, they alone do not constitute the transformation of total being, the constitution of a new consciousness that sparks new meanings of life that are endemic to religion as feeling for complex subjectivity and to religion as historical manifestation of this feeling in the form of institutions, doctrines, and practices.

Why Is This Religion?

Even if the presence of this impulse is acknowledged, why consider it religion? This impulse and its manifestations constitute black religion because of the goal associated with this quest and its manifestations. Sociopolitical and psychological health are only two of the dimensions of this commitment and the space in which this "wholeness" develops. There is also an element that is not definable in those terms, a component that is not fully understood. It is this continual unfolding that pushes this beyond the level of philosophy or mere community activism. It entails a recognition of deeper levels of being reflected in sociopolitical circumstances but is not fully captured through these circumstances. That is to say, as Charles Long has argued, it is not defined and limited to the liberal tradition and democratic principles that consume religion as institutions and doctrine as well as the work of sociopolitical and economic organizations and activism. This impulse is larger, more expansive, and it addresses the very meaning of our existence in ways that tie or bind together historical struggles. Hence, it involves more than just a correction of material inequality, more than political struggle, because it is concerned with the very meaning of existence.

Such must be the case because, turning again to Long, the creation of the negro as a project of modernity entailed a "second creation," a new mode of restricted meaning extending beyond socioeconomic abuse that cannot be fully corrected for through aggressive measures to promote equality of socioeconomic and political opportunity. In Long's words: "The locus for this structure is the mythic consciousness which dehistoricizes the relationship for the sake of creating a new form of humanity—a form of humanity that is no longer based on the master-slave dialectic. The utopian and eschatological dimensions of the religions of the oppressed is the negation of the image of the oppressor and the discovery of the first creation. It is thus the negation that is found in community and seeks its expression in more authentic forms of community, those forms of community which are based upon the first creation, the original authenticity of all persons which precedes the master-slave dichotomy."[55] Long continues: "The problem of identity for colonized and neocolonized societies is the same issue of consciousness, but it is not simply an attempt to create a new consciousness among the oppressed but a new form of human consciousness and thus a new historical community."[56]

The problem is deeper, and the feeling or impulse defining religion's elemental nature addresses this ontological terror by pushing for, in Long's words, "the original authenticity," or what I refer to as subjectivity premised upon agency and defined by a new consciousness.[57] This impulse, a type of deep stirring that I am defining as the elemental nature of black religion, is the framework for a world system, a new way of conceiving of the wholeness of being that cannot be contained in schemes of meaning premised merely upon the acquisition of rights as payment for the historical workings of white supremacy. A new world system, of course, has implications for any and all who are willing to fall under its sway; in this sense, it has the potential to involve a new way of being, a new mode of meaning that affects more than those with black skin. I believe this is what Charles Long had in mind when writing these words: "Human intercourse with the world of sacred realities is, hermeneutically speaking, one way, and probably the most profound way of meeting and greeting our brothers and sisters who form and have formed our species for these several millennia. . . . The visibility of the black community in America is our opening to a wider humanity, historically and contemporaneously."[58]

Black religion, then, is not a transhistorical mode of reality but, rather, a creative and bold wrestling with history in order to place black bodies in healthier spaces, with a greater range of possibilities. What are the implications of this statement? For example, does it mean the gods and their stories are illusions, figments of our imagination? No. The language used by the oppressed in developing their stories has a materiality of its own that renders the gods true. In pragmatic terms, *they are real and present to believers*; this gives them a validity that I am not motivated to question in this book. However, drawing from the work of historians of religions, I argue that gods are mythic—as opposed to fictitious—figures whose stories and rites explain something about the core feelings revolving around subjectivity and provide examples of how to extend agency in beneficial (and sometimes harmful) ways. Hence, gods, spirits, and the like that inhabit religious doctrine and stories model ways of being in the world, modalities from which members of a given tradition are able to draw in developing their own consciousness.[59] This is why black Christians talk in terms of being followers of Christ and why members of the Nation of Islam discipline themselves to embrace the model of agency presented by the Honorable Elijah Muhammad, the Christ figure for the modern age. It is why being the "son" or "daughter" of a particular *orisha* or god says something about the characteristics or talents of practitioners of Santería. Accordingly, the gods and other divine beings, through their actions and words, point to modes of consciousness that imply *more*—more possibilities, more complexity, more vitality. This is metaphorically presented in song lyrics of old, such as "I know I've been changed; God in heaven done changed my name."

8

FINDING THE CENTER

Methodological Issues Considered

As demonstrated previously, an understanding of religion as historical liberation does not entirely capture the elemental nature of
black religion. Rather, a common root impulse—a yearning or feeling for a new and complex subjectivity—forms religion in history.
Attention to this particular theory of religion is important for the
selection of sources and resources used to study religion, but theory
alone does not constitute such a study. A method, a process, a strategy is needed. This theory of black religion as impulse or feeling for
complex subjectivity cannot be adequately addressed through the
methodology presented in chapter 6 because that method is best
equipped to interpret historical materials. Another method is necessary, if articulating religion's center is the goal.

Psychology of Religion and Centering

Using William James's *The Varieties of Religious Experience* as a
starting point, I begin by applying psychology of religion to the conversion experience, discussed in the previous chapter. Keep in mind

that James's work is at least familiar within, if not a major source for, black religious studies.[1] For example, the scholar whose work had a major impact on the development of W. E. B. DuBois must have had some influence on the philosophical sensibilities, and by extension the study of black life, DuBois inspired.[2] Although a bit too centered on the individual for my concern with corporate corruption and group oppression, James's pragmatic sensibilities, crudely reduced to the "cash value of ideas" in many cases, works with the existential concerns and the experiential basis of truth found in much black religious studies scholarship. Furthermore, Cornel West's work on pragmatism, which includes DuBois, and James to a lesser degree, gives further credence to philosophical inquiry's ability to address challenging social ills. As West notes, pragmatism gives philosophy done in America a "political and moral side."[3]

According to James in chapters 9 and 10 of *The Varieties of Religious Experience*, conversion entails the experience by which the "self" is made whole. Psychological health is intact; life has meaning. Such a wholeness resembles what I have referred to as meaningful existence premised on a liberative consciousness, through which new possibilities of fruitful agency are made real because the feeling or aching for more humanity is no longer superseded by the terror of dehumanization. Through conversion, then, blacks begin to act out of their own consciousness. To make use of modified Jamesian language and a crude construction of his psychological categories, through conversion—whether quick or the result of a long process—blacks no longer simply wonder if they are more than objects of history. A recognition that they are much more than this becomes the "real self," the center of consciousness.

Although the ghosts of dehumanization may not be completely removed, they become peripheral to the center of consciousness—or what some might refer to as the soul, the core from which meaning and behavior emerge.[4] In this respect, conversion fosters a blooming of consciousness whereby new modalities of being are recognized and made real, through what James calls the "habitual centre of personal energy." Whether described in mystical terms or as a response to historical events, conversion entails the framing of a yearning for complex subjectivity as dominating one's consciousness and energy. And this is played out in a new sense of being and a vibrant system of ethics.[5] I suggest once again that this experience is grounded in consideration of an historical predicament—in its full array of problems and prospects—although developments resulting from conversion may have an initial tone of transcendental dealings. At its worst, conversion might involve a theodicy by which converts reflect on their American heritage in ways that simply muddy important issues of responsibility, accountability, and power regarding what has happened during any number of horrific historical moments.

Redemptive suffering theodicy, the idea that collective moral evil has benefit for the sufferers either as justified punishment or as pedagogical moment, is an example.[6] In such instances, conversion can involve mutation of religious feeling into regressive sentimentalism that reinforces myopic modes of being and doing. Those who theologically frame their conversion in these terms might be prone to "otherworldly" and "deradicalized" modes of religious expression, as critiqued by scholars such as Gayraud Wilmore.[7] But at its best, conversion entails forming and acting out a creative set of values that promote and demand behaviors stemming from a strong regard for humanity and human dignity. Conversion, in this case, is an initial step toward humanity reconstituted, a loud and strong "yes!" to transformation—to the flexible reorganization of psychic, social, economic, cultural, political, geographic, and intellectual space. Writer Beverly Hall Lawrence speaks to this point when reflecting on reasons her generation (the black baby boomers) is returning to the Black Church. "Now that we're nearing middle age and are raising families," she writes, "[baby] boomers are beginning to contemplate the meaning of life. We are returning, therefore, in part, because religion can provide a framework for basic questions regarding the origin, purpose, and meaning of life."[8] Another example given in Lawrence's book is worth presenting before moving on. Although well educated and relatively successful, Pam Shaw experienced existential angst. Reflecting on Shaw's situation, Lawrence remarks:

The longing not to be "nothing" is among the sharpest hungers
a human can know. It is not unlike the heart stab one feels in
seeing one's own reflection fade from a lover's eye. But at times,
even with those we know only casually—or not at all—this
hunger not to be nothing can be just as crippling. To be denied
a name or anything distinguishing is among the most dehumanizing of conditions—the death of the ego. It is a common
tool of torturers of prisoners during war and of slavers in robbing the spirit of their captives. The need to be special, to stand
out, is an urge we all feel. . . . Most of us will mercifully never
know loss of personhood in the extreme, but what of the many
subtle ways in which each day we can be denied? The hunger
gnawing at Pam Shaw by the mid-1980s brought her to her
knees in Bethel African Methodist Episcopal Church. Foremost among her pleas: "I am somebody! . . . aren't I?"[9]

If one perceives a sense of ontological and psychological defiance
in William James's work, it is squarely lodged in a preoccupation with
individuals and the importance of individuality. But there is more to
the impulse that gives rise to consciousness and defiance. One also
must take into consideration communal intercedents and historical
situations for the feeling of religion. For the purposes of this book, the
psychology of conversion offered by James must be supplemented by
a recognition of the African's presence and its ramifications for North
America. For this, I turn to work in the psychology of black religion,
particularly a modified presentation of Edward Wimberly's thought
because he is able to blend religious concern with the individual psyche and communal integration.[10] According to a text coauthored with
Anne Streaty Wimberly, titled *Liberation and Human Wholeness: The
Conversion Experiences of Black People in Slavery and Freedom*, conversion experiences have a "holistic function of facilitating growth,"
which allow beleaguered blacks to transcend fixed forms of identity
and develop more complex modalities of lived meaning as both individuals and members of community.[11] Through this process, perceptions of what is real are suspended through contact with a "greater"

reality, often discussed in terms of a transcendent being. While having a mystical component, this conversion process is also wed to historical reality; it provides a space in which the convert is able to reflect upon and critique socioeconomic and political conditions as a basis for developing a new consciousness. Social context can be briefly suspended through an appeal to mystical unions and visions, but it can never be escaped—nor should it. Even the meanings of mystical experience and visions are socially driven and culturally defined; metaphors, signs, and symbols are less than useful without interpretation in light of history and the language of history.[12]

Psychology of Religion and the Hermeneutic of Inner Meaning

Although brief, my presentation of the psychology of religious conversion as done by James and the Wimberlys helps to highlight promising points on the methodological front and promotes attention to the hermeneutical value of modalities of reality that are not confined to the formal structures we are most comfortable with, those we can touch and handle. Put differently, the work of figures like the Wimberlys allows for a method of study sensitive to the "shakeup in customary patterns of consciousness . . . [that] resulted from experiences coming from sources that were extrasensory, transpersonal, transcendent, and supernatural."[13] And while the language of transcendence is not my preferred terminology, it does point to the presence of "something" that influences historical perceptions but is not consumed by these historical developments, similar to the impulse, yearning, or feeling discussed in chapter 7. This, by extension, affords an opportunity to examine black religious reality for both its inner workings and its external structures, which in turn allows conversion accounts, through what amounts to an hermeneutic of inner meaning, to be examined for what they say about the inner urges that inform practice, as opposed to simply concentrating on the socioeconomic and political consequences of these inner urges. This hermeneutic of inner meaning promoted by James and the Wimberlys can be further described as an interpretation focused on cutting through layers of historical modalities to the core of experience. It entails an examination of events, activities, and other realities in light of a nagging question: what is underneath this happening? Through this mode of interpretation, we are pushed to dig into experience and expose, as best we can, the presence of an elemental impulse. The Wimberlys refer to this impulse as the "need" underlying and informing religious experiences.[14] A useful shift occurs here, a move to explore the religious context of blacks in terms of their experience of inner meaning as opposed to simply describing religious institutions and doctrines that stem from this experience of encounter.

This hermeneutic of inner meaning operating in psychology of religion resists a reduction of religion to the historical manifestations presented in chapters 4 and 5. Such resistance, in turn, fosters attention to the meaning of events as opposed to concern only with how religious reality plays existentially. The Wimberlys' comments concerning the feelings that lead to conversion within the slave and ex-slave accounts make my point. They too believe that modes of interpretation are needed that penetrate to the depths of the feeling marking religious life, while being cognizant of the origin of these feelings outside "social expectations," because "genuine conversion goes beyond social expectations."[15] This is not a flight from history but, rather, is a wrestling through historical arrangements and structures in search of an elemental form of religion, best described not as esoteric knowledge and mystery—for religious realities limited to a few are not the essential nature of religion—but as a core impulse or feeling for complex subjectivity that informs black religious institutions and doctrines of all types. At stake in this type of investigation is religion's referent.

History of Religions and the Hermeneutic of the Ontological Dimension

The Wimberlys' psychology of religious conversion, and James's to a lesser degree, provide useful questions: What are the inner struggles involved in the process of conversion? How does the individual's feeling of need manifest in conversion relate to communal sensibilities and relationships? In this way, their psychology of religion offers hermeneutical sensibilities important for the type of study I have proposed. Yet I suggest that the Wimberlys' hermeneutic of inner meaning be supplemented by Charles Long's approach so as to balance the Christian assumptions that inform the Wimberlys' hermeneutic with Long's comparative sensibilities that oppose reliance on narrow theological concepts.[16] A Christian apologetics lurking in the work of the Wimberlys is corrected, to our advantage, by the more critical engagement of religion expressed in Long's work. Hence, while the Wimberlys speak in terms of encounter with the Christian God drawn from Christian narratives, and of what is a rather impotent theodicy, Long speaks in terms of a more general encounter with the "sacred." As we shall see, such a move gets us conceptually and methodologically closer to recognition of the impulse or feeling for complex subjectivity.

Here we turn to an explication of Long's hermeneutic of the ontological dimension. This approach works from the presupposition that the sacred—the referent for religion—is manifest in the context of history and gives depth to all modalities of human consciousness and experience. Therefore, resources for the "study of religion as religion" are found embedded in cultural production and the natural environment encountered during the course of human life. It is because of these natural and historically bound objects that "sacred reality" is kept from being "merely the fantastic and the bizarre."[17] These objects and the ability of language to somewhat grasp these realities allow the elemental meaning of religion to be discussed as a type of clarification, an ordering of social structures and realities or means for monitoring human experience. The hermeneutic of the ontological dimension interprets the social as experience and expression to promote clearer vision regarding the issues of meaning and purpose that plague humans.

In short, a better understanding of self, or a richer self-consciousness, in relationship to communal realities emerges. Recognizing that the organization or structure of social reality is, in fact, an effort to communicate certain underlying impulses, this hermeneutic probes cultural structures for what they say about their source.[18] And this information, in turn, helps us to live fuller lives through a critical engagement with the world, because it involves "a return to the roots of human perception and reflection undertaken so that we might grasp anew and reexamine the fundamental bases of the human presence."[19] Such a move requires that this hermeneutic hold in tension the "positionality" of humans in relationship to the structures, ideas, and practices interpreted. The odd thing about history, however, is that it entails a contradiction: it represents the recording of things, but at the same time it amounts to a type of forgetfulness. Thus, a hermeneutic of the ontological dimension helps sensitize us to that which through history we often ignore. For our purposes, this means a movement beyond the obvious structures of life—churches, sporting events, and so forth—to the elemental structure, the impulse, motivating us to seek greater consciousness and more meaning through various modes of lived "architecture." It is an act of *re*-membering, a rooting of structures and practices in a more central "something," acknowledging all the while that interpretive work entails coming to grips with "one's being . . . mirrored in the reality of life and history and simultaneously created in the moment of interpretation."[20]

Charles Long's sensibilities allow for fine-tuning the methodological questions proposed by the Wimberlys. So, for example, rather than asking about the inner struggles manifest in the process of conversion, we ask, how does the language of conversion speak to inner and elemental modes of reality and meaning? When the Wimberlys' work and Long's approach are combined, we are able to better ascertain how religion should be discussed in terms of inner and less easily discernible encounters with an elemental impulse. Why such discernment is vital stems from the way it holds this inner "something" in tension with historical structures and activities. Such a step is an important methodological development because it explores consciousness and historical action in terms of an underlying genius, the prevalent feeling or impulse as genesis of the black liberation struggle broadly conceived. Other approaches to the study of black religion, such as the hermeneutic of suspicion or the hermeneutic of liberation, are sensitive to historical action. However, they are not as committed to investigation of this genius in terms that extend beyond the existential and doctrinal: the Black Church holds as a primary theological principle the equality of all humanity, or the Nation of Islam provides a theology of status that promotes blacks to think of themselves as special and capable of socioeconomic and religious autonomy from whites. While useful to some extent, these more popular approaches, and the assertions involved, leave unaddressed the questions that are primary for a method combining the best of the Wimberlys' work and Long's analysis: What is the genesis of doctrinal assertions? What is the elemental genius of black religion? What is *religious* about black religion?

Art History and the Meaning of Things

As I hope is obvious at this point, I find methodologically appealing the push toward the center of religion offered by history of religions and psychology of religion—presented here as a type of digging into the tender core impulse that shapes what we encounter or forge in history. However, I think the blending of their hermeneutical sensibilities with a continuation of attention to the arts is even more promising. In chapter 6, I promoted the arts, particularly the decorative and visual arts, for the way they present the movement toward liberation that marks institutional and doctrinal religious developments. This is because, as also noted in that chapter, through art blacks find themselves as they are and as they wish to be. In order to properly understand this role of the arts, I argued for a hermeneutic of style. Although useful in the study of religion as historical manifestation, this particular method is of little use for understanding the central impulse that informs religion so conceived. Historical context is significant here because, as art historians remind us, much art prior to the twentieth century is an attempt to represent the world in convincing ways, to provide the pictorial equivalents of objects of the world. However, with the development of cinematography, representation was to some extent perfected with respect to technique and form. As a result, it is no longer necessary for the art world to concentrate so intensely on faithful representation of historical perceptions. The changing function raised an ontological question played out and fought over through various art movements: what is art?[21]

Early North American society contained people with little awareness of major works of art and trends in artistic production.[22] This is not to suggest that they were devoid of artistic sensibilities and that their environment lacked visual interest. But when produced, much North American art was concerned with depicting popular values and attitudes. Art as revolutionary act was not the norm; rather, direct and precise depictions of commonly held beliefs and truths were the standard, and depiction of nature was viewed as a way to increase sensitivity to the richness of life. Art was "good," so to speak, if it was easily recognized and interpreted by viewers and thereby could serve as a pedagogical device not requiring much formal education. Museums that begin to emerge during the late nineteenth century, governmental buildings, and public spaces gave place to artistic renditions of national themes, values, and attributes.[23] Art was "bad" if it was too complex and obscure. However, this would change.

The stage was set for rethinking the form and content of art during the Great Depression of the 1930s, when, according to art critic Barbara Rose, the Federal Art Project sponsored by the government to keep artists creating changed the artistic taste of the country because "by making no formal distinction between abstract and representational art, the Project helped to make abstract art respectable." This effect carried over to the 1940s.[24] Abstract expressionism emerged during the 1940s, resulting in a shift in the art world's center from Paris to New York City. As developed in the work of Jackson Pollock (1912–1956), its technique rejected standard use of traditional tools and approaches combining surrealism and a philosophy of transcendental reality. This mode of painting was at times called "action painting" because of the style utilized by Jackson Pollock, marked as it was by an aggressive "takeover" of the canvas. Referring to his work in abstract expressionism, Pollock said: "My painting does not come from the easel. I hardly ever stretch my canvas before painting. I prefer to tack the unstretched canvas on the hard wall or floor. I need the resistance of a hard surface. On the floor I feel more at ease. I feel nearer, more part of the painting, since this way I can walk around it, work from the four sides and literally be in the painting. This is akin to the Indian sand painters of the West. I continue to get further away from the usual painter's tools such as easel, palette, brushes, etc. I prefer sticks, trowels, knives and dripping fluid paint. . . . I have no fears about making changes, destroying the image, etc., because the painting has a life of its own. I try to let it come through."[25]

For Pollock, the inner reality—the hidden consciousness—was most important—in fact, it was the only reality—and it is this sole real-ness that is present in abstract expressionism. Material reality remained vital—Pollock did use canvas and paints—while the hidden layers of consciousness expressed through new applications of these materials remained central. It was this theory of nonmaterial reality that allowed critics such as Harold Rosenberg to describe abstract expressionism as a "conversion phenomenon" or a type of "religious movement."[26] Pollock's working philosophy also seems informed by the rugged individualism that marked much of the United States's ideological history from the cultivation of the frontiers moving forward into Pollock's own historical context. While the general idea of something real underneath the work of art is useful for my project here, the manner in which for Pollock social or communal developments and demands are often ignored in favor of the individual does not allow for an embrace of both historical reality and inner meaning necessary for the study of religion as I propose it. This is not to say that abstract expressionism must be defined in terms of social isolation. But even when the social and historical are considered, it is usually in terms of individual personality. Like the psychology of conversion drawn from William James, abstract expressionism's sensibilities and methodological contribution to this project must be supplemented with sensibilities that recognize the impact of historical realities on art. For this I turn to pop art.[27]

Jackson Pollock died in a car accident in 1956, but abstract expression as a movement continued to live through other artists until roughly 1962. And like the quick pace of socioeconomic and political developments during the decade of the 1960s, the art world also experienced rapid turnover through new art movements and theories.[28] During this turbulent time, pop art developed as history and social norms were ruptured by the demands of oppressed and once-silenced communities, with cultural production trying to keep pace with changing sensibilities. What distinguished pop art from abstract expressionism is nicely presented by Andy Warhol (1928–1987), one of pop art's major figures: "The Pop Artist did images that anyone walking down Broadway could recognize in a second—comics, picnic tables, men's trousers, celebrities, shower curtains, refrigerators, Coke bottles—all the great modern things the Abstract Expressionists tried so hard not to notice at all."[29] Many within the context of the United States—typical "Joes" and "Janes," as it were—had contrived a functioning definition of art: it's that which I cannot create. But the pop artist raised questions about this test of authenticity: What makes some art high and some low? What is the use of such a distinction anyway? By encouraging viewers to see their world differently, pop art spoke to both the source and the work of transformation underlying much of my focus in this book. This new act made it difficult at best to think strictly in terms of form or content as the mark of art—content entailing "aboutness" and form as the embodiment of this content, external portrayal of something and the inner meaning of something.[30] Yes, art might be on some level a "picture of reality" in literal or abstract terms, but what do we make of a series of Brillo boxes housed in a gallery? Can art simply be a "picture of reality," or must we think in terms of both form and content? These are the sort of issues forced upon the art world and popular imagination by pop art.

Art Criticism —
Talking about Things Hidden from Sight

Artists like Warhol did not rule out the possibility of "good" and "bad" art. Pop art—using images of popular icons, food labels, and other items seen daily in many venues—signified stylistic categorizations into superior and inferior form and challenged established modes of interpretation. As Susan Sontag alleges, pop art uses "a content so blatant, so 'what it is.'"[31] Some found it almost impossible to accept pop art because it offended their sensibilities and confused the manner in which they sought to neatly categorize and arrange things. This being the case, it was much easier to dismiss pop art as a surrender to bad taste and novelty that should amount to nothing more than a scam perpetrated against the art world. By 1964, critics looked at pop art—for example, at Warhol's Brillo box or cans of soup—and saw no way of distinguishing it from grocery store products.[32] How could just anything be art? An altered photo of Marilyn Monroe might be beautiful, to the extent that she was considered attractive, but does that make it art? Answering no to this question, critics waited for these so-called artists and their work to fade away, forgetting that a similar attitude had at one point been voiced concerning the "real" art they championed. Realism had its moments with abstract expressionism, and abstract expressionism with pop art.

Warhol challenged accepted notions of art's visual markers of value in a way that merits Arthur Danto's referring to art after 1960 as "art after the end of art." This was Danto's way of capturing the philosophical shift taking place, a movement to aggressively challenge long-accepted notions of the nature and meaning of art.[33] Art, of course, continued; do not take Danto's words literally. But viewers were pushed to "look" *at it* but, more importantly, to "look" *to it* for what it reveals, and this became the pattern of exploration and criticism: content says something about form.[34] The nature of art was questioned, and the boundaries of what constitutes art were pushed. This move is expressed by Arthur Danto's explanation of Andy Warhol's seriousness, for example, as "almost otherworldly."[35] Consequently, and this is important for our discussion, the rupturing of aesthetic sensibilities enhanced the ability of artistic expression to flow more easily between form and content; and art criticism was caught up in its currents. Turning again to Andy Warhol's 1964 sculpture of the Brillo box, exhibited at the Stable Gallery in New York City, we have a fine example of the creative dilemma of content and form. The visual alone could no longer be used to judge the presence of art, because the eye could not really distinguish between Warhol's art and the Brillo boxes lining the shelves of too many grocery stores. Prices were certainly different between the two, but nothing of real visual significance distinguished them.[36] One could not approach pop art with unwavering certainty and fixed formulas: chairs were not just chairs, wine racks were not just wine racks, and so on. The chair and the wine rack, when carefully considered, reveal something underneath the literal content. Meaning had to be addressed as a mode of transfiguration, thus demonstrating an appreciation for material reality while recognizing its limitations and holding it suspect.[37] Then, perhaps in more general terms, material reality can be said to be a picture of the elemental or nonmaterial impulse discussed in chapter 7.[38] From the perspective of pop artists, any material, any substance, could be used to activate our awareness and speak about issues of inner meaning.

How does one mark the difference between the two—the material and what lurks behind it? How does one then speak to and about the underlying reality? The response of art critics to these questions is helpful in regards to my theory of black religion and an applicable method of study. I claim no expertise in art history or art criticism, and I make no pretense of being able to provide new insights into philosophical theory of art. Rather, my task is to glean material from those with such expertise and to use this information to better formulate an approach to the study of religion as conceived in this book.[39] My theory of religion requires the type of attention to both content and form that is marked to some extent by abstract expressionism and even more forcefully in pop art. Inspiring recognition and expression of this elemental feeling or impulse is a purpose

inherent in religious structures and doctrines. This is the same purpose one finds in the work of such artists as Jackson Pollock and
Andy Warhol, who challenged viewers to think beyond the concrete
presence of particular colors and shapes, to see inner reality as a
sphere of meaning lurking behind what is existentially obvious. In
this way, viewers are encouraged to look at "mundane" items in two
ways: for what they are as ordinary objects, and to also see beyond
this to what they are as works of art. The importance of this is the
question it raises: what makes something art? This query relates to
the questions underlying the development of method for the study of
religion: What makes something religiously significant? What makes
something religion? Is there more to historical structures than what
readily meets the eye?

Such questions train students of religion—in this case, black religion—to approach materials with a sensitivity to the links between
content and form, between identity and aesthetics. Nicholas Davey,
using a hermeneutic of aesthetics, raises a similar point: "Art works
do not merely reinterpret and represent subject matters but extend
and alter their being. . . . It is in the notion of subject-matter . . . [that
we gain] insight into how an art work can transcend the temporal
restrictions of its historical origin and affect the contemporary world
. . . and it can only do so if it successfully enables us to understand
that there is something more to be seen in it than what is immediately before the eyes."[40] Seeing involves more than meets the eye
because it requires recognizing the deep value of what visual realities
do not give up right away but, rather, present as opaque influences.
But the exploration is worth it because, as feminist scholar bell hooks
notes, "experiencing art can enhance our understanding of what it
means to live as free subjects in an unfree world."[41]

Art holds in tension material existence and nonmaterial impulses,
and it brings to the mind of the viewer the presence of this nonmaterial impulse in ways that influence relationships with historical
realities and materials. Turning again to Davey: "Each aesthetic revelation not only extends the map of our seeing but also, in so doing,
alters and extends our sense of self and how we understand our exis-

tential concerns and predicaments."[42] Art has the ability to affect us by drawing into the open concealed realities, possibilities, and meanings, thereby teaching us about connections between historical developments and inner urges. Or, as Hilton Als, staff writer for the *New Yorker*, remarks: "The art that affects us and attacks us with the artist's passion and dreams is something we've seen before, somewhere, if only we could place it. It's a matter of how deeply one has ever looked at one's interior world: it's been there all along."[43] Content and form, material history and elemental impulses, bleed into each other. Art so conceived points to an underlying reality, and by extension art criticism sheds light on how to discuss and explore elemental reality and its relationship to the historical material through which it is manifest.

An Interdisciplinary Venture, or Introducing Relational Centralism

Nigel Whiteley suggests that art criticism prior to the 1960s shift to pop art was concerned with authorship. The critic provided assessments, with little explanation, that were considered solid and authoritative. Criticism so conceived left room for artists to speak of their vision, but without a substantial degree of analysis or rebuttal by the critic. Circular in nature, this mode of artist-centered criticism did little to explore art in its historical context, to seek out and present various possibilities without an air of certainty. Contrary to this take on criticism, Whiteley speaks of "new art criticism" as a more aggressively interpretive process through which the critic is held responsible for deciphering and deconstructing the meaning implicit within the work, all in light of historical and social context. In moving to this mode of art criticism, one experiences a shift from judgments of visual quality as the hallmark of art criticism to a preoccupation with deconstructing the artist's attitudes, assumptions, and values.[44] In other words, it is a paradigm shift from historical material to nonmaterial impulses and meaning.

Whiteley's suspicion of "new" criticism aside, I believe it offers, when the significance of actual historical material—the visual—is not forgotten, an insightful approach to the always present interaction between material and intent. Questioning the art, so to speak, requires attention to both the visual dimensions of all art and how it signifies nonmaterial realities. Some might suggest that this criticism is a blending of anthropological, philosophical, and theological sensibilities, with perhaps a hint of Susan Sontag's erotics (or sensory appreciation) of art. But regardless of theoretical labels, what is important here is how mindfulness of both content and form allows for the exploration of connected concerns: what art is, and what it means or signifies, as well as how it is made, its history of production.[45] Those who undertake this exploration, according to Arthur Danto, are involved in art criticism because addressing content and form without segregating one from the other is not only possible but plausible, and "putting all that into words is what art criticism is."[46] This is where I part company with those who say art must be encountered quickly, taken in all at once, and digested just as quickly.[47] How can we quickly move through the layers of historical reality to sense, or perhaps have a stronger reaction to, an impulse deeply embedded in a nonmaterial reality we do not have the skills to fully capture? Weaving together content and form—and art should have both—requires a type of patient examination, a sustained looking at and looking to.

I call this methodological result of my thinking thus far *relational centralism*.[48] It is an interdisciplinary method of study—combining insights from psychology of religion's work on conversion, history of religions, and art criticism focused on abstract expressionism and pop art—through which the relationship or resemblance between modes of black religion is explored in terms of their shared referent. Relational centralism allows us to decipher patterns and layers of meaning and movement in order to help us put in perspective the past, present, and future possibilities for more fulfilled existence. This approach fosters a recognition of the deep commonality between groups—the elemental nature of all religious experience—

that links us. It may help move us toward what Charles Long refers to as "hermeneutically speaking, one way, and probably the most profound way, of meeting and greeting our brothers and sisters who form and have formed our species for these several millennia."[49] This, however, is not meant to suggest that my work includes universalizing tendencies.[50] This is not the only plausible way of addressing black religion. Rather, I am arguing for a healthy tension between the distinctive manner in which religion operates within particular historical moments and the common impulse undergirding all historical manifestations of religion. It is because of this attention to both particularity and the shared impulse that marks all humans that I refer to this approach as relational centralism.

As an approach to the study of black religion, relational centralism operates based on a set of theoretical assumptions and interpretative questions, both of which serve not only to collect and observe resources for evaluation but also to analyze these resources. The assumptions help to contextualize our study through the formation of language as a tool of interpretation as well as through promoting awareness of nuance and detail. First, utilizing this approach requires an understanding that the self, community, and the world constructed by humans all serve as resources for our study. Attention to religious institutions, doctrines, and other historically situated realities does not assume them to be insular, but they are important because they entail encounter with the manifestations of a deeper "something." Therefore, they reveal more than just a particular moment in human history and social interaction. Such a study reveals, as historians of religions might note, realities hidden from "immediate experience."[51] Second, this underlying "something" is best described as an impulse or feeling for complex subjectivity that is, through attention to its rupturing of historical situations, open to investigation. Third, one must also recognize that this feeling or impulse is the genius behind all forms of black religious practice. Fourth, relational centralism requires an assumption that better understanding this underlying impulse and how it operates will also generate better knowledge of what it means to be human in terms not restricted to race. Finally, this approach requires a realism with respect to outcome, recognizing that religion as elemental impulse cannot be fully captured by the exploratory tools available to us. While being accessible through historical realities that generate high potential for deeper understanding, it does not allow for full comprehension.

When taken together, these theoretical assumptions urge methodological humility along the lines of what Arnold Hauser says about art criticism: "Works of art . . . [are] like unattainable heights. We do not go straight towards them, but circle round them."[52] As a consequence, we must think about religion's core, the feeling for complex subjectivity, as entailing movement toward *More*, a term I use to designate a continual unfolding. Limitations of this kind are not a problem but, rather, a necessity, in part because this method seeks to clarify the nature and meaning of religion while recognizing such clarification must also mean a troubling complexity. Perhaps it is for this reason that historians of religion often talk about religion in terms of opacity and define the study of religion as an oblique process that "provides us with hints that remain too fragile to bear the burden of being solutions."[53]

With the theoretical assumptions briefly outlined, we turn to some questions that inform our interpretative process. Guided by the interdisciplinary sensibilities drawn from psychology of religion, history of religions, and art criticism, relational centralism poses questions revolving around the extraction of meaning. The first question seeks to pull away layers of history to expose the internal impulse by asking: Can the present reality be reduced to a common denominator, or does the reality point to itself as the genius of black religion? So, for example, when applied to the Black Church or to the Nation of Islam, the answer must be no because both religious organizations can be reduced to individuals who have had a certain "encounter," and this can be further reduced to a source for this encounter. When the first question is applied, it forces a move through historical developments to the source of these developments. By so doing, the importance of both the historical (or external) and the elemental impulse (or center) are considered. Or, in other words, it promotes a productive tension between what might resemble historian of religion Jonathan Z. Smith's interpretation as a "centripetal" view and "centrifugal" view by which both the center and the periphery of religious life are valued.[54]

Using this approach also requires a sensitivity to comparison as an element of interpretation. And so, the next several questions: What is to be made of the various incarnations of the elemental nature of religion? Does the arrangement of black life and its priorities point to the "texture" of this elemental yearning? Do the diverse manifestations and the context of each manifestation say something about the nature of this elemental impulse? Do similarities and differences in modalities of manifestation point to particular attributes and characteristics of this impulse? These questions appeal to the relational nature of this approach by seeking to put in better focus our understanding of what is religious about black religion through a framework of analogy. Comparison, however, in itself is far from enough in that the generalizations upon which comparison is based do not provide focused insights; some comparisons are awkward at best, based on the limits of our theoretical language. For example, to say that manifestations of religion in black contexts share a concern with worship is partially useful in that it might point to how the body figures in religious practice. Yet it shows a bias toward particular modes of religious expression insofar as talk of worship is a poor fit with communities such as the Nation of Islam. Furthermore, only an extremely loose definition of sacred text as a mode of expressing the elemental nature of religion can make it applicable for analogy between traditions such as the Black Church and traditions in black communities that are more oral in orientation (that is, Yoruba-based traditions).[55]

In any case, the comparative component of the approach I suggest here runs the risk of ranking traditions as superior and inferior based upon the categories used to undertake the analogy. Being mindful of this, relational centralism must be concerned with uncovering dimensions of religion's elemental impulse while seeking to hold in tension value judgments based on the interpreter's own cultural sensibilities and commitments. Such value judgments are useless because they assume some manifestations are better than others, when in reality no one cultural product through which the elemental nature of religion emanates is more "sacred," to use popular terminology, than another. As historians of religions have argued, manifestation of the sacred is a situational affair that is flexible and subject to change based on historical need and materials available. In this sense, religion's features are much more ordinary than extraordinary.[56]

We, in the long run, will come to discover that black religion in fundamental terms feels much more familiar than anticipated and seems much closer than we wanted to believe. Perhaps it is at this point that we recognize the making of meaning when it is most meaningful, and humanity when it is at its best.

NOTES

Preface

1. For this approach, see Anthony B. Pinn, *Varieties of African American Religious Experience* (Minneapolis: Fortress Press, 1998).

2. Willie Jennings, in his review of *Varieties of African American Religious Experience*, highlighted concerns and questions my subsequent work needed to address. See *Interpretation* 53.4 (October 1999): 436–38.

1. "Look, a Negro!" How the New World African Became an Object of History

1. Charles Long, *Significations: Signs, Symbols, and Images in the Interpretation of Religion* (Philadelphia: Fortress Press, 1986), 7.

2. See, for example, Anthony B. Pinn, *Varieties of African American Religious Experience* (Minneapolis: Fortress Press, 1998).

3. I will give attention to other traditions in two projects currently under development: *Varieties of African American Religious Experience*, vol. 2 (to be published by Fortress Press); *The Encyclopedia of African American Religious Culture* (to be published by ABC-CLIO).

4. I must stress that this presentation does not attempt a systematic and detailed history of the slave trade. In fact, historians may be bothered by my quick movement, a leaping through history of sorts, which marks this presentation. Yet, as will become clear, my goal is not the same as the historian's objective. Different research sensibilities and tactics are at play. And so, the work of historians provides the context for my work, but their questions and concerns do not define my project. Those seeking the type of statistical and more detailed analysis entailed by such a history may find this frustrating but should be comforted by the many volumes already available on this subject.

5. Although the focus is limited to the United States, readers interested in a broader analysis of race as a category should see, for example, the works of George Fredrickson. See below, nn. 16, 28, 29.

6.   Cornel West, *Prophesy Deliverance! An Afro-American Revolutionary Christianity* (Philadelphia: Westminster, 1982), 58.

7.   For a good discussion using literary modes of the idea of whiteness, see Toni Morrison, *Playing in the Dark: Whiteness and the Literary Imagination* (Cambridge: Harvard University Press, 1992).

8.   Winthrop D. Jordan, *White over Black: American Attitudes toward the Negro, 1550–1812* (Chapel Hill: University of North Carolina Press, 1968). Jordan gives the poetry of Robert Baker as an example. Regarding his travel to west Africa in 1562 and 1563, he wrote:

> And entering in [a river], we see
> a number of black soules,
> Whose likelinesse seem'd men to be,
> but all as blacke as coles.

The stanza is quoted from "The First Voyage of Robert Baker to Guinie . . . 1562," in Richard Hakluyt, *The Principall Navigations, Voiages, and Discoveries of the English Nation . . .* (London, 1589), 132.

9.   Jordan, *White over Black,* 5, 6–7.

10.   Ibid., 5.

11.   Ibid., 7–8. On the origins of color prejudice in early Christian writers, see Robert E. Hood, *Begrimed and Black: Christian Traditions on Blacks and Blackness* (Minneapolis: Fortress Press, 1994), 73–90.

12.   Jordan, *White over Black,* 22–25, 40–43.

13.   Genesis 1:25-27 kjv.

14.   Genesis 2:7-8, 18-25 kjv.

15.   It is of interest to note here that the term *creature* often used in reference to Africans in the slave trade is drawn from the biblical notion of creation. There are, according to Patricia Romero, at least two possible connotations for the term *creature*. The first was used by slave traders and others to imply the inferiority of blacks. The second use of the term is in a show of sympathy, as if to say "poor soul." See Patricia Romero, "The Slave Traders' Image of Slaves," in Vera Rubin and Arthur Tuden, eds., *Comparative Perspectives on Slavery in New World Plantation Societies,* Annals of the New York Academy of Sciences, vol. 292 (New York: New York Academy of Sciences, 1977).

16.   George M. Fredrickson, *The Black Image in the White Mind: The Debate on Afro-American Character and Destiny, 1817–1914* (New York: Harper & Row, 1971), 321. Readers will want to also consider David B. Davis, *In the Image of God: Religion, Moral Value, and Our Heritage of Slavery* (New Haven: Yale University Press, 2001).

17.   Genesis 9:20-22, 24-25 rsv.

18. Alden T. Vaughan, *New England Frontier: Puritans and Indians, 1620–1675* (Boston: Little, Brown and Company, 1965), 96.

19. Vaughan, *New England Frontier*, 186.

20. Ibid., 207.

21. There are examples of Indians and Europeans being sentenced to slavery as early as 1636, but this was not a common practice. Furthermore, slavery in these instances was punishment for crime or war. With Africans, the justification for slavery was more theological and physiological.

22. John Hope Franklin, *From Slavery to Freedom: A History of Negro Americans*, 5th ed. (New York: Knopf, 1980), 31. Sir John Hawkins is given credit for starting England's trading of Africans.

Ivan Van Sertima provides an interesting study of the African presence in the Americas prior to the slave trade. See *They Came before Columbus* (New Brunswick: Rutgers University, 1983). Also see Lerone Bennett's *They Came before the Mayflower* (Baltimore: Penguin, 1966). For studies of African civilization and its impact on world culture and civilization, see Cheikh Anta Diop, *The African Origin of Civilization: Myth or Reality*, translated by Mercer Cook (New York: L. Hill, 1974); and Martin Burnell, *Black Athena: The Afroasiatic Roots of Classical Civilization*, vols. 1–2 (New Brunswick, N.J.: Rutgers University Press, 1987).

23. Ronald Segal, *The Black Diaspora: Five Centuries of the Black Experience outside Africa* (New York: Farrar, Straus & Giroux, 1995), 22–23.

24. Franklin, *From Slavery to Freedom*, 58.

25. Ibid., 132.

26. Jordan, *White over Black*, 27.

27. Ibid., 28; George M. Fredrickson, *The Arrogance of Race: Historical Perspectives on Slavery, Racism, and Social Inequality* (Middletown, Conn.: Wesleyan University Press, 1988), 201–2.

28. George M. Fredrickson, *White Supremacy: A Comparative Study in American and South African History* (New York: Oxford University Press, 1981), 70, 73–74. Fredrickson tends to place more emphasis on religious difference as an early factor in the enslavement of Africans than do Orlando Patterson, Cornel West, and Winthrop Jordan.

29. Fredrickson, *The Arrogance of Race*, 191.

30. Franklin, *From Slavery to Freedom*, 54–55, 56–58. I limit my examples to middle and southern states because slavery in northern areas such as New England begins to decline by the late eighteenth century. Nonetheless, New England continued to play a role in supplying human cargo until importation was outlawed.

31. Jordan, *White over Black*, 82.

32. Ibid., 95.

33. Orlando Patterson, *Slavery and Social Death: A Comparative Study* (Cambridge: Harvard University Press, 1982), 11–12.

34. Fredrickson, *The Arrogance of Race*, 23. It should be noted that the arguments for slavery differed from state to state based upon the size of the black population and the degree of dependence on slave labor. So, for example, one would during this period find more aggressive defenses of slavery in South Carolina than Virginia. Nonetheless, white supremacy was the pervasive doctrine throughout the states.

35. For information on the mechanisms of capture and the rates of exportations in the slave trade, see these works: W. E. B. Dubois, *The Suppression of the African Slave-Trade to the United States of America, 1638–1870* (New York: Russell and Russell, 1965); John Hope Franklin, *From Slavery to Freedom*; Philip Curtin, *The Atlantic Slave Trade: A Census* (Madison: University of Wisconsin, 1969); Robert William Fogel, *Without Consent or Contract: The Rise and Fall of American Slavery* (New York: Norton, 1989); Stanley L. Engerman and Joseph E. Inkori, eds., *The Atlantic Slave Trade: Effects on Economies, Societies, and Peoples in Africa, the Americas, and Europe* (Durham: Duke University Press, 1992); Eugene Genovese, *The Slave Economy of the Old South: Selected Essays in Economic and Social History* (Baton Rouge: Louisiana State University Press, 1968) and *Roll, Jordan, Roll: The World the Slaves Made* (New York: Vintage, 1976).

36. Hussein Abdilahi Bulhan, *Frantz Fanon and the Psychology of Oppression* (New York: Plenum, 1985), 101.

37. According to Patterson, when viewed comparatively, slavery is an exchange of servitude for life. In *The Black Diaspora*, Ronald Segal also gives attention to this idea and the manner in which the Atlantic slave trade played into this practice. He writes:

> The Atlantic trade battened on the societies, large and small, of western-central Africa by distorting a crucial element of their functioning. In the competition of "big men" for prestige and authority, the decisive factor was the number of people they controlled, both as the measure of wealth and as the means of producing it, through procreation and labor. People, not goods, were the prize, and the goods acquired through production or trade were invested in acquiring the allegiance or dependence of more people. In kingdoms such as that of the Kongo, powerful provincial lords required correspondingly large gifts to secure their allegiance, though they might then mitigate their obligations by dispatching tribute in return. At the other extreme, those arriving as captives or as refugees from drought and famine required no further gifts for their subordination, since they were already being given their lives. (12)

38. Patterson, *Slavery and Social Death*, 21, 24–28.

39. Bulhan, *Frantz Fanon and the Psychology of Oppression*, 103.

40. Fredrickson, *The Black Image in the White Mind*, 64.

41. Abbot Emerson Smith, *Colonists in Bondage: White Servitude and Convict Labor in America, 1607–1776* (Gloucester, Mass.: Peter Smith, 1965), 234, 235. The distinction between indentured servants and black slaves presented by Ronald Segal is worth noting:

> These whites were individually bound for a stipulated period to their masters, and indentures could be sold by one master to another without the consent of the laborers concerned. The ownership of the service was not, however, the ownership of the servant. The person was not property. This was implicit both in the term of the indenture and in the nature of most indentures as voluntary contracts. [Many, however, were kidnapped or brought to the colonies under false pretenses.] In fact, as reports circulated at home about conditions in the colonies, recruitment required the concession of ever shorter terms and became increasingly difficult all the same. Black slaves had no choice. (Segal, *The Black Diaspora*, 17)

42. H. Hoetink, *Slavery and Race Relations in the Americas: Comparative Notes on Their Nature and Nexus* (New York: Harper & Row, 1973), 15.

43. Patterson, *Slavery and Social Death*, 38–48, 96–100. Even when one considers the presence of free blacks in North America, the importance of blackness as a marker of social death and justification for enslavement remains strong. One need only keep in mind that free blacks anywhere in the colonies (and later the United States) ran the risk of becoming slaves simply because of skin color. Even blacks who owned slaves were never free of the social stigma of blackness because blackness remained a justification for slavery; could never exercise fully the liberties and privileges associated with life as a white person. Furthermore, blacks' owning slaves was allowed in that it did not damage the social system because it was an implicit acceptance of existing social arrangements. In fact, it was the most powerful acceptance of the social order.

44. Fredrickson, *The Black Image in the White Mind*, 54–55.

45. Ibid., 56–57.

46. Patterson, *Slavery and Social Death*, 22.

47. Ira Berlin, Marc Favreau, and Steven F. Miller, eds., *Remembering Slavery: African Americans Talk about Their Personal Experiences of Slavery and Emancipation* (New York: New Press/Library of Congress, 1998), 15–16.

48. Segal, *The Black Diaspora*, 43.

49. If slaves did not possess something that resembled personhood but

were merely property in a strict sense, would not masters of slaves be punished for the crimes committed by slaves? Patterson, *Slavery and Social Death*, 196; Bulhan, *Frantz Fanon and the Psychology of Oppression*, 122. This tension between two given identities is found in the fact that while slaves were dehumanized, whites also depended on them for more than their labor. They were also forced to provide sexual partnership, child care, and so forth. Segal, *The Black Diaspora*, 17–18.

50. Frantz Fanon, *Black Skin, White Masks* (New York: Grove, 1967), 60.

51. Ibid., 34.

52. Concerning this point, Mary Douglas provides a helpful anthropological discussion of the body and its meaning. Chapters 6–8 of this work draw heavily on her theory of the body. See Mary Douglas, *Natural Symbols: Explorations in Cosmology* (New York: Routledge, 1996).

53. Fanon, *Black Skin, White Masks*, 116.

54. Howard Thurman, *The Luminous Darkness: A Personal Interpretation of the Anatomy of Segregation and the Ground of Hope* (Richmond, Ind.: Friends United Press, 1989), 7.

55. Alice Walker, *The Color Purple* (New York: Washington Square, 1982), 187.

56. Richard Wright, *Black Boy* (New York: Harper & Row, 1945), 66.

57. Readers interested in the problematic of image and imagery with respect to black women should see, for example, K. Sue Jewell, *From Mammy to Miss America and Beyond: Cultural Images and the Shaping of U.S. Social Policy* (New York: Routledge, 1993).

58. West, *Prophesy Deliverance!* 47.

2. "How Much for a Young Buck?" Slave Auction and Identity

1. Cornel West, *Prophesy Deliverance! An Afro-American Revolutionary Christianity* (Philadelphia: Westminster, 1982), 47.

2. I am not convinced that Herbert Klein's rationale for rethinking the nature of the Middle Passage is sufficient. For example, he gives little attention to the description of the events by Africans; although these reports are limited in number, they are important. I also wonder if statistics concerning mortality rates provide a solid basis for his argument in that statistics were often altered by captains in order to maximize profits. Yet it is important to recognize his argument. According to Klein, it is likely that attention to the Middle Passage as the primary image of dehumanization of the African stems in part from the importance placed on this event by early abolitionists, whose work influenced historical writings. It is also likely, according to Klein, that

the availability of information on the Middle Passage has also made possible the preoccupation with it in literature on slavery. See Herbert S. Klein, *The Atlantic Slave Trade* (New York: Cambridge University Press, 1999), 130–33.

3. Michael Gomez, *Exchanging Our Country Marks: The Transformation of African Identities in the Colonial and Antebellum South* (Chapel Hill: University of North Carolina Press, 1998), 13–14, 158.

4. Nathan Irvin Huggins, *Black Odyssey: The Afro-American Ordeal in Slavery* (New York: Pantheon, 1977), 27.

5. Richard Jobson, *The Golden Trade* (London, 1623), 122, as quoted in Edward Reynolds, *Stand the Storm: A History of the Atlantic Slave Trade* (New York: Allison & Busby, 1985), 28.

6. Michael Gomez notes that available materials suggest that the British colonies imported slaves from the southeastern portion of Africa in substantial numbers. According to Gomez, Elizabeth Donnan (in *Documents Illustrative of the History of the Slave Trade to America*) "makes reference to three ships from Madagascar (totaling seven hundred people) arriving in the British West Indies in 1678, and further states that during this same period the colonies of Massachusetts, New York, and Virginia were all receiving 'East African' slaves." (Gomez, *Exchanging Our Country Marks*, 29.) Patricia Romero notes that the mechanics and conditions of the slave trade in East Africa strongly resembled what emerged on the West coast. See Patricia Romero, "The Slave Traders' Images of Slaves," in Vera Rubin and Arthur Tuden, eds., *Comparative Perspectives on Slavery in New World Plantation Societies*, Annals of the New York Academy of Sciences, vol. 292 (New York: New York Academy of Sciences, 1977), 332–33.

7. Hugh Thomas, *The Slave Trade: The Story of the Atlantic Slave Trade, 1440–1870* (New York: Simon & Schuster, 1997), 155.

8. This would include persons found guilty of adultery or witchcraft. In many cases, rather than being killed, those found guilty of such crimes were sold into slavery. This is in keeping with Orlando Patterson's notion of social death versus physical death presented in chapter 1.

9. Reynolds, *Stand the Storm*, 35.

10. For information on the ships used in the slave trade see, for example, Ulrich Bonnell Phillips, *American Negro Slavery: A Survey of the Supply, Employment and Control of Negro Labor as Determined by the Plantation Regime* (New York: Appleton, 1918), 34–35; and Klein, *The Atlantic Slave Trade*, 132–60.

11. Reynolds, *Stand the Storm*, 45, 46.

12. Donnan, *Documents Illustrative of the Slave Trade to America*, I: 399, quoted in Thomas, *The Slave Trade*, 396.

13. This was an extreme moment of anxiety based on the social and cultural significance of tattoos in many areas of Africa.

14. Gustavus Vassa, *The Life of Olaudah Equiano or Gustavus Vassa, the African—Volume One* (London: n.p., 1789; London: Dawsons of Pall Mall, 1969), 79.

15. Donnan, *Documents Illustrative of the History of the Slave Trade to America*, I: 402–3, quoted in Gomez, *Exchanging Our Country Marks*, 159.

16. This is a rethinking of my earlier opinion on the significance of the Middle Passage presented in the introductory essay of my edited volume *Moral Evil and Redemptive Suffering: A History of Theodicy in African-American Religious Thought* (Gainesville: University Press of Florida, 2002).

17. Reynolds, *Stand the Storm*, 55.

18. Abbot Emerson Smith, *Colonists in Bondage: White Servitude and Convict Labor in America, 1607–1776* (Gloucester, Mass.: Peter Smith, 1965), 3–5.

19. Patricia Romero, "The Slave Traders' Images of Slaves," 333.

20. Vassa, *The Life of Olaudah Equiano*, 70–71, 77.

21. Gomez, *Exchanging Our Country Marks*, 14, 158 (italics added).

22. Vassa, *The Life of Olaudah Equiano*, 86–87, 88.

23. Phillips, *American Negro Slavery*, 187.

24. Frederick Bancroft, *Slave Trading in the Old South* (New York: Frederick Ungar, 1959), 22–23.

25. Ibid., xi, xiii. For information on the illegal slave trade, see Thomas, *The Slave Trade*, 561–785.

26. Ibid., 69. The central location for this internal trade was, until the mid-1800s, Washington, D.C., because its location made transport of slaves both by land to other areas and by sea easier to manage. Other important locations included Charleston, South Carolina, and Richmond, Virginia.

27. Ibid., 273, 271–72; Michael Tadman, *Speculators and Slaves: Masters, Traders, and Slaves in the Old South* (Madison: University of Wisconsin Press, 1989), 83–108.

28. Ibid., 282.

29. Traders made an effort to limit the stay of slaves in these jails and pens in order to keep costs of trading low and profits high.

30. Bancroft, *Slave Trading in the Old South*, image found between pp. 32 and 33.

31. George P. Rawick, ed., *The American Slave: A Composite Autobiography*, vol. 18, *Unwritten History of Slavery: Autobiographical Account of Negro Ex-slaves* (1941; reprint, Westport, Conn.: Greenwood, 1972), 45, 46–47.

32. James Mellon, ed., *Bullwhip Days: The Slaves Remember* (New York: Weidenfeld & Nicolson, 1988), 291.

33. Bancroft, *Slave Trading in the Old South*, 106–7.

34. It was not uncommon for traders to allow buyers to have a trial period with both male and female slaves who were marketed as having special skills before the final sale was made. This policy did not apply to field

hands. The quotation is from John W. Blassingame, ed., *Slave Testimony: Two Centuries of Letters, Speeches, Interviews, and Autobiographies* (Baton Rouge: Louisiana State University Press, 1977), 74.

35. For a narrative that touches on the use of slaves for sexual pleasure, see Linda Brent, *Incidents in the Life of a Slave Girl, An Authentic Historical Narrative Describing the Horrors of Slavery as Experienced by Black Women,* edited by L. Maria Child (New York: Harcourt Brace Jovanovich, 1973).

36. Mellon, ed., *Bullwhip Days,* 291.

37. Rawick, ed., *The American Slave: A Composite Autobiography,* vol. 16 "Kansas, Kentucky, Maryland, Ohio, Virginia, and Tennessee Narratives," (1941; reprint, Westport, Conn.: Greenwood, 1972), 8.

38. L. A. Chamerovzow, ed., *Slave Life in Georgia: A Narrative of the Life, Sufferings, and Escape of John Brown, A Fugitive Slave, Now in England* (London, 1855), quoted in Tadman, *Speculators and Slaves,* 98–99.

39. Tadman, *Speculators and Slaves,* 72.

40. Ibid., 294, 302.

41. Edmund L. Drago, *Broke by the War: Letters of a Slave Trader* (Columbia: University of South Carolina Press, 1991), 49.

42. Blassingame, ed., *Slave Testimony,* 96–97. Slaves who could write would draft their own letters. In other cases, they would secure the services of a white who was willing to write on their behalf.

43. Ibid., 108.

44. For information on the various figures—agents, speculators, and so forth—involved in the interstate trade as well as the mechanics of the trade see, for example, Tadman, *Speculators and Slaves,* especially ch. 7. Also see Daniel P. Mannix and Malcolm Cowley, *Black Cargoes: A History of the Atlantic Slave Trade, 1518–1865* (London: Longmans, Green, 1963).

45. Ulrich Bonnell Phillips, *American Negro Slavery* (New York: Appleton, 1918), 200, 192. This text, while useful in some ways, should be read with caution because of the often racist overtones.

46. Thomas, *The Slave Trade,* 254F, 254L.

47. Walter Johnson, *Soul by Soul: Life inside the Antebellum Slave Market* (Cambridge: Harvard University Press, 1999), 149–50.

48. Blassingame, ed., *Slave Testimony,* 185.

49. Ibid., 218.

50. Ibid., 697.

51. Ibid., 347.

52. Readers interested in this sort of manipulation of the body will find Mary Douglas's work on the body as symbol of society useful. See Mary Douglas, *Purity and Danger: An Analysis of the Concepts of Pollution and Taboo* (New York: Ark, 1966); and Mary Douglas, *Natural Symbols: Explorations in Cosmology* (New York: Routledge, 1996).

53. Blassingame, ed., *Slave Testimony,* 138.

54. Leslie Howard Owens, *This Species of Property: Slave Life and Culture in the Old South* (New York: Oxford University Press, 1976), 183–85.

55. Saidiya V. Hartman, *Scenes of Subjection: Terror, Slavery, and Self-Making in Nineteenth Century America* (New York: Oxford University Press, 1997), 38.

56. Ibid., 25.

3. Rope Neckties: Lynching and Identity

A slightly modified version of this chapter will be published as "Rope Neckties and Lynchings: A Discussion of Terror as an Impetus for Black Religion," *Journal of Black Theology in Britain* 1.1 (2002): 10–27.

1. Richard Wright, *Native Son* (1966; reprint, New York: Perennial Library, 1987), 359.

2. John Hope Franklin, *From Slavery to Freedom: A History of Negro Americans*, 5th ed. (New York: Knopf, 1980), 214.

3. When Abraham Lincoln's administration began its term of service in 1861, the friction between northern states and southern states had no easy resolution. Many southern states quickly left the union over the issue of slavery, and others threatened to follow. Lincoln's effort to maintain the authority of the federal government and the integrity of the union would eventually result in the Civil War. A careful reading of the war effort makes clear that this battle did not center on the slave question; this was not the federal government waging war against the institution of slavery. In fact, many in the North feared a mass movement of blacks into northern states as a result of emancipation, and others in the North argued that slavery was the best position for blacks because it was in keeping with their ontologically derived station. Yet the decision Lincoln would make was premised not upon social sensibilities but upon political expediency. He had made an appeal for the gradual freeing of slaves even before his presidency, and as president he offered pro-slavery advocates in the South compensation if they would undertake a gradual emancipation of their slaves, who once freed would be settled outside the United States. With the failure of this plan, freeing the slaves was, from Lincoln's perspective, a strategic military move to preserve the union by weakening the economic and social fabric of the slave-holding states. Franklin, *From Slavery to Freedom*, 205–13.

4. In Ira Berlin, Marc Favreau, and Steven F. Miller, eds., *Remembering Slavery: African Americans Talk about Their Personal Experiences of Slavery and Emancipation* (New York: New Press; Washington, D.C.: Library of Congress, 1998), 267.

5. Ibid., 269.

6. Stewart E. Tolnay and E. M. Beck, A *Festival of Violence: An Analysis of Southern Lynching, 1882–1930* (Urbana: University of Illinois Press, 1995), 4. In response to these codes, the Civil Rights Act of 1866 was established, along with the fourteenth and fifteenth amendments. According to the former, blacks were citizens and attempts to deny life, liberty, or property without due process of law were prohibited. It also enforced equal protection under the law. The latter gave blacks legal right to "enjoy all the entitlements accorded white citizens."

7. Henry McNeal Turner, *Respect Black: The Writings and Speeches of Henry McNeal Turner,* edited by Edwin Redkey (New York: Arno, 1971), 42. Originally printed in *African Repository* 51:2 (April 1875): 39. For additional information on emigration see, for example, Edwin S. Redkey, *Black Exodus: Black Nationalist and Back-to-Africa Movements, 1890–1910* (New Haven, Conn.: Yale University Press, 1969).

8. Lawrence Levine, *Black Culture and Black Consciousness: Afro-American Folk Thought from Slavery to Freedom* (New York: Oxford University Press, 1979), 264, quoted in Leon F. Litwack, *Trouble in Mind: Black Southerners in the Age of Jim Crow* (New York: Knopf, 1998), 482.

9. Litwack, *Trouble in Mind,* 489.

10. Milton C. Sernett, *Bound for the Promised Land: African American Religion and the Great Migration* (Durham, N.C.: Duke University Press, 1997), 18.

11. Reverdy C. Ransom, *The Pilgrimage of Harriet Ransom's Son* (Nashville, Tenn.: Sunday School Union, 1949), 49.

12. Wright, *Native Son,* 326.

13. Joel Williamson, *The Crucible of Race: Black-White Relations in the American South since Emancipation* (New York: Oxford University Press, 1984), 323, quoted in Sernett, *Bound for the Promised Land,* 23.

14. Franklin, *From Slavery to Freedom,* 265.

15. Arthur F. Raper, *The Tragedy of Lynching* (Chapel Hill: University of North Carolina Press, 1933), 49.

16. Berlin, Favreau, and Miller, eds., *Remembering Slavery,* 324.

17. These means came into vogue shortly after the emancipation of slaves when it was argued that blacks freed from the good constraints of the slave system reverted to their bestial and barbaric tendencies and that this jeopardized American society.

18. James Elbert Cutler, *Lynch-Law: An Investigation into the History of Lynching in the United States* (1905; reprint, New York: Negro Universities Press, 1969), 19–21, 41, 48–49.

19. Ibid., 57. Also see W. Fitzhugh Brundage, *Lynching in the New South: Georgia and Virginia, 1880–1930* (Urbana: University of Illinois Press, 1993), ch. 1.

20. Cutler, *Lynch-Law*, 30, 82. The exact date of "Lynch's Law" as a phrase is uncertain in this text. On page 37, Cutler gives a date of 1818, but on page 98 he provides a date of 1833.

21. Ibid., 28. Also see Walter White, *Rope and Faggot: A Biography of Judge Lynch* (New York: Knopf, 1929).

22. Increased abolitionist fervor during the mid-1800s sparked episodes of lynching because talk of freeing slaves threatened the delicate social system. Also, slaves who took seriously abolitionist ideals and participated in insurrections or were rumored to be involved in rebellious plots were punished and in some cases killed, and blacks accused of threatening the welfare of the white community in other ways faced severe punishment.

23. Cutler, *Lynch-Law*, 108, 113, 126–27, 212–13.

24. While white supremacy is the overall philosophy that makes possible the lynching of blacks in large numbers, particular challenges to white supremacy marked by the emancipation of slaves account for the freedom with which lynchings took place. These particulars include agricultural hardships, inadequate legal procedures in rural areas of the South, the provincial ethos of the rural South, and economic uncertainty. Walter T. Howard, *Lynchings: Extralegal Violence in Florida during the 1930s* (London: Associated University Presses, 1995), 19.

25. Brundage, *Lynching in the New South*, 4. It should be noted that on a less frequent basis blacks also participated in lynching as a means of maintaining an agreed-upon moral code. According to Brundage: "In 1883, a cavalier regard for moral standards, including the taboo against incest, by Bully Roberson, a black farmer in Decatur County, Georgia, provoked a mob of blacks to mete out justice by flogging him to the point of death." The scope of this practice cannot be discussed with any certainty because of a lack of recorded accounts of lynchings conducted by blacks against blacks—never against whites. Brundage, *Lynching in the New South*, 22, 30.

26. David N. Lyons, "The Minstrel Show as Ritual: Surrogate Black Culture," in Ray B. Browne, ed., *Rituals and Ceremonies in Popular Culture* (Bowling Green, Ohio: Bowling Green University Popular Press, 1980), 150.

27. For an interesting study of lynching that gives primary attention to psychosexual origins for lynching, deeply embedded in a fear of black male prowess, see Trudier Harris, *Exorcising Blackness: Historical and Literary Lynching and Burning Rituals* (Bloomington: Indiana University Press, 1984).

28. Ralph Ginzburg, *100 Years of Lynchings* (1962; reprint, Baltimore, Md.: Black Classic Press, 1988), 24, 27.

29. Ida B. Wells-Barnett, *Selected Works of Ida B. Wells-Barnett*, compiled with an introduction by Trudier Harris (New York: Oxford University Press, 1991), 36.

30. Ginzburg, *100 Years of Lynchings*, 102.

31. Ibid., 96.

32. See Richard Maxwell Brown, ed., *American Violence* (Englewood Cliffs, N.J.: Prentice-Hall, 1970). In this text (p. 73), it is argued that there were actually three Klans. The first developed to respond to Reconstruction (1865–1871); the second emerged in the 1920s, during the Great Migration; and the third developed during the civil rights struggle, the 1950s and 1960s. For more history related to the Ku Klux Klan, see Gladys-Marie Fry, *Night Riders: In Black Folk History* (Nashville: University of Tennessee Press, 1975).

33. In reviewing charges used to rationalize the lynching of blacks, particularly that of rape, readers must exercise a hermeneutic of suspicion. So, for example, while I have found the Cutler text useful with respect to the genealogy of lynching, I believe it seems to easily accept the overall legitimacy of the charge of rape against blacks in that Cutler does not raise a strong critique. As Ida B. Wells-Barnett notes in *On Lynching*, such charges were most usually groundless and really served as an excuse for violence. See Ida B. Wells-Barnett, *On Lynching: Southern Horrors, a Red Record, Mob Rule in New Orleans* (New York: Arno, 1969).

34. Tolnay and Beck, *A Festival of Violence*, 23.

35. Thomas Dixon, *The Leopard's Spots: A Romance of the White Man's Burden, 1865–1900* (1902; reprint, Ridgewood, N.J.: Gregg, 1967), 196, 244.

36. Quoted in George M. Fredrickson, *The Black Image in the White Mind: The Debate on Afro-American Character and Destiny, 1817–1914* (New York: Harper & Row, 1971), 279.

37. Dixon, *The Leopard's Spots*; Thomas Dixon, *The Clansman: An Historical Romance of the Ku Klux Klan* (1905; reprint, Ridgewood, N.J.: Gregg, 1967).

38. Dixon, *The Leopard's Spots*, 137.

39. Dixon, *The Clansman*, 263–64, 268.

40. Dixon, *The Leopard's Spots*, 109.

41. Ibid., 128.

42. Dixon, *The Clansman*, 272.

43. Ibid., 152.

44. Ibid., 2.

45. Dixon, *The Leopard's Spots*, 442–43.

46. Michel Foucault, *Discipline and Punish: The Birth of the Prison* (New York: Vintage, 1979), 25–26.

47. In addition to the threat of physical violence, black women suffered from another form of abuse related to the cult of true womanhood or domesticity. Stemming from the idealization of white women, this philoso-

phy restricted the proper role of women to the domestic sphere; the political and economic (public) spheres were the areas of male interaction. Espoused by both local and national black leaders, it created an impossible situation for black women in that the economic situation of blacks after emancipation did not typically allow black women to remain in the home. Yet work outside the home often came with the peril of possible physical and sexual assault by white men. Furthermore, this philosophy limited the life options afforded women in ways that stymied the attainment of leadership roles in prominent organizations in black communities such as the church. For a more detailed study of this dilemma, see Paula Giddings, *When and Where I Enter: The Impact of Black Women on Race and Sex in America* (New York: William Morrow, 1984); and Angela Davis, *Women, Race, and Class* (New York: Random House, 1981).

48. Frantz Fanon, *Black Skin, White Masks* (New York: Grove, 1967), 9.

49. Saidiya V. Hartman, *Scenes of Subjection: Terror, Slavery, and Self-Making in Nineteenth Century America* (New York: Oxford University Press, 1997), 10.

50. Raper, *The Tragedy of Lynching*, 111–12.

51. Tolnay and Beck, *A Festival of Violence*, 113.

52. Hilton Als, "GWTW [Gone With The Wind]," in James Allen et al., *Without Sanctuary: Lynching Photography in America* (Santa Fe, N.M.: Twin Palms, 2000), 42.

53. Robert L. Zangrando, *The NAACP Crusade against Lynching, 1909–1950* (Philadelphia: Temple University Press, 1980), 5; White, *Rope and Faggot*, 20–21; Howard, *Lynchings*, 18. Also see National Association for the Advancement of Colored People [NAACP], *Thirty Years of Lynching in the United States, 1889–1918* (New York: Arno Press and the *New York Times*, 1969). The decrease in lynchings by the 1950s may be the result of several factors: resistance from individual blacks as well as by organizations such as the NAACP, radio-dispatched police patrols, and increasing negative press coverage. Yet, while the number of lynchings decreased by the mid-1900s, this form of violence never vanished. Clear examples of its continued use include the lynching of Michael Donald in Alabama in 1981.

54. Foucault, *Discipline and Punish*, 8. See pp. 33–34 for Foucault's definition of torture; readers will find that lynching easily fits within his definition.

55. NAACP, *Thirty Years of Lynching in the United States*, 21–22.

56. Ginzburg, *100 Years of Lynchings*, 115.

57. Foucault, *Discipline and Punish*, 25. It is worth noting that, while Foucault was aware of the racialized nature of the U.S. prison system, he does not give real attention to this in his study. For information on the race and class dimensions of imprisonment, see Mark Lewis Taylor, *The Exe-*

cuted God: The Way of the Cross in Lockdown America (Minneapolis: Fortress Press, 2001).

58. Leon F. Litwack, "Hell Hounds," in James Allen et al., *Without Sanctuary*, 12.

59. For information on "second creation," see Charles Long, "Conquest and Cultural Contact in the New World" and "The Oppressive Elements in Religion and the Religions of the Oppressed," in Charles H. Long, *Significations: Signs, Symbols, and Images in the Interpretation of Religion* (Philadelphia: Fortress Press, 1986). This book as been reissued with introductory statements by other scholars (Denver: Davies Group, 1999).

60. This term, "feast of blood," and the accompanying description are used in Orlando Patterson's *Rituals of Blood: Consequences of Slavery in Two American Centuries* (New York: Basic, 1998), ch. 2. Patterson argues that only a small percentage of lynchings qualified as ritual murder because they contained "torture, mass attendance, and burning" (179). However, I assert that rituals, such as lynchings, are rituals not because of attendance or of particular elements they contain. To this extent I am in agreement with W. Fitzhugh Brundage's analysis in *Lynching in the New South*. However, I disagree with him in that the existence of various forms of lynching—the lack of one particular structure—does not mean that lynchings are not significant communal rituals or "metasocial commentary . . . organizing collective existence" (Brundage, 18). Perhaps Brundage's definition of communal is too narrow. I would suggest that lynchings were communal at times because of the large number of people involved in their organization and performance. More importantly, lynchings—regardless of "audience" size—were communal events because they held the sanction of the larger community. Would not the lack of prosecution of lynchers, who were known in most cases, be a testament to community sanction of the deed?

I draw from Ronald Grimes's work on ritual to suggest that these lynchings are rituals—despite difference in presentation and number of participants—because they are repeated activities in found spaces. Furthermore, I argue that lynching by its very nature entails torture. It is not the quickest nor the most humane form of death; a quick shot to the head would be faster and without the same level of psychological manipulation and pain. Granted, those lynchings highlighted by Patterson more graphically highlight the ritual nature of lynching; yet the most explicit examples are not the only examples. In short, I believe Patterson's criteria for ritual murder are much to narrow. In other cases, scholars are concerned with the rituals utilized in lynchings, whereas my concern here is with lynchings as a ritual.

61. Orlando Patterson goes so far as to argue that cannibalism takes place because the senses of smell and taste are connected and are actually the "same sensation." Hence, to smell the burning victim is to taste the victim.

In addition, victims were often forced to eat pieces of their own flesh. See Patterson, *Rituals of Blood*, 198–202.

62. Ruth E. Hill, ed., *The Black Women Oral History Project*, vol. 8 (Westport, Conn.: Meckler, 1991), 14, quoted in Litwack, *Trouble in Mind*, 13.

63. Fanon, *Black Skin, White Masks*, 116.

64. This is not to say that all victims of mob violence were innocent. However, lynchers were not really concerned with justice for crimes proven. Rather, the motivation was different, as the full range of charges suggests—from murder and rape to signs of disrespect such as being "uppity" or successful.

65. Foucault, *Discipline and Punish*, 45–46, 47.

66. Patterson, *Rituals of Blood*, 185.

67. NAACP, *Thirty Years of Lynching in the United States*, 13.

68. Litwack, "Hellhounds," 16.

69. Ibid., 14.

70. Foucault, *Discipline and Punish*, 34.

71. Litwack, "Hellhounds," 11.

72. Fanon's comment on desire is worth quoting here because of the light it sheds on the relationship between blacks and whites over the issue of being: "When it encounters resistance from the other, self-consciousness undergoes the experience of desire—the first milestone on the road that leads to the dignity of the spirit. Self-consciousness accepts the risk of its life, and consequently it threatens the other in his physical being." Fanon, *Black Skin, White Masks*, 218.

73. It is worth noting that, according to Winthrop Jordan, both free and enslaved blacks were castrated as punishment for certain crimes. Castration was seldom inflicted on white men, which leads Jordan to comment as follows: "Castration of negroes clearly indicated a desperate, generalized need in white men to persuade themselves that they were really masters and in all ways masterful, and it illustrated dramatically the ease with which white men slipped over into treating their Negroes like their bulls and stallions whose 'spirit' could be subdued by emasculation." Winthrop Jordan, *White over Black: American Attitudes toward the Negro, 1550–1812* (Chapel Hill: University of North Carolina Press, 1968), 156.

74. Mary Douglas, *Purity and Danger: An Analysis of the Concepts of Pollution and Taboo* (New York: Ark, 1966), 115. Also see Mary Douglas, *Natural Symbols: Explorations in Cosmology* (New York: Routledge, 1996), particularly "Two Bodies."

75. Litwack, "Hell Hounds," 12.

76. Some argue that the innocence of the scapegoat must go unrecognized by the participating community for the event to truly involve scapegoating. See Robert G. Hamerton-Kelly, ed., *Violent Origins: Walter*

Burkert, René Girard, and Jonathan Z. Smith on Ritual Killing and Cultural Formation (Stanford, Calif.: Stanford University Press, 1987), 74–79. However, I would like to modify this argument by suggesting that recognition of the scapegoat's innocence can take several forms. The most common with respect to lynching involves a reluctance to even investigate innocence, to render innocence and guilt of no consequence, to blur the distinction between the two.

77. Eddie Glaude makes a related point regarding the development of communal solidarity and "nation" over against what I will call American democratic hypocrisy. His concern, however, is limited to the political—in the sphere of politicized communal and individual identity. See Eddie Glaude, *Exodus! Religion, Race, and Nation in Early Nineteenth-Century Black America* (Chicago: University of Chicago Press, 2000).

4. Houses of Prayer in a Hostile Land: Responses of Black Religion to Terror

1. This is not to suggest, however, that this terror or dread is a "positive" or useful thing simply because it results in manifestations of religion. To make this assertion would be to support notions of redemptive suffering that I have rejected elsewhere. See, for example, Anthony B. Pinn, *Why, Lord? Suffering and Evil in Black Theology* (New York: Continuum, 1995); and Anthony B. Pinn, ed., *Moral Evil and Redemptive Suffering: A History of Theodicy in African-American Religious Thought* (Gainesville: University Press of Florida, 2002). Instead, this terror or dread are historical realities that must be fought. Furthermore, this dread or terror results in a historical manifestation of religion that is relevant on the individual level and the collective level. With respect to the former, personal encounters with dread result in affiliation with a particular religious tradition. I think work on ritual killing points to the validity of my argument. Take, for example, this statement from Robert G. Hamerton-Kelly, ed., *Violent Origins: Walter Burkert, René Girard, and Jonathan Z. Smith on Ritual Killing and Cultural Formation* (Stanford, Calif.: Stanford University Press, 1987): "Religion arises in relation to some human activity fundamental to social life, and for each of them, religion in all its manifestations is essentially a human construction" (4).

2. Richard Wright, *Native Son* (1966; reprint, New York: Perennial Library, 1987), xxv.

3. See Paul Gilroy, *The Black Atlantic: Modernity and Double Consciousness* (Cambridge: Harvard University Press, 1993). Although I disagree with Gilroy's limited application of the idea of nation resulting from his tendency to take black theological formulations and language (that is,

black Christian tradition) at face value and as normative, I think this rather liberal application of Gilroy's critique is made possible in this chapter, in part at least, through the critique of Gilroy's position offered by Eddie S. Glaude Jr. in *Exodus! Religion, Race, and Nation in Early Nineteenth-Century Black America* (Chicago: University of Chicago Press, 2000), chs. 5–6.

4. It should be noted concerning this chapter and chapter 5 that I am not interested in exploring the cultural origins of these religions. That is to say, I do not explore the syncretism process giving birth to these traditions in cultural terms; the content of "africanisms" or European sensibilities is not the focus of these chapters.

5. See Hans Baer, *The Black Spiritualist Movement: A Religious Response to Racism* (Knoxville: University of Tennessee Press, 1984); Hans A. Baer and Merrill Singer, *African-American Religion in the Twentieth Century: Varieties of Protest and Accommodation* (Knoxville: University of Tennessee Press, 1992); and Cheryl J. Sanders, *Saints in Exile: The Holiness-Pentecostal Experience in African American Religion and Culture* (New York: Oxford University Press, 1996).

6. For additional information on the history of black churches, see Albert J. Raboteau, *Slave Religion: The "Invisible Institution" in the Antebellum South* (New York: Oxford University Press, 1978); Gayraud S. Wilmore, *Black Religion and Black Radicalism: An Interpretation of the Religious History of Afro-American People*, 2nd ed. (Maryknoll, N.Y.: Orbis, 1983). For a short, reader-friendly history of the major black denominations, see Anne H. Pinn and Anthony B. Pinn, *Fortress Introduction to Black Church History* (Minneapolis: Fortress Press, 2001).

7. See Genesis 9:20-26 KJV.

8. Ira Berlin, Marc Favreau, and Steven F. Miller, eds., *Remembering Slavery: African Americans Talk about Their Personal Experiences of Slavery and Freedom* (New York: New Press; Washington, D.C.: Library of Congress, 1998), 197–98.

9. Ibid., 205.

10. Walter F. Pitts Jr., *Old Ship of Zion: The Afro-Baptist Ritual in the African Diaspora* (New York: Oxford University Press, 1993), 50.

11. James Weldon Johnson and J. Rosamond Johnson, *The Books of American Negro Spirituals, including the Book of American Negro Spirituals and the Second Book of Negro Spirituals* (New York: Da Capo, 1969), 183–84.

12. Albert J. Raboteau, *A Fire in the Bones: Reflections on African-American Religious History* (Boston: Beacon, 1995), 17–18. For additional attention to the idea of Exodus sensitive to Raboteau's work while extending it, see Glaude, *Exodus!*

13. Johnson and Johnson, *The Books of American Negro Spirituals*, 52–53.

14. Benjamin E. Mays and Joseph W. Nicholson, "The Genius of the Negro Church," in Milton C. Sernett, ed., *Afro-American Religious History: A Documentary Witness* (Durham, N.C.: Duke University Press, 1985), 340.

15. See Anthony B. Pinn, *The Black Church in the Post–Civil Rights Era* (Maryknoll, N.Y.: Orbis, 2002), 3.

16. Frederick Douglass, *Narrative of the Life of Frederick Douglass, an American Slave, Written by Himself* (New York: New American Library, 1968), appendix, 120–21.

17. For additional information on Black Church activism, see Pinn, *The Black Church in the Post–Civil Rights Era*; Frederick C. Harris, *Something Within: Religion in African-American Political Activism* (New York: Oxford University Press, 1999); Peter J. Paris, *The Social Teaching of the Black Churches* (Philadelphia: Fortress Press, 1985); and Stephen W. Angell and Anthony B. Pinn, eds., *Social Protest Thought in the African Methodist Episcopal Church, 1862–1939* (Knoxville: University of Tennessee Press, 2000).

18. C. Eric Lincoln and Lawrence H. Mamiya, *The Black Church in the African-American Experience* (Durham, N.C.: Duke University Press, 1990); Andrew Billingsley, *Mighty like a River: The Black Church and Social Reform* (New York: Oxford University Press, 1999); Baer and Singer, *African-American Religion in the Twentieth Century*; Wilmore, *Black Religion and Black Radicalism*; F. C. Harris, *Something Within*.

19. Billingsley, *Mighty like a River*, 198–206.

20. Paris, *The Social Teaching of the Black Churches*, 2.

21. While I acknowledge the important role the Black Church has played in the development of black Americans, I find much of its theological framework faulty. This is particularly the case with respect to its theodicy. For information on this, see Pinn, *Why, Lord?*; and Anthony B. Pinn, ed., *Moral Evil and Redemptive Suffering: A History of Theodicy in African-American Religious Thought* (Gainesville: University Press of Florida, 2002). Also see Anthony B. Pinn, ed., *By These Hands: A Documentary History of African American Humanism* (New York: New York University Press, 2001).

22. Much of the material on the Back-to-Africa Movement presented here is drawn from the first chapter of my book *The Black Church in the Post–Civil Rights Era*.

23. Charles V. Hamilton, "Our Nat Turner and William Styron's Creation," in John Henry Clarke, *William Styron's Nat Turner*, (Boston: Beacon, 1968), 74, quoted in Wilmore, *Black Religion and Black Radicalism*, 63.

24. Wilmore, *Black Religion and Black Radicalism*, 70.

25. Daniel Alexander Payne, "Welcome to the Ransomed," in Sernett, ed., *Afro-American Religious History*, 223.

26. Alexander Crummell, "The Regeneration of Africa," in Sernett, ed., *Afro-American Religious History*, 255.

27. Henry McNeal Turner, *Respect Black: The Writings and Speeches of Henry McNeal Turner*, edited by Edwin Redkey (New York: Arno, 1971), 91.

28. Psalms 68:31 KJV.

29. Lawrence S. Little, *Disciples of Liberty: The African Methodist Episcopal Church in the Age of Imperialism, 1884–1916* (Knoxville: University of Tennessee Press, 2000), 70.

30. For additional information, see Pinn, *The Black Church in the Post–Civil Rights Era*. Also see Victor Anderson, *Beyond Ontological Blackness: An Essay in African American Religious and Cultural Criticism* (New York: Continuum, 1995); and Kelly Brown-Douglas, *Sexuality and the Black Church: A Womanist Perspective* (Maryknoll, N.Y.: Orbis, 1999).

31. For an interesting discussion of this idea of the "responsible self" within the context of a marginalized community, see Darryl M. Trimiew, *Voices of the Silenced: The Responsible Self in a Marginalized Community* (Cleveland, Ohio: Pilgrim, 1993).

32. Paris, *The Social Teaching of the Black Churches*, 7.

33. In making this point, I draw from Patricia J. Williams's challenging discussion "On Being the Object of Property," in Micheline R. Malson, Elisabeth Mudime-Boyi, Jean F. O'Barr, and Mary Wyer, eds., *Black Women in America: Social Science Perspectives* (Chicago: University of Chicago Press, 1988), 19–38.

34. Clayborne Carson, ed., *The Autobiography of Martin Luther King, Jr.* (New York: Warner, 1998), 200–201.

35. Cheryl Townsend Gilkes, "'Together and in Harness': Women's Traditions in the Sanctified Church," in Malson, Mudime-Boyi, O'Barr, and Wyer, eds., *Black Women in America*, 228.

36. Shane White and Graham White, *Stylin': African American Expressive Culture from Its Beginnings to the Zoot Suit* (Ithaca, N.Y.: Cornell University Press, 1998), 127.

37. Helen Bradley Foster, *"New Raiments of Self": African American Clothing in the Antebellum South* (New York: Berg/Oxford International Publishers, 1997), 2, 4. Readers interested in the sociology and psychology of clothing during the period of slavery will find this study, based on slave narratives, useful. Whereas no attention is given in this chapter to the class distinctions—or general differences in status—within the black community connoted by dress, Foster's book provides information on this topic.

38. Linda B. Arthur, introduction to *Undressing Religion: Commitment and Conversion from a Cross-Cultural Perspective* (New York: Berg/Oxford International Publishers, 2000), 2–3.

39. Michael Cunningham and Craig Marberry, *Crowns: Portraits of Black Women in Church Hats* (New York: Doubleday, 2000), 40.

40. Ibid., 46.

41. It is acknowledged in current scholarship that some members of the Black Church also participated in traditions such as hoodoo as a supplement to enhance their ability to deal with both visible and invisible forces. For those in hoodoo, the importance of body would have been attested to through, for example, the use of hair, nails, and body fluids as items with spiritual power. Such use of black bodies and its elements attest to the body's importance, and it provides a critique or inversion of the typical depiction of the black body as of no inherent value, without power, socially dead. The power of the black body was also demonstrated through negation in that hoodoo could also be used to attack the physical body and destroy its strength and vitality.

42. This is based on a loose application of Michel Foucault's understanding of soul as a reality created within and on the body through power relationships between the individual and culture. See Michel Foucault, *Discipline and Punish: The Birth of the Prison*, (New York: Vintage, 1979).

43. For an interesting introductory and comparative approach to worship, see Pedrito U. Maynard-Reid, *Diverse Worship: African-American, Caribbean and Hispanic Perspectives* (Downers Grove, Ill.: InterVarsity, 2000). This text should be read in the context of Joseph Murphy's more substantive treatment (though still meant as an introduction) in Joseph M. Murphy, *Working the Spirit: Ceremonies of the African Diaspora* (Boston: Beacon, 1994).

44. This text is from Elizabeth Ware Pearson, ed., *Letters from Port Royal Written at the Time of the Civil War* (Boston, 1906), 27, quoted in Joseph M. Murphy, *Working the Spirit: Ceremonies of the African Diaspora* (Boston: Beacon, 1994), 148.

45. For a comparative study of possession as well as a discussion of the African influence on black religion, see Pitts, *Old Ship of Zion*.

46. Elsie W. Mason, "Bishop C. H. Mason, Church of God in Christ," in *The Man, Charles Harrison Mason (1866–1961)* (Memphis, Tenn.: Church of God in Christ, 1979), quoted in Sernett, ed., *Afro-American Religious History*, 291.

47. Some churches also accept as evidence of the indwelling of the Spirit dancing, emotional release through tears, or being "slain by the spirit," which entails passing out in response to the overwhelming power of the Spirit.

48. Murphy, *Working the Spirit*, 162.

49. Connected to this is the pentecostal doctrine of healing present in the Church of God in Christ, and other pentecostal churches and charismatic churches within Methodist denominations and Baptist conventions. Through healing rituals, black bodies bent and broken by objectification and its ramifications are renewed and strengthened. For information on

healing practices, see, for example, Albert J. Raboteau, "The Afro-American Traditions," in Ronald and Darrel W. Amundsen, eds., *Caring and Curing: Health and Medicine in the Western Religious Traditions* (New York: Macmillan, 1986).

50. See Sheila S. Walker, *Ceremonial Spirit Possession in Africa and Afro-America: Forms, Meanings, and Functional Significance for Individuals and Social Groups* (Leiden, The Netherlands: Brill, 1972), 97–103. Readers will find the analysis of ritual activities such as the ring shout an important addition to the discussion presented here. See Sterling Stuckey, *Slave Culture: Nationalist Theory and the Foundations of Black America* (New York: Oxford University Press, 1987).

51. Examples of this early thought include David Walker, *David Walker's Appeal to the Coloured Citizens of the World, but in Particular, and Very Expressly, to Those of the United States of America*, edited with an introduction by Charles M. Wiltse (1829; reprint, New York: Hill & Wang, 1965); Maria Stewart, *Maria W. Stewart: America's First Black Woman Political Writer*, edited by Marilyn Richardson (Bloomington: Indiana University Press, 1987); Sernett, ed., *Afro-American Religious History*; and Angell and Pinn, eds., *Social Protest Thought in the African Methodist Episcopal Church*.

52. For additional information in concise form, see Lincoln and Mamiya, *The Black Church in the African American Experience*, 164–235; Wilmore, *Black Religion and Black Radicalism*, 135–241; Gayraud S. Wilmore and James H. Cone, eds., *Black Theology: A Documentary History, 1966–1979* (Maryknoll, N.Y.: Orbis, 1979); and Gayraud S. Wilmore and James H. Cone, eds., *Black Theology: A Documentary History, 1980–1992* (Maryknoll, N.Y.: Orbis, 1992).

53. The early development of black theology has been documented in several texts. See, for example, Wilmore and Cone, eds., *Black Theology: A Documentary History, 1966–1979*; Dwight N. Hopkins, *Introducing Black Theology of Liberation* (Maryknoll, N.Y.: Orbis, 2000); Anthony B. Pinn and Benjamin Valentin, eds., *The Ties That Bind: African American and Hispanic American/Latino/a Theologies in Dialogue* (New York: Continuum, 2001), ch. 1.

54. The 1970 text is James H. Cone, *A Black Theology of Liberation* (1970; reprint, Maryknoll, N.Y.: Orbis, 1985). Themes concerning doctrine of God are continued in James H. Cone, *God of the Oppressed* (1975; reprint, Maryknoll, N.Y.: Orbis, 1998). For this critique, see V. Anderson, *Beyond Ontological Blackness*.

55. Gil Scott-Heron, "The Revolution Will Not Be Televised." *The Best of Gil Scott-Heron* (New York: Arista, 1974, 1975, 1976, 1978, 1979, 1981, 1984).

56. James H. Cone, "Black Theology and the Black Church: Where Do We Go From Here?" in James H. Cone, *Risks of Faith: The Emergence of a Black Theology of Liberation, 1968–1998* (Boston: Beacon, 1999), 48.

57. Derrick Bell, of New York University Law School, provides a creative depiction of black religious thought (particularly as expressed in music) in the struggle for civil rights and liberties. See Derrick Bell, *Gospel Choirs: Psalms of Survival in an Alien Land Called Home* (New York: Basic, 1996).

58. For reactions to Cone's work, see Dwight N. Hopkins, ed., *Black Faith and Public Talk: Critical Essays on James H. Cone's Black Theology and Black Power* (Maryknoll, N.Y.: Orbis, 1999).

59. James H. Cone, "Preface to the 1989 Edition," in *Black Theology and Black Power*, 20th anniversary edition (1969; reprint, San Francisco: Harper & Row, 1989), vii. Albert Cleage first makes this assertion concerning the blackness of God and Christ. See Albert Cleage, *The Black Messiah* (New York: Sheed & Ward, 1968).

60. Cone, *Black Theology and Black Power*, quoted in Wilmore and Cone, eds., *Black Theology*, 116–17.

61. Ibid., 217.

62. Ibid.

63. The best work on black theology and social theory has been done by Cornel West. See *Prophesy Deliverance! An Afro-American Revolutionary Christianity* (Philadelphia: Westminster, 1982). As part of this early critique, West states that "an undisputable claim of black theology is America's unfair treatment of black people. What is less apparent is the way in which black theologians understand the internal dynamics of liberal capitalist America, how it functions, why it operates the way it does, who possesses substantive power, and where it is headed. As noted earlier, black theologians do not utilize a social theory that relates the oppression of black people to the overall makeup of America's system of production, foreign policy, political arrangement, and cultural practices" (113).

64. James H. Cone, "New Roles in the Ministry: A Theological Appraisal," in James H. Cone, *Risks of Faith: The Emergence of a Black Theology of Liberation, 1968–1998* (Boston: Beacon, 1999), 114.

65. Katie Cannon, "Moral Wisdom in the Black Woman's Literary Tradition," in *Katie's Canon: Womanism and the Soul of the Black Community* (New York: Continuum, 1995), 59–60.

66. V. Anderson, *Beyond Ontological Blackness*, 17.

5. Covert Practices:
Further Responses of Black Religion to Terror

1. I know some will argue the Nation is insignificant and does not merit this type of consideration. These critiques will suggest that attention be given to "orthodox" Islam and the 2 million black Americans practicing

it. My attention to the Nation, however, is not meant to suggest it has the same numerical significance. It does not claim the same seven-figure membership. Rather, study of the Nation here is premised on the radical manner in which it addresses subjectivity and object status. In later work, attention, however, should be given to black Americans who are orthodox Muslims.

2. E. D. Beynon, "The Voodoo Cult among Negro Migrants in Detroit," *American Journal of Sociology* (May 1938). Reprinted in pamphlet form with commentary by Prince A. Cuba as *Master Fard Muhammad: Detroit History* (Stone Mountain, Ga.: The Universal Truth, 1996), 3.

3. Elijah Muhammad, *The Supreme Wisdom*, vol. 2 (Hampton, Va.: United Brothers and U. S. Communications Systems, n.d.), 11–12; Louis E. Lomax, *A Report on Elijah Muhammad, Malcolm X, and the Black Muslim World* (Westport, Conn.: Greenwood, 1963), 41. Concerning the name Fard, the following is said by Mr. Elijah Muhammad:

> He came to us in the name of Fard. What is that? It's a name that is absolutely, (well, to make it clear to you) you're compelled to observe and do this in the prayer service of Islam. That morning prayer service, it's called Fard and that it is made absolutely binding upon you and I to say. Because in the last days, a man is coming by that name, and it is going to be binding upon you and I to bow down to that man or else. The Fard, it is said by the commentators, is a name that means Independent and a name that is absolutely made binding and compulsive. We are compelled to submit to. But nevertheless, it is not one of the ninety-nine attributes, yet this is an independent name outside of these one hundred. What and why you should choose such names? He is a God that is not associated with any other God. He's a God that the others before him have no, absolutely no association with him. (Elijah Muhammad, *The True History of Master Fard Muhammad* [Atlanta: M.E.M.P.S. Publications, 1996], 21–22)

Furthermore,

> Master Fard Muhammad, also called the Great Mahdi, is a world traveler. . . . He had traveled the world over and . . . that He had visited North America for 20 years before making Himself known to us, His people whom He came for. He had visited the Isle of the Pacific, Japan and China, Canada, Alaska, the North Pole, India, Pakistan, all of the Near East and Africa. He had studied the wild life in the jungles of Africa and learned the language of the birds. He could speak 16 languages and could write 10 of them. He visited every inhabited place on the

earth and had pictured and extracted the language of the people on Mars and had a knowledge of all life in the universe. He
could recite by heart the histories of the world as far back as
150,000 years and knew the beginning and end of all things."
(E. Muhammad, *The True History*, 50–51)

4. For information on the Honorable Elijah Muhammad, see Jabril
Muhammad, *This Is the One: Messenger Elijah Muhammad, We Need Not
Look for Another!* (Phoenix, Ariz.: Book Company, 1996); Claude Andrew
Clegg III, *An Original Man: The Life and Times of Elijah Muhammad*
(New York: St. Martin's, 1997).

5. Although not discussed in this book, the nationalist movement (the
Universal Negro Improvement Association) started by Marcus Garvey is
extremely important. It represents the largest mass movement of black
Americans in the history of the United States, and it entailed another push
against the terror of dehumanization. But rather than framing it in terms of
full humanity and citizenship within the context of the United States, as the
Church suggested, it argued—more in keeping with some of the Nation of
Islam's rhetoric—for a form of sociopolitical nationalism with the establishment of community (composed of the diasporic Africans) in Africa as the
ultimate outcome. According to a Garveyite: "We are not a social club. We
must press the issue of nationalism. We have the right to resolve the universal conflict of the Negro people of the world. We've got to redeem Africa.
We must be radical and nationalistic. We are hungry for freedom and liberty. This is not a private club, not a private society. It is a universal business.
It is not a religious organization. It is a nationalist organization to stop everything that prevents black people everywhere from enjoying their freedom.
Garvey was sent by God to tell the people what they needed. Ninety percent
of the Negroes do not want anything important. We have been praying too
long. You've got to be hungry for freedom" (Richard B. Moore, *The Name
"Negro"—Its Origin and Evil Use* [New York: Afroamerican Publishers,
1960], quoted in E. U. Essien-Udom, *Black Nationalism: Search for an
Identity in America* [Chicago: University of Chicago Press, 1962], 42).

For additional information on the Garvey Movement, see Tony Martin,
*Race First: The Ideological and Organizational Struggles of Marcus Garvey
and the Universal Negro Improvement Association* (Westport, Conn.: Greenwood, 1976); Amy Jacques-Garvey, ed., *The Philosophy and Opinions of
Marcus Garvey* (New York: Arno Press and the *New York Times*, 1969); Randall K. Burkett, *Garveyism as a Religious Movement* (Metuchen, N.J.:
Scarecrow, 1978); Randall K. Burkett, ed., *Black Redemption: Churchmen
Speak for the Garvey Movement* (Philadelphia: Temple University Press,
1978); Robert Hill, ed., *The Marcus Garvey and Universal Negro Improvement Association Papers* (Berkeley: University of California Press, 1983).

6. Elijah Muhammad, *The True History*, 123.

7. Malcolm X at the Boston University Human Relations Center, 15 February 1960, quoted in C. Eric Lincoln, *The Black Muslims in America*, 3rd ed. (Grand Rapids, Mich.: Eerdmans, 1994), 64–65.

8. Essien-Udom, *Black Nationalism*, 199.

9. Elijah Muhammad, *The Fall of America* (Chicago: Muhammad's Temple of Islam, No. 2, 1973), 48.

10. Malcolm X at Boston University Human Relations Center, 15 February 1960, quoted in Lincoln, *The Black Muslims in America*, 77.

11. It was also argued that the whites, having their rightful home in Europe, stole land from the Indians to develop the United States. Indians and blacks are related in that the former are, in fact, the descendants of a segment of the original people who rejected Islam and were exiled to North America. Hence, because the land does not belong to whites, blacks, because they are related ontologically to those who first possessed the land, have a right to self-determination and nationhood in North America.

12. See Elijah Muhammad, *Message to the Blackman in America* (Chicago: Muhammad's Temple of Islam, No. 2, 1965), 220–42.

13. While wanting to separate from whites in the United States, members of the Nation speak of a deep connection with the world Muslim community and claim good relations with their Islamic brothers and sisters, particularly those of the Middle East.

14. Quoted in Essien-Udom, *Black Nationalism*, 153.

15. The principles are symbolized on the Nation's flag by the sun, five-pointed star, and moon: the sun represents freedom, the moon symbolizes equality, and the star stands for justice. Furthermore, the five points of the star stand for the human's five senses. See Elijah Muhammad, *The Flag of Islam* (Chicago: self-published, 1974).

16. Elijah Muhammad, *How to Eat to Live, Book No. 1* (Atlanta: M.E.M.P.S. Publications, 1967), 14. The hog was developed to help with the diseases affecting whites because of their weak genetic structure: "The hog was made, Allah taught me, for medical purposes, to cure the white man's many diseases, since he had been grafted out of the black man, and he attracted germs and diseases easily that were possibly incurable. At that time, the Arab medical scientists did not have anything that would kill most, or probably all, of his diseases, so they made a medicine for him—that is the hog. The hog contains, Allah said to me, 999 poisonous germs. This is what makes up the hog. And, the Christian will look at you, with a Bible at home and in his pocket, and say, if you do not eat it, 'what is wrong with the hog?'" E. Muhammad, *How to Eat to Live*, 98. The Nation, however, provides no details concerning the mechanics of using the hog for medicinal purposes.

17. In addition to shorter fasts of one to three days to clean the body, Mr.

Muhammad required members of the Nation to fast during the month of Ramadan. See E. Muhammad, *How to Eat to Live*, 45–46.

18. E. Muhammad, *How to Eat to Live*, 17. According to the Nation of Islam, whites partake of pork and other foods prohibited in Scripture out of a complete disrespect for Allah and his teachings.

19. Ibid., *How to Eat to Live*, 102.

20. Elijah Muhammad, *The Supreme Wisdom*, 52–53. Also see pp. 63–65 for information on prayer, as well as in E. Muhammad, *Message to the Blackman in America*, 135–60.

21. One debate concerns whether the Nation of Islam is a religion or a black nationalism organization. From my perspective, such a discussion is of little value. How many religious traditions in the black community, including the Black Church, have not engaged in some form of community building based upon racial identification as an extension of their religious obligation? It strikes me that the existential and ontological situation of blacks in the United States has required religious organization to take this two-pronged approach. I think this debate, at least in part, stems from a Christian bias in depictions of religion within black communities. For a concise statement on the nature and meaning of Islam, see E. Muhammad, *Message to the Blackman in America*, 68–85.

The wants and beliefs of the Nation can be concisely stated as follow. Wants: (1) freedom, (2) justice, (3) equality of opportunity, (4) a separate nation, (5) freedom of imprisoned Muslims, (6) end to police brutality, (7) equal justice and employment until a separate nation is developed, (8) exemption from taxes for all blacks, (9) equal education in separate facilities for boys and girls, and (10) prohibition on interracial relationships. Beliefs: (1) Allah is the only God; (2) recognize the Qur'an and other scriptures of the prophets; (3) recognize the Bible as containing truth, but tampered with by whites; (4) the prophets of God must be acknowledged; (5) mental resurrection of the dead; (6) judgment by God; (7) separation of blacks and whites; (8) justice for all; (9) rejection of integration; (10) pacifism; (11) protection of women is mandatory; and (12) Master Fard Muhammad is Allah. E. Muhammad, *Message to the Blackman in America*, 161–64.

22. Quoted in Essien-Udom, *Black Nationalism*, 219.

23. See, for example, "Detroit's University of Islam," *SALAAM* 1.1 (July 1960): 6–13. For an interesting narrative on the Nation of Islam using discovery and education as the basic framework, see Sonsyrea Tate, *Little X: Growing Up in the Nation of Islam* (New York: HarperSanFrancisco, 1997).

24. E. Muhammad, *The Fall of America*, 3.

25. Tate, *Little X*, 2–3.

26. Quoted in Lincoln, *The Black Muslims in America*, 70.

27. E. Muhammad, *Message to the Blackman in America*, 109.

28. Albert J. Raboteau, "'How Far the Promised Land?': Black Religion and Black Protest." In Albert J. Raboteau, *A Fire in the Bones: Reflections on African-American Religious History* (Boston: Beacon, 1995), 66.

29. The Nation preaches a clear distinction between Christianity and Islam, arguing that the former is the proper religion for those made by Yakub but Islam is the proper religion for the descendants of the original people: "The answer to this question 'Why not Islam for all Mankind?' is simple: All mankind can't believe and obey the teachings of Islam. All mankind are not members [*sic*] of the Righteous. Islam is righteousness and he who would believe in it and do the Will of Allah (God) must be by nature one born of Allah. The only people born of Allah is the Black Nation of which the so-called Negroes are descendants. That is why Islam is offered to them." E. Muhammad, *The Supreme Wisdom*, 50–51.

30. Mattias Gardell, "The Sun of Islam Will Rise in the West: Minister Farrakhan and the Nation of Islam in the Latter Days," in Yvonne Yazbeck Haddad and Jane Idleman Smith, eds., *Muslim Communities in North America* (Albany: State University of New York Press, 1994), 17. Also of interest is Gardell's recent book *In the Name of Elijah Muhammad: Louis Farrakhan and the Nation of Islam* (Durham, N.C.: Duke University Press, 1996).

31. Lincoln, *The Black Muslims in America*, 69.

32. E. Muhammad, *The Supreme Wisdom*, 9. While Mr. Muhammad argues that whites created the Christian faith as a tool of mastery over blacks, the idea of a spirit God is much older: "The belief in a God other than man (a spirit) Allah has taught me goes back into the millions of years—long before Yakub (the father of the devils)—because the knowledge of God was kept as a secret from the public. This is the first time that it has ever been revealed, and we, the poor rejected and despised people, are blessed to be the first of all the people of earth to receive this secret knowledge of God. If this people (the white race) would teach you truth which has been revealed to me, they would be hastening their own doom—for they were not created to teach us the truth but rather to teach us falsehood (just contrary to the truth)." Whites developed a certain form of this doctrine, but they do not create the doctrine itself. The genealogy of this particular doctrine of God as spirit remains, however, unclear. E. Muhammad, *Message to the Blackman in America*, 9.

33. Elijah Muhammad, *Our Saviour Has Arrived* (Newport News, Va.: United Brothers Communications Systems, n.d.), 39.

34. Although a group of twenty-four gods or wise scientists worked as a collective in developing history within 35,000-year cycles, only one of the twenty-four is supreme during the writing of each cycle. In the current cycle, the Nation's theology states, Master Fard Muhammad is the Supreme

Being. This does not mean that Master Fard was present during the initial creation from the single atom because the gods are human and do not live forever. Rather, it means he possesses the same knowledge and power as the original Allah. E. Muhammad, *The True History of Master Fard Muhammad*, xxxix–xl. Elsewhere, we are told that there are twenty-five scientists; twenty-four of them do the actual writing, and the twenty-fifth is the judge. E. Muhammad, *Our Savior Has Arrived*, 12.

35. E. Muhammad, *The Supreme Wisdom*, 14.

36. See Malcolm X, *Yacub's History* (Stone Mountain, Ga.: T. U. T. Publications, 1997); also in Malcolm X, *The End of White World Supremacy: Four Speeches by Malcolm X* (New York: Arcade, 1971), 23–66. It is interesting to note that "the first two thousand years was the period between Yakub, the father and grafter of the white race, to the birth of Musa (Moses) to the birth of Isa (Jesus), the last Great Prophet to the white race. The third two thousand year period is from the birth of Isa (Jesus) to the coming of Allah, often referred to by the Christians as 'The coming of God, the Christ, the Messiah, the Son of Man,' or the 'second coming of Jesus.' In Islam, it is referred to as the 'coming of the Great Madhi, the coming of Allah' to the birth of Muhammad." E. Muhammad, *Our Savior Has Arrived*, 14. For additional information on the genealogy of white people, see E. Muhammad, *Message to the Blackman in America*, 103–34.

37. According to the Nation, this is the meaning behind the Book of Revelations found in the Christian Bible.

38. E. Muhammad, *Message to the Blackman in America*, 105.

39. E. Muhammad, *The True History of Master Fard Muhammad*, 100–101.

40. E. Muhammad, *Message to the Blackman in America*, 105.

41. E. Muhammad, *Our Savior Has Arrived*, 42–43.

42. According to the Messenger, 2 Thessalonians 2 explains why God would allow the development and rule of the white race. The hermeneutic of destiny used by the Nation suggests that God allowed this because it is part of the destiny of the original people to be ruled for a certain amount of time. The theodical formulation attached to this implies that through this white rule, the original people are prepared for their destiny and are punished for past sins against Allah, such as rejecting Islam. For information on the final destruction of white supremacy, see E. Muhammad, *The Fall of America*, 68–73, 112–202, 225–57. For information on the "Mother Plane" used to destroy the earth, see E. Muhammad, *The Fall of America*, 236–47.

43. E. Muhammad, *The Supreme Wisdom*, 23; E. Muhammad, *Our Savior Has Arrived*, 10. For the Nation's take, in comparative terms, on the Bible and the Qur'an as scripture, see E. Muhammad, *Message to the Blackman in America*, 86–99.

44. E. Muhammad, *The Supreme Wisdom*, 36.

45. February 26 is Savior Day for the Nation of Islam, a large gathering during which the birth of Allah is celebrated. It is unclear whether whites can really embrace Islam and hence be redeemed. In some cases, it appears the Nation says no (see E. Muhammad, *Message to the Blackman in America*, 131). In other cases, it seems possible but highly unlikely. But at other times, the Honorable Elijah Muhammad clearly states that some whites have embraced Islam and will be blessed, meaning they will not be destroyed during judgment: "There are white people in Europe who believe in Islam. They are Muslim by faith and not by nature. They believe in righteousness and have tried, and are still trying, to practice the life of a righteous Muslim. Because of their faith in Islam, Allah (God) blesses them and they will see the Hereafter. There are quite a few white people in America who are Muslim by faith. Good done by any person is rewarded and these white people who believe in Islam will receive the blessing of entering into the Hereafter."

There is epistemological tension here, however, because after saying this Mr. Muhammad proclaims that "the white people who believe in Islam will not enter the Hereafter that is Promised to the Lost-Found Black People. The Lost-Found People will take on a new birth. But the white people who believe in Islam will not take on a new birth because they will not be the people to live forever. Because of their belief in Islam, they will escape the great world destruction that we now face." But, if redemption entails escape from the destruction of the old world and whites who accept Islam achieve redemption in this sense, how is it they do not live forever? It is clear that the Nation does not believe in resurrection from the dead or individuals living forever; not even Allah lives forever. Yet, if the whites who embrace Islam survive the destruction, and this is the final purging of the earth, how is it they do not live forever through their descendants? E. Muhammad, *Our Savior Has Arrived*, 89. Also see E. Muhammad, *The Fall of America*, 102–4.

46. Clegg, *An Original Man*, 66.

47. E. Muhammad, *The Supreme Wisdom*, 30, 32. See pp. 40–42 for information on "heaven" and "hell." Also see the New Testament Book of Revelations. For details on the battling leading to this new world, see E. Muhammad, *Message to the Blackman in America*, 290–94.

48. Scholars such as Robert Beckford have raised questions concerning the exclusion of Malcolm X's organizational efforts after his break with the Nation of Islam. While I recognize the importance of Malcolm X's work for a rethinking of Islamic faith and activism in the context of the United States, this chapter is limited to the Nation of Islam and its development as a response to dehumanization.

49. For information on Wallace Deen Muhammad, see Imama W.

Deen Muhammad, *Challenges That Face Man Today* (Chicago: W. D. Muhammad Publications, 1985). For information on Farrakhan's ministry as a continuation of Mr. Muhammad's work, see Jabril Muhammad, *This Is the One,* ch. 10 and appendix. For biographical information on Farrakhan, see Mattias Gardell, *In the Name of Elijah Muhammad;* and Arthur J. Magida, *Prophet of Rage: A Life of Louis Farrakhan and His Nation* (New York: Basic, 1996).

50. Gardell, *In the Name of Elijah Muhammad,* 131–32, quoted in Anthony B. Pinn, *Varieties of African American Religious Experience* (Minneapolis: Fortress Press, 1998), 139.

51. Pinn, *Varieties of African American Religious Experience,* 139–40.

52. Louis Farrakhan, *A Torchlight for America* (Chicago: FCN Publishing Co., 1993), 29. Other books of interest related to Minister Farrakhan include Louis Farrakhan, *Let Us Make Man: Select Men Only and Women Only Speeches* (New York: Uprising Communications, 1996).

What is not clear in Farrakhan's book *A Torchlight for America* is the ultimate benefit of accepting his prescription. That is to say, Farrakhan seems to maintain Mr. Muhammad's eschatology. If this is the case, what benefit do whites receive for following Farrakhan's agenda? Does it prevent judgment? Does it merely delay judgment? If the former is not the case, what is the real motivation for transformation?

53. Farrakhan, *A Torchlight for America,* 34. This perspective also resulted in a revised approach to the issue of reparations. Gone is the explicit demand for payment now because "even though this country owes us reparations, in her present condition what she owes will stay on the back burner or not on the stove at all. We must work harder to address our own problems. We must also provide the country with solutions that benefit us as well as the whole, to pull the country to a state of strength. Perhaps, when the country's condition improves, we can speak more effectively about what is owed to us for our services, past and present, to repair our condition." Farrakhan, *A Torchlight for America,* 41. Yet, in the section "Make Good on 40 Acres and a Mule" (87–94), Farrakhan calls for a form of reparations revolving around distribution of land to blacks and the provision of resources for the acquisition of new skills. Furthermore, in chapter 6 of his book, Farrakhan promotes a more explicit mode of nationhood by suggesting that the Nation of Islam be allowed to work with black prisoners, reform them, and develop a new nation in Africa composed of these reformed prisoners and other blacks who are interested in the project (done with the cooperation of African Nations).

54. Ibid., 34.

55. Ibid., 47.

56. Ibid., 141. The basic approach to proper health is (1) prayer; (2)

proper knowledge through sources such as Mr. Muhammad's *How to Eat to Live*; (3) eat with moderation and avoid harmful items such as pork; (4) exercise; (5) avoid addictions such as drugs; (6) proper rest; (7) connection with nature; and (8) regular dental and physical examinations (Farrakhan, *A Torchlight for America*, 145–48).

57. E. Muhammad, *Our Savior Has Arrived*, 8 (italics added).

58. Farrakhan, *A Torchlight for America*, 25. Chapter 6 of Farrakhan's book, "Developing America's Moral Backbone," outlines the remedy for the ills noted in this quotation. In this chapter, issues such as homosexuality are treated in keeping with the typical perspective found in American society and the Church: it is considered an aberration, a problematic mode of sexual expression.

Concerning women in the Nation, see Amina Beverly McCloud, *African American Islam* (New York: Routledge, 1995); and Tate, *Little X*.

59. A brief, interesting discussion of the changes in the Nation of Islam over the past twenty-five years is provided in the postscript to the third edition of C. Eric Lincoln's *The Black Muslims in America*. It is interesting to note that Farrakhan, while keeping to the spirit of the Messenger's teachings, has made structural changes. For example, he appointed Sister Ava Muhammad a minister in the Nation, and her theological work has been of significance to the Nation. Also, under Minister Farrakhan, the ethnic makeup of the Nation has changed to include Hispanics and others. And while there are still questions about orthodoxy, it cannot be denied that Minister Farrakhan was accepted into the Continental Muslim Council based on his confession of the faith.

6. "I'll Make Me a World": Black Religion as Historical Context

1. Although I share a preoccupation with black religion at its best as being a complex form of protest, a major concern for me with respect to traditional discussions of black religion and black religious studies is how both are confined, for the most part, to the Black Church. That is to say, Black Church studies and black religious studies are usually understood as synonymous enterprises. When alternate forms of religious expression in black communities are discussed, they are typically referred to as "cults" and "sects" and are viewed as implicitly of less value and relevance than the Black Church. While a discussion and analysis of black religious studies as a mode of investigating black life is merited, the focus of this chapter is on outlining my particular method. For those interested in more general information and other methods of exploring black religion see, for example, Gayraud S. Wilmore,

ed., *African American Religious Studies: An Interdisciplinary Anthology* (Durham, N.C.: Duke University Press, 1989), particularly the introduction; Donald H. Matthews, *Honoring the Ancestors: An African Cultural Interpretation of Black Religion and Literature* (New York: Oxford University Press, 1998); Will Coleman, *Tribal Talk* (College Station: Pennsylvania State University, 1999); Cornel West, *Prophesy Deliverance! An Afro-American Revolutionary Christianity* (Philadelphia: Westminster, 1982); Anthony B. Pinn, *Varieties of African American Religious Experience* (Minneapolis: Fortress Press, 1998); Victor Anderson, *Beyond Ontological Blackness: An Essay in African American Religious and Cultural Criticism* (New York: Continuum, 1995); Marcia Y. Riggs and Barbara Holmes, eds., *Can I Get a Witness? Prophetic Religious Voices of African American Women: An Anthology* (Maryknoll, N.Y.: Orbis, 1997), introduction; Katie Cannon, *Katie's Canon: Womanism and the Soul of the Black Community* (New York: Continuum, 1995); and Delores S. Williams, *Sisters in the Wilderness: The Challenge of Womanist God-Talk* (Maryknoll, N.Y.: Orbis, 1993).

2. This is an appeal for careful and calculated attention to materials for study that I first made several years ago, but one that I have refined since working on the present book. See Pinn, *Varieties of African American Religious Experience*, ch. 5. A version of this essay was published as "In the Raw: African American Cultural Memory and Theological Reflection," in Delwin Brown et al., eds., *Converging on Culture: Theologians in Dialogue with Cultural Analysis and Criticism (Reflection and Theory in the Study of Religion)* (New York: Oxford University Press, 2001).

3. A very useful collection resulting from this work is Savannah Unit, Georgia Writers' Project, Work Projects Administration. *Drums and Shadows: Survival Studies among the Georgia Coastal Negroes* (1940. Reprint, Athens: University of Georgia Press, 1986).

4. Pierre Nora, "Between Memory and History: Les Lieux de Mémoire," in Geneviève Fabre and Robert O'Meally, eds., *History and Memory in African-American Culture* (New York: Oxford University Press, 1994), 284.

5. Frantz Fanon, *Black Skin, White Masks* (New York: Grove, 1967), 237.

6. Susan Willis, "Memory and Mass Culture," in Fabre and O'Meally, eds., *History and Memory in African-American Culture*, 184.

7. Toni Morrison, "The Site of Memory," in Russell Ferguson et al., *Out There: Marginalization and Contemporary Cultures* (Cambridge: MIT Press, 1990), 302.

8. Karen Fields, "What One Cannot Remember Mistakenly," in Fabre and O'Meally, eds., *History and Memory in African-American Culture*, 150.

9. Cornel West provides one of the few examples of attention to this area

by one who has done substantial work in black religious studies. See Cornel West, *The Cornel West Reader* (New York: Basic Civitas, 1999), 456–62.

10. Leland Ferguson, *Uncommon Ground: Archaeology and Early African America, 1650–1800* (Washington, D.C.: Smithsonian Institution Press, 1992), 58.

11. Ibid., 58.

12. Ibid., xliv; Theresa A. Singleton, ed., *"I, Too, Am America": Archaeological Studies of African-American Life* (Charlottesville: University of Virginia Press, 1996), 5. I also address the potential value of archaeology for the study of black religion in Pinn, *Varieties of African American Religious Experience*, ch. 5.

13. Peter Gathercole, introduction to Peter Gathercole and David Lowenthal, eds., *The Politics of the Past* (Boston: Unwin Hyman, 1990), 1.

14. Singleton, ed., *"I, Too, Am America,"* 17.

15. Ibid., 1.

16. Several scholars are moving toward a reevaluation of resources and sources for the study of religion, particularly with respect to theological inquiry. However, their efforts are often premised on a rather narrow depiction of religion, theology, and theology's mission and proper focus. See, for example, Dwight N. Hopkins and Sheila Greeve Davaney, eds., *Changing Conversations: Religious Reflection and Cultural Analysis* (New York: Routledge, 1996). I understand that my movement beyond the written word is useful but troubled by the continued use of terms such as *text* and *reading*, which draw the mind back to the written text.

17. Hopkins and Davaney, eds., *Changing Conversations*, 4.

18. James H. Cone, "Black Theology and the Black Church: Where Do We Go From Here?" in *Risks of Faith: The Emergence of a Black Theology of Liberation, 1968–1998* (Boston: Beacon, 1999), 48.

19. Hazel V. Carby, *Race Men* (Cambridge: Harvard University Press, 1999), 157.

20. Singleton, ed., *"I, Too, Am America,"* 6. My concern here is not to reconstruct the African nature of black cultural production. Rather than address issues of "africanisms," I am more concerned with how cultural production in the United States speaks to black religion as the struggle for liberation, regardless of the origin of the style and expression of these cultural forms.

21. Anthony B. Pinn, *Why, Lord?: Suffering and Evil in Black Theology* (New York: Continuum, 1995), 116.

22. Marcia Muelder Eaton, *Basic Issues in Aesthetics* (Belmont, Calif.: Wadsworth, 1988), 4.

23. Although the idea of aesthetics is brought up here, my concern is limited to how art is and represents the struggle for liberation. Attention is given to the *experience* of art in chapter 8.

24. Nicholas Davey, "The Hermeneutic of Seeing," in Ian Heywood and Barry Sandywell, eds., *Interpreting Visual Culture: Explorations in the Hermeneutics of the Visual* (New York: Routledge, 1999), 22, 26.

25. The phrase "aesthetic experience" is from Davey, "The Hermeneutics of Seeing," 21.

26. I am not the first to point out the body's significance for religious studies. For example, black theology has given attention to the body, but this has often been expressed in less than liberating ways. Think, for example, of black theology's early preoccupation with the presence of the black male body and its need for liberation against racism. The preoccupation of necessity meant little attention to black female bodies and the sexism implicitly excepted by black male theologians and the churches they represent. Furthermore, on both fronts, black male and female theologians have often observed the pleasures of the body strictly in terms of heterosexual orientation and in this way buttressed a long history of homophobia within black theology and the churches it speaks for. In part, the notion of liberation impressed by black theology generally promoted and enforced these preoccupations. Pointing this problematic out is the strong point of Victor Anderson's work. With this in mind, I would like to suggest a more complex understanding of liberation and of the multidimensionality of black bodies by posing liberation as the free range of locations and positions for human bodies. That is to say, to be liberated is to have the freedom and resources to exist in a variety of locations simultaneously. It is to not be defined by skin color or sexual orientation alone. It is to be self-conscious with a tangled identity. This, to be sure, is not a quest for disembodiment, but a freedom of movement or position for the body.

27. Paula M. Cooey, *Religious Imagination and the Body: A Feminist Analysis* (New York: Oxford University Press, 1994), 110. In part, my agreement with Cooey on this point stems from both of us having been trained by Gordon Kaufman, whose students tend to exhibit historicist sensibilities.

28. Readers interested in examples of how the body is discussed within the context of liberation theology and ethics, projects that differ from my effort to construct a theory of black religion, should see Katie Cannon, "Womanist Perspectival Discourse and Canon Formation," in *Katie's Canon*; and Emilie M. Townes, *In a Blaze of Glory: Womanist Spirituality as Social Witness* (Nashville, Tenn.: Abingdon, 1995).

29. The importance of the body was recognized early in the context of North America. One need only reflect on various forms of evangelical and reform activities in the North American colonies and the young United States for evidence of this. During the early to mid-1800s, many within the United States turned reformers' attention to the importance of the body in the development of a strong and morally upstanding country. Fueled by the

first Great Awakening, reformers such as Lyman Beecher recognized that the health of the physical body was connected to spiritual and societal renewal. In accordance, the manual labor movement sought to enhance seminary training through attention to physical activity, which kept the body strong and ministers alive. That is to say: "Consciousness of the importance of physical strength as part of a ministerial ideal led many in the church to perceive a tragedy unnoticed before: it appeared that the heavy intellectual demands of theological seminary life were turning potentially fine ministers into . . . sickly souls hardly capable of hobbling away from the graduation rostrum" (Robert H. Abzug, *Cosmos Crumbling: American Reform and the Religious Imagination* [New York: Oxford University Press, 1994], 118. Hence, it was understood that the body served as an outward sign of inner strength and vitality, which were both necessary to actually do the will of God. The religious, in other words, live through the body, not in spite of the body. The recent book *Race Men*, by Hazel Carby, points to the manner in which this attention to black bodies can devolve into attention to the black male body—black masculinity—thereby rendering black women invisible. In Carby's words, the intellectual and academic ramifications of this preoccupation with masculinity is clear: "It is true that, superficially, the situation appears to have improved. The words 'women and gender' are frequently added after the word 'race' and the appropriate commas, and increasingly the word 'sexuality' completes the litany. . . . But the intellectual work of black women and gay men is not thought to be of enough significance to be engaged with, argued with, agreed or disagreed with" (5). That is to say, attention to the body as an important religious site can—if one is careless—regress into a gendered conversation that reifies notions of masculinity. And what then becomes incorporated into our theological dialogue is problematic and misrepresentative of the body's role in the various religious worlds of concern.

This points to a larger problem of the black body as a negative symbol. Not much attention needs to be given to this here because the literature on this is well known and often cited. Yet, it also points to another noteworthy notion: the body has long been an important symbol.

30. I am just as interested in the body lived as I am in the body as metaphor. Therefore, I am not suggesting that experience is simple physiological data; rather, I understand the body as complex. Because of this, I make no attempt to talk in terms of the body as a universal symbol or as representing a universally lived history. Hence, the body may mean something different in each cultural and historical context. My discussion is concerned with the body (both meanings) in the particular context of black culture and history in the United States. I find Paula Cooey's work helpful with some of these concerns. See Cooey, *Religious Imagination and the Body*.

31. Some of my discussion of the body presented here is also found in a shorter article that summarizes some of what is in this book: Anthony B. Pinn, "Black Bodies in Pain and Ecstasy: Terror, Subjectivity, and the Nature of Black Religion," special issue of *Nova Religio*, edited by Anthony B. Pinn (scheduled for spring 2003). My formulation of the body was first presented in a lecture titled "Is Black (Church) Theology Enough?: Thoughts on the Reformulation of a Liberation Theology," Harvard Divinity School, Cambridge, Mass., 12 April 2000.

32. Mary Douglas, *Natural Symbols: Explorations in Cosmology* (New York: Routledge, 1996), 67–69. Also see Mary Douglas, *Purity and Danger: An Analysis of the Concepts of Pollution and Taboo* (New York: Ark, 1966). Readers will note that I tie Douglas's theory of the body to Cornel West's genealogy of white supremacy by suggesting that the social system as body carries out the construction of power dynamics and a restricted discourse that promotes the development and maintenance of white supremacy. See West, *Prophesy Deliverance!*, 47–61.

33. Skip James, "Hard Time Killin' Floor Blues," in Eric Sachheim, comp., *The Blues Line: A Collection of Blues Lyrics from Leadbelly to Muddy Waters* (New York: Ecco, 1969), 176. Lyrics reprinted here copyright 1968 Wynwood Music Co. Inc. Used by permission.

34. Ralph Ellison, *Invisible Man* (New York: Vintage, 1972), xviii.

35. Ibid., 3.

36. Quoted in Townes, *In a Blaze of Glory*, 48.

37. Ellison, *Invisible Man*; Alice Walker, *The Color Purple: A Novel* (New York: Harcourt Brace Jovanovich, 1982); Richard Wright, *Black Boy: A Record of Childhood and Youth* (New York: Harper, 1945); Richard Wright, *Native Son* (New York: Harper, 1940).

38. Richard Wright, "Introduction: How 'Bigger' Was Born," in *Native Son*, xv.

39. Michele Wallace, "Afterword: 'Why Are There No Great Black Artists?' The Problem of Visuality in African American Culture," in Michele Wallace and Gina Dent, eds., *Black Popular Culture* (Seattle: Bay Press, 1992), 335; Michele Wallace, *Invisibility Blues: From Pop to Theory* (London: Verso, 1990), 2.

40. I draw from a discussion of Spiller's idea in G. M. James Gonzalez, "Of Property: On 'Captive' 'Bodies,' Hidden 'Flesh,' and Colonization," in Lewis R. Gordon, editor, *Existence in Black: An Anthology of Black Existential Philosophy* (New York: Routledge, 1997). I have made use of Spiller's depiction elsewhere because of its importance for my understanding of the cultural and religious significance of the body. See Anthony B. Pinn, "How Do We Talk About Religion?: Religious Experience, Cultural Memory, and Theological Method," in Pinn, *Varieties of African American Religious Experience*.

However, I must say that I am not convinced by Spiller's distinction between body and flesh. I am not certain it is a necessary distinction for my purposes. Rather, I would argue that the nature of liberation as meant here entails a turning of bodies into flesh. Put another way, it is a movement from a corporeal object controlled and tortured by oppressive, essentializing forces to a complex conveyer of cultural meaning—from object to subject.

One could also include here the imagery provided by Toni Morrison concerning emotional memory housed in the inner body: "Writers are like that [water]: remembering where we were, what valley we ran through, what the banks were like, the light that was there and the route back to our original place. It is emotional memory—what the nerves and the skin remember as well as how it appeared." Toni Morrison, "The Site of Memory" in Russell Ferguson et al., *Out There: Marginalization and Contemporary Cultures* (Cambridge, Mass.: MIT Press, 1990), 305. Also see James Perkinson, "Ogou's Iron or Jesus' Irony: Who's Zooming Who in Diasporic Possession Cult Activity?" *Journal of Religion* 81:4 (October 2001): 585–86.

41. This connection between religion and culture has become of concern to scholars of religious studies, and it is expressed through a growing turn toward cultural studies as a resource for the study of religion. Examples include Hopkins and Davaney, eds., *Changing Conversations*; Delwin Brown, Sheila Greeve Davaney, and Kathryn Tanner, eds., *Converging on Culture: Theologians in Dialogue with Cultural Analysis and Criticism* (New York: Oxford University Press, 2001). Also of importance here is ritual studies for how it, through such figures as Ronald Grimes, speaks to the religious and ritual value of overlooked activities and moments. See, for example, Ronald L. Grimes, *Beginnings in Ritual Studies* (Washington, D.C.: University Press of America, 1982), where Grimes says: "Ritual studies asserts the priority of persons-in-action and interprets words and cultural objects in the light of this acting. . . . Ritual studies pays its fullest attention to the performative, non-verbal elements of action" (3). Readers will also be interested in Tom F. Driver, *Liberating Rites: Understanding the Transformative Power of Ritual* (Boulder, Colo.: Westview, 1991).

42. Matthews, *Honoring the Ancestors*, 8. It must be acknowledged that not all efforts toward liberation are positive in conduct and outcome. For example, the folklore surrounding what are referred to as "badmen" speaks to efforts toward liberation from dehumanization that in fact only reinforce this dehumanization through a rejection of the responsibilities that accompany participation in the human community. Some might argue that this misguided mind-set and activity is also present in some strands of contemporary folktales, such as those in gangsta rap music. I argue that these efforts are flawed because they arise from a warped understanding of what it means to be fully human, one that is preoccupied with the exercise of indiscrimi-

nate power in ways that merely buttress systems of discrimination and abuse. In so doing, these "badmen" simply substitute one form of terror for the ability to inflict another. This is not the liberation meant within the best traditions of black religion. For additional information, see Lawrence Levine, *Black Culture and Black Consciousness: Afro-American Folk Thought from Slavery to Freedom* (New York: Oxford University Press, 1977); John Roberts, *From Trickster to Badman: The Black Folk Hero in Slavery and Freedom* (Philadelphia: University of Pennsylvania Press, 1989); Anthony B. Pinn, "Gettin' Grown: Gangsta Rap Music and Notions of Manhood," *Journal of African-American Men* 2:1 (summer 1996): 61–73; and Anthony B. Pinn, "How Ya Livin'?: Notes on Rap Music and Social Transformation," *Western Journal of Black Studies* 23:1 (1999): 10–21.

43. Houston A. Baker Jr., *Afro-American Poetics: Revisions of Harlem and the Black Aesthetic* (Madison, Wis.: University of Wisconsin Press, 1988), 13.

44. Shane White and Graham White, *Stylin': African American Expressive Culture from Its Beginnings to the Zoot Suit* (Ithaca, N.Y.: Cornell University Press, 1998), 154.

45. Ibid., 176.

46. Ibid., 84. Some of my discussion on the decorative and visual arts presented here is also found in summary form in Pinn, "Black Bodies in Pain and Ecstasy."

47. White and White, *Stylin'*, 94.

48. Floyd Coleman, "A Foreword," and Maude Southwell Wahlman, "A Foreword," in Jacqueline L. Tobin and Raymond G. Dobard, *Hidden in Plain View: A Secret Story of Quilts and the Underground Railroad* (New York: Anchor, 2000), 6, 8; Gladys-Marie Fry, *Stitched from the Soul: Slave Quilts from the Ante-bellum South* (New York: Dutton Studio Books in association with the Museum of American Folk Art, 1990), 1. Robert Farris Thompson, *Flash of the Spirit: African and Afro-American Art and Philosophy* (New York: Vintage, 1983), remains an important text for those interested in the expressive or material culture of African Americans. Sterling Stuckey speaks to this with respect to music and literature in *Going through the Storm: The Influence of African American Art in History* (New York: Oxford University Press, 1992), 17.

49. John Michael Vlach, *The Afro Tradition in Decorative Arts* (Athens: University of Georgia Press, 1990), is helpful with this point. For example, Vlach says: "My findings helped complete the picture of black American cultural history by revealing that the full account must include things as well as words and deeds" (ix).

50. Cited in Wahlman, "A Foreword," 8–9. Also see Raymond G. Dobard, "Stitching Ideas into Patterns," in Tobin and Dobard, *Hidden in Plain View*, 30–31. For additional information on quilts, including ties to

African sensibilities, see Fry, *Stitched from the Soul*; Vlach, *The Afro Tradition in Decorative Arts*; and Sharon F. Patton, *African-American Art* (New York: Oxford University Press, 1998).

51. Judith Wilson raises questions concerning the existence of a black aesthetic in part because such an aesthetic would be "defined in terms of race. Underlying the terminology is the assumption that race itself is a valid cultural category. And this is where things get sticky" (24). Even so, she suggests the possibility of such an aesthetic when it is premised on more "substantive" categories that link those of African descent to particular geographic and historical locations—"U.S. Black Aesthetic," "African-American Aesthetic," even an "African Diasporic Aesthetic." See Judith Wilson, "The Myth of the Black Aesthetic," in Southeastern Center for Contemporary Art, *Next Generation: Southern Black Aesthetic* (Chapel Hill: University of North Carolina Press, 1990), 24–25. This does not remove the notion of race she finds so problematic because the qualifiers she promotes still speak to the curse of modernity—the dehumanization of Africans through the creation of the negro. Contextualizing this tragedy is vital, but it does not lessen the impact of race as a category of "being."

52. See Studio Museum in Harlem, *Memory and Metaphor: The Art of Romare Bearden, 1940–1987* (New York: Oxford University Press, 1991); Romare Bearden and Harry Henderson, *A History of African-American Artists from 1792 to the Present* (New York: Pantheon, 1993); and Ralph Ellison, "The Art of Romare Bearden," in Ralph Ellison, *Going to the Territory* (New York: Vintage, 1986). Cited in Wahlman, "A Foreword," 10.

53. Ellison, "The Art of Romare Bearden, 234–35.

54. Mary Schmidt Campbell, "History and the Art of Romare Bearden," In Studio Museum in Harlem, *Memory and Metaphor*, 9.

55. Sharon F. Patton, "Memory and Metaphor: The Art of Romare Bearden, 1940–1987," in Studio Museum in Harlem, *Memory and Metaphor*, 39–40.

56. This phrase is taken from Ann Gibson, "The African American Aesthetic and Postmodernism," in David C. Driskell, ed., *African American Visual Aesthetics: A Postmodernist View* (Washington, D.C.: Smithsonian Institution Press, 1995), 94.

57. Guy C. McElroy, "Introduction: Race and Representation," in Guy C. McElroy, ed., *Facing History: The Black Image in American Art, 1710–1940* (San Francisco: Bedford Arts; Washington, D.C.: Corcoran Gallery of Art, 1990), xi. A similar argument is made by Judith Wilson: "For the most part, however, we must speak of the black body as 'haunting' the artistic production of both white and black artists in modern times—either in the form of what George Nelson Preston has dubbed 'the peripheral Negro' (in reference to the legions of black servants who loom in the shadows of

European and Euro-American aristocratic portraiture and to those blacks perpetually cast in supporting roles in allegorical works like William Blake's 1793 print "Europe Supported by Africa and America"), or, as a set of compulsively repeated stereotypes (such as nineteenth-century American painting's genial watermelon eaters and banjo pluckers, or the twentieth-century electronic media's favorite emblems of poverty, physical prowess, and emotional abandon)." Judith Wilson, "Getting Down to Get Over: Romare Bearden's Use of Pornography and the Problem of the Black Female Body in Afro-U.S. Art," in Wallace and Dent, eds., *Black Popular Culture*, 113–14.

58. McElroy, "Introduction: Race and Representation," xiii.

59. Carby, *Race Men*, 56, 62.

60. White and White, *Stylin'*, 90.

61. Albert C. Barnes, "Negro Art and America," in Alain Locke, ed., *The New Negro* (New York: Atheneum, 1986), 19, 20.

62. See Marcia Muelder Eaton, *Merit, Aesthetic and Ethical* (New York: Oxford University Press, 2001).

63. However, I disagree with Welch's assumption that traditional "others" in the United States—women, African Americans, and so forth—have power and now must rethink their approach to social transformation based on their altered positions within the existing power structures. From my perspective, the "enemies" are the same; only their tactics and conversation have changed. Her appeal to discontent and disillusioned "baby boomers" does not, I believe, accurately note the way many of those who represent the "other" continue to have little control over their surroundings. Sharon Welch, *A Feminist Ethic of Risk* (Minneapolis: Fortress Press, 2000), 70.

64. Albert Camus, *The Myth of Sisyphus and Other Essays* (New York: Vintage, 1991), 120–21, 123.

65. Stuart Hall, "What Is This 'Black' in Black Popular Culture?" in Michele Wallace and Gina Dent, eds., *Black Popular Culture* (New York: New Press, 1999), 29, 30.

7. Crawling Backward:
Toward a Theory of Black Religion's Center

Those familiar with the history of religions will recognize that the title of this chapter is drawn from Charles Long's notion of "crawling back" and Mircea Eliade's idea of religion's center.

1. It is important to be in conversation with Charles Long's work in a project like this because Long (along with William R. Jones) provides the

most important challenge to black religious studies in the late twentieth century. Long—in regard to the nature of black religion and modes of exploration that challenge black theology—and William Jones—in terms of a critique of black theological responses to theodicy—pose the problem of modernity as the major contention black religious studies must wrestle with. In this way, Long and Jones pose the negro as a modern creation as the underlying issue students of black religion must address.

2. I imagine some readers might be disappointed or at least slightly anxious over the rather functional definition of religion that has guided the previous three chapters. While I think a functional understanding of religion is appropriate when considering religion's attempt to address the terror of fixed identity through the creation of liberative structures and practices, I want to suggest in this chapter another layer to my understanding of religion's nature and meaning that extends well beyond functionalism.

3. Paget Henry, "African and Afro-Caribbean Existential Philosophies," in Lewis R. Gordon, ed., *Existence in Black: An Anthology of Black Existential Philosophy* (New York: Routledge, 1997), 15.

4. Robert Birt, "Existence, Identity, and Liberation," in Gordon, ed. *Existence in Black*, 205.

5. Lewis R. Gordon, "Existential Dynamics of Theorizing Black Invisibility," in Gordon, ed., *Existence in Black*, 72.

6. Birt, "Existence, Identity, and Liberation," 206.

7. The inner sense of consciousness, the psychological angle on subjectivity, is moderated by responsibilities to external commitments. At play here is a measured sense of autonomy; it is an autonomous existence in that it is associated with freedom from oppressive constraints, yet it does not entail freedom from relationship and the obligations entailed by relationship. The key is individual subjectivity in creative tension with the demand for quality of relationships (community).

8. James Baldwin, *Go Tell It on the Mountain* (New York: Dell, 1953).

9. Ibid., 200–201.

10. Ibid., 201.

11 W. E. B. DuBois, *The Souls of Black Folk* (New York: Vintage Books/ Library of America, 1990), 7.

12. Baldwin, *Go Tell It on the Mountain*, 204.

13. Ibid., 221.

14. Clifton H. Johnson, ed., *God Struck Me Dead: Religious Conversion Experiences and Autobiographies of Ex-slaves* (Philadelphia: Pilgrim, 1969).

15. C. Johnson, ed., *God Struck Me Dead*, 45.

16. Ibid., 40–41.

17. Ibid., 81.

18. Ibid., 85.

19. Mrs. Julia A. J. Foote, "A Brand Plucked from the Fire: An Autobiographical Sketch," in William L. Andrews, ed., *Sisters of the Spirit: Three Black Women's Autobiographies of the Nineteenth Century* (Bloomington: Indiana University Press, 1986), 174.

20. Ibid., 175.

21. Ibid., 176, 177.

22. Ibid., 180.

23. Ibid., 208.

24. Some might argue that this movement from one tradition to another with respect to a theory of conversion is problematic. While this might be the case in many instances, the common contextual link to black Christianity makes the comparison here possible. Both those who accept the Black Church and are converted to Christianity and those who leave the Black Church to join the Nation of Islam share a common knowledge base.

25. E. U. Essien-Udom, *Black Nationalism: A Search for Identity in America* (Chicago: University of Chicago Press, 1962), 201.

26. The "X" refers to the unknown as well as to "ex"—the rejection of the former self.

27. C. Eric Lincoln, *The Black Muslims in America*, 3rd ed. (Grand Rapids, Mich.: Eerdmans, 1994), 106.

28. Minister Lucius X, "Why I Believe in Islam," *SALAAM* 1:1 (July 1960): 28.

29. Sonsyrea Tate, *Little X: Growing Up in the Nation of Islam* (New York: HarperSanFrancisco, 1997), 3.

30. Some scholars have raised questions concerning this text as an accurate depiction of Malcolm X's early life. Some believe he manipulates and in some cases alters events in order to prove the merits of the Nation of Islam. See, for example, Bruce Perry, *Malcolm: The Life of a Man Who Changed Black America* (Barrytown, N.Y.: Stations Hill, 1991). While there may be merit to such arguments, for my purposes the autobiography is adequate because my concern is with Malcolm X's perceptions of his experience.

31. Malcolm X, *The Autobiography of Malcolm X* (New York: Ballantine, 1973), 1.

32. Ibid., 27.

33. Ibid., 36.

34. Ibid., 27.

35. Ibid., 37.

36. Ibid., 155.

37. Ibid., 156.

38. Ibid., 164. Malcolm X would undergo another conversion in Mecca, which would result in his embrace of Sunni Islam, also a way of

addressing his inner desire or yearning for complex subjectivity—this time stemming beyond blackness.

39. Quoted in Eugene V. Gallagher, *Expectation and Experience: Explaining Religious Conversion* (Atlanta: Scholars Press, 1990), 29.

40. The language of "telling" as it relates to conversion and the sharing of this experience is from Glenn Hinson, *Fire in My Bones: Transcendence and the Holy Spirit in African American Gospel* (Philadelphia: University of Pennsylvania, 2000), 15.

41. Joseph Washington, "How Black is Black Religion?" in James J. Gardiner and J. Deotis Roberts Sr., eds., *Quest for a Black Theology* (Philadelphia: Pilgrim, 1971), 28.

42. My project is certainly open to a critique of functionalist definitions of religion. But I believe my attention to religion as triadic, while not resolving this issue, does provide a complexity to black religion that sidesteps some of the criticisms of functionalism. Besides Trulear, readers will be interested in the discussion of functionalism offered by Arthur E. Paris, *Black Pentecostalism: Southern Religion in an Urban World* (Amherst: University of Massachusetts, 1982), ch. 4.

43. Harold Dean Trulear, "A Critique of Functionalism: Toward a More Holistic Sociology of Afro-American Religion," *Journal of Religious Thought* 42:1 (spring 1985): 39.

44. Robert G. Hamerton-Kelly, ed., *Violent Origins: Walter Burkert, René Girard, and Jonathan Z. Smith on Ritual Killing and Cultural Formation* (Stanford, Calif.: Stanford University Press, 1987), 5. For additional information on the centrality and irreducibility of the "Sacred," see: Mircea Eliade, *Patterns in Comparative Religion* (New York: Meridian Books/New American Library/Sheed & Ward, 1958); Mircea Eliade, *The Sacred and the Profane: The Nature of Religion* (New York: Harvest Books/Harcourt, Brace & World, 1959).

45. This point is raised by Charles Long in Charles H. Long, "The Oppressive Elements in Religion and the Religions of the Oppressed," in Charles H. Long, *Significations: Signs, Symbols, and Images in the Interpretation of Religion* (Philadelphia: Fortress Press, 1986), 164–68.

46. The "human sciences" approach terminology is from Hamerton-Kelly, ed., *Violent Origins*, 4; Peter J. Paris, *The Social Teachings of the Black Church* (Philadelphia: Fortress Press, 1985), 17. While having some agreement on the importance of transcendence, Trulear and Paris do not go so far as to label opponents of this position "nonreligious" as does Eliade:

> But it is only in the modern societies of the West that nonreligious man has developed fully. Modern nonreligious man assumes a new existential situation; he regards himself solely as

the subject and agent of history, and he refuses all appeal to transcendence. In other words, he accepts no model for human- ity outside the human condition as it can be seen in the various historical situations. Man makes himself, and he only makes himself completely in proportion as he desacralizes himself and the world. The sacred is the prime obstacle to his freedom. . . . He will not be truly free until he has killed the last god. (Eliade, *The Sacred and the Profane*, 202–3)

While Trulear and Paris do not go this far, some critiques of humanism within black communities express a similar rejection of nontheistic orienta- tions. This was certainly the reaction to William R. Jones, *Is God a White Racist? A Preamble to Black Theology* (Garden City, N.Y.: Anchor, 1973). I met a milder version of this reaction with the publication of my first book, *Why, Lord? Suffering and Evil in Black Theology* (New York: Continuum, 1995).

47. Cornel West, "The Historicist Turn in Philosophy of Religion," in *The Cornel West Reader* (New York: Basic Civitas, 1999), 360, 367. I believe black theology provides numerous examples of this restricted range of possi- bilities through the way positions that fall outside the "accepted" frame- work—such as humanism—are met with great resistance, in part because such frameworks are not considered black. See James H. Cones's response to William R. Jones in James H. Cone, *God of the Oppressed*, rev. ed. (Maryknoll, N.Y.: Orbis, 1997).

48. Birt, "Existence, Identity and Liberation," 211.

49. Eliade, *The Sacred and the Profane*, 64.

50. Wayne L. Proudfoot, *Religious Experience* (Berkeley: University of California Press, 1985).

51. I draw on Wayne Proudfoot's text *Religious Experience* here (see pp. 155–227).

52. I have in mind here William James regarding the first definition pre- sented and Mircea Eliade with respect to the second definition.

53. Proudfoot, *Religious Experience*, secs. 5 and 6; Ann Taves, *Fits, Trances and Visions: Experiencing Religion and Explaining Experience from Wesley to James* (Princeton, N.J.: Princeton University Press, 1999), intro- duction and pt. 3.

54. Edward P. Wimberly and Anne Streaty Wimberly, *Liberation and Human Wholeness: The Conversion Experiences of Black People in Slavery and Freedom* (Nashville, Tenn.: Abingdon, 1986), 19, 20, 21.

55. Long, "The Oppressive Elements in Religion," 170.

56. Ibid., 166.

57. Charles H. Long, "Assessment and New Departures for a Study of Black Religion in the United States of America," in Gayraud Wilmore, ed.,

African American Religious Studies: An Interdisciplinary Anthology (Durham, N.C.: Duke University Press, 1989), 44–46; Long, "The Oppressive Elements in Religion," 170.

58. Long, *Significations*, 25, 140. A new edition of this book, with reflections by numerous historians of religion, including David Carasco, was published in 1999 by the Davies Publishing Group of Denver, Colorado.

59. In my work on black humanism, I raise questions concerning the importance of God or the gods. But for the purposes of this general theory of black religion's nature and meaning, this question is unimportant.

8. Finding the Center: Methodological Issues Considered

1. As readers will quickly note, my concern with psychology of religion is rather limited in this project. I do not address the issues currently debated within the field, nor do I give attention to the full range of theoretical and methodological concerns. I make limited use of this field to support my work in my primary areas of disciplinary interest—religious history, theology, and ethics. For a useful collection of documents on psychology of religion, see Diane Jonte-Pace and William B. Parsons, eds., *Religion and Psychology: Mapping the Terrain, Contemporary Dialogues, Future Prospects* (New York: Routledge, 2001). My book *Varieties of African American Religious Experience* (Minneapolis: Fortress Press, 1998) is one example of recognition of James's work by black religious studies.

2. See Cornel West, *The American Evasion of Philosophy: A Genealogy of Pragmatism* (Madison: University of Wisconsin Press, 1989).

3. West, *The American Evasion of Philosophy*, 146.

4. My thinking about the soul is influenced by my reading of Michel Foucault, *Discipline and Punish: The Birth of the Prison* (New York: Vintage, 1979).

5. William James, *The Varieties of Religious Experience: A Study in Human Nature* (New York: Collier, 1961), 163–65.

6. For information on redemptive suffering, see Anthony B. Pinn, *Why, Lord? Suffering and Evil in Black Theology* (New York: Continuum, 1995); and Anthony B. Pinn, ed., *Moral Evil and Redemptive Suffering: A History of Theodicy in African-American Religious Thought* (Gainesville: University Press of Florida, 2002).

7. Gayraud Wilmore, *Black Religion and Black Radicalism: An Interpretation of the Religious History of Afro-American People*, 2nd ed. (Maryknoll, N.Y.: Orbis, 1983).

8. Beverly Hall Lawrence, *Reviving the Spirit: A Generation of African Americans Goes Home to Church* (New York: Grove, 1996), 16.

9. Lawrence, *Reviving the Spirit,* 28–29.

10. It is a modification of his work because I am less comfortable with a transhistorical basis, or catalyst, for religious experience than he is. Furthermore, his paradigm is more heavily indebted to Christian doctrine and sensibilities than is my more general theory of black religion's nature and meaning. In this respect, his perspective is much more dependent upon black liberation theology, its categories and biblical leanings, than I would like to be in this particular study. I prefer to think about religious experience and religion as being historically and culturally situated and dependent. In this respect, my work is more in line with that of Wayne Proudfoot, Paula Cooey, Sheila Davaney, and Delwin Brown. Yet the Wimberlys' work is a helpful way of thinking through the communal consequences of conversion, particularly in light of the black community.

11. Edward P. Wimberly and Anne Streaty Wimberly, *Liberation and Human Wholeness: The Conversion Experiences of Black People in Slavery and Freedom* (Nashville, Tenn.: Abingdon, 1986), 16.

12. Wimberly and Wimberly, *Liberation and Human Wholeness,* 68. The following quotation is also helpful here: "The ability to describe in detail the events of the encounter presupposed an existing language and symbol system capable of making sense out of the encounter or experience. Biblical imagery and African symbolism provided interpretive tools for the experiencer of conversion. Although the conversion encounter was private, it was by no means static or divorced from context" (107).

The Wimberlys talk in terms of the "social symbols for translating the experience definitely influenced the person's response. In very real ways, the religious experience, although inward and personal, pushed the person toward community. It was expected that the community would influence the response to the conversion experience. The influence of the community was evident in that persons often sought out community to help them to understand and to interpret the experience" (73).

13. Ibid., 19.

14. Ibid., 22.

15. Ibid., 60.

16. The conceptual limitations of traditional theological formations is evident in the dominant mode of discourse in black circles—black theology of liberation. According to Dwight N. Hopkins: "The foundation of the African American community's heartbeat for emancipation comes from the black church. . . . Though God moves in diverse ways within the African Americans' freedom journey, the black church is the oldest, most organ-

ized, and most influential gathering of justice-loving folk among black people." Dwight N. Hopkins, *Shoes That Fit Our Feet: Sources for a Constructive Black Theology* (Maryknoll, N.Y.: Orbis, 1993). Or, in the words of James H. Evans Jr.: "Theological reflection is central to the ongoing life of the African-American Christian church. Theology is essentially the church's response to the autobiographical impulse, and it grows out of the need to proclaim with authority and commitment the identity and mission of the church in the world. . . . Because there was no precedent for the experience of people of African descent, they created distinctive ways of conceptualizing and speaking about their ultimate concerns. Black theology is a continuation of that discursive tradition." James H. Evans Jr., *We Have Been Believers: An African-American Systematic Theology* (Minneapolis: Fortress Press, 1997), 1, 2.

17. Charles H. Long, "Prolegomenon to a Religious Hermeneutic," in Charles H. Long, *Significations: Signs, Symbols, and Images in the Interpretation of Religion* (Philadelphia: Fortress Press, 1986), 32.

18. Long, "Archaism and Hermeneutics," 46.

19. Ibid., 46.

20. Ibid., 51.

21. Preben Mortensen, *Art in the Social Order: The Making of the Modern Concept of Art* (Albany: State University of New York Press, 1997), 37–40.

22. Neil Harris, in *The Artist in American Society*, suggests that the absence of industrialism, nationalism, and urbanization in the early United States prevents the fine arts from taking hold. Cited in Sally M. Promey, "Pictorial Ambivalence and American Protestantism," in Alberta Arthurs and Glenn Wallach, eds., *Crossroads: Art and Religion in American Life* (New York: New Press, 2001), 197.

23. Arthurs and Wallach, eds., *Crossroads*, 1–27.

24. Barbara Rose, *American Art since 1900*, quoted in Edward Lucie-Smith, *Movements in Art since 1945* (New York: Thames & Hudson, 2001), 16.

25. Quoted in Lucie-Smith, *Movements in Art since 1945*, 21, 23.

26. Cited in Lucie-Smith, *Movements in Art since 1945*, 24. There is no consensus on this opinion, however. In fact, according to Laurie Fendrich, "abstract painting cannot offer much of what we call Deep Hidden Meaning, in the way that religion or philosophy can. Put bluntly, abstract painting cannot provide a substitute for God—the loss of whom is the earmark of modernism. Indeed, the ability of abstract painting to move people at all is much weaker than that of other arts, such as music, theater, novels, or poetry." Laurie Fendrich, "Why Abstract Painting Still Matters," in Deborah Chasman and Edna Chiang, eds., *Drawing Us In: How We Experience Visual Art: A Beacon Anthology* (Boston: Beacon, 2000), 69.

I would agree that abstract painting is a different modality for meaning, with a different language and sensibilities than one finds in theology. It does not phrase ontological questions, issues of meaning, in the same manner as philosophy. But theology and philosophy are to some extent bound to texts, to written expression. But this does not mean, from my perspective, that abstract art has nothing to say concerning the opaque layers of meaning. Rather, it entails a different approach to meaning, one not confined to the grammar and textual needs of theology and philosophy.

27. The term was coined by Lawrence Alloway, art critic for the *Nation*. Arthur C. Danto, *After the End of Art: Contemporary Art and the Pale of History* (Princeton, N.J.: Princeton University Press, 1995), 128.

28. Danto, *After the End of Art*, 13.

29. Kyneston McShine, ed., *Andy Warhol: A Retrospective* (New York: Museum of Modern Art, 1989), 416, quoted in Arthur C. Danto, *Philosophizing Art: Selected Essays* (Berkeley: University of California Press, 1999), 74. In subsequent work on this topic, it will be important to move beyond Warhol to such figures as Jean-Michael Basquiat (1960–1988) and his graffiti art.

30. Danto, *Philosophizing Art*, 8–9.

31. Susan Sontag, "Against Interpretation," *Evergreen Review*, 1964, reprinted in Eric Fernie, ed., *Art History and Its Methods: A Critical Anthology* (London: Phaidon, 1999), 220.

32. Arthur Danto gives this date as the turning point in pop art, from "drips and dribbles of paint in the manner of abstract expressionism" to 1964, when "it had thrown off the disguises and stood, in its full reality, as what it was." Danto, *After the End of Art*, 122.

33. Danto, *After the End of Art*, 25, 27.

34. Wassily Kandinsky, *Concerning the Spiritual in Art*, translated by M. T. H. Sadler (New York: Dover, 1977), 29.

35. Danto, *Philosophizing Art*, 68.

36. Ibid., 50.

37. See Danto, *After the End of Art*, 128–29.

38. Wittgenstein is the source of this statement. Cited in Danto, *Philosophizing Art*, 45.

39. While some might concern themselves with the politics of art, discussing the manner in which both abstract expressionism and pop art represent white western domination of artistic creativity in the United States, this is not of interest to me here. Although I recognize the manner in which these two forms had little to say explicitly to black America, that does not mean these art forms offer nothing of value in the formation of an approach to the study of black religion. My use of hermeneutical resources gained from art criticism of these modes of artistic production should not suggest acceptance of their elitism. Rather, I am simply arguing that there exist

materials not produced by black Americans that might be useful in the formation of a better understanding of black life. Yes, the "master's tools" can be used to "dismantle the master's house."

40. Nicholas Davey, "The Hermeneutics of Seeing," in Ian Heywood and Barry Sandywell, eds., *Interpreting Visual Culture: Explorations in the Hermeneutics of the Visual* (New York: Routledge, 1999), 4, 8.

41. bell hooks, "Art Is for Everybody," in Chasman and Chiang, eds., *Drawing Us In*, 104.

42. Davey, "The Hermeneutics of Seeing," 25.

43. Hilton Als, foreword to Chasman and Chiang, eds., *Drawing Us In*, ix.

44. Nigel Whiteley, "Readers of the Lost Art: Visuality and Particularity in Art Criticism," in Heywood and Sandywell, eds., *Interpreting Visual Culture*, 101, 103–4.

45. While a concern for social and historical context would suggest a need to also explore the "audience" for art, I believe technological advances, for example, make works of art available beyond many traditional restrictions. That is to say, the potential audience is quite expansive.

46. Possession of both content and form broadly define art. According to Danto: "An artwork must have content, that is, it must possess aboutness; and it must embody that content." Danto, *Philosophizing Art*, 6. Quotation from Danto, *After the End of Art*, 98.

47. Jed Perl lists Clement Greenberg as one who espouses this philosophy. See Jed Perl, "The Art of Seeing," in Chasman and Chiang, eds., *Drawing Us In*, 58–63.

48. I understand that my presentation of art's importance with respect to issues of subjectivity and transformation naturally raises questions: Can art also make negative connections to this inner impulse; that is, can art support dehumanization and objectification? What is the relationship between art and ethics? While these questions are important, addressing them is beyond the scope of this book. I leave detailed discussion of the latter to scholars better equipped to address it, such as Marcia Eaton. Regarding the former, I acknowledge the significance of the issue and simply suggest that my discussion of art has involved a presentation of art at what I consider its optimal function in light of my concern with a method for studying black religion. This, however, does not suggest that art cannot function in other ways, some of which do not promote the type of revelation or consciousness raising I am interested in. Similarly, not all religious institutions and doctrines can be considered solely liberating in their impact. Otherwise, there is no way to explain the homophobia of black churches and the Nation of Islam. Recognition of this inner impulse toward complex subjectivity is one thing; acting on it is another.

49. Charles H. Long, "The Study of Religion: Its Nature and Its Discourse," in Long, *Significations*, 51.

50. I say this in response to Talal Asad's argument for the impossibility of universal definitions: "My argument is that there cannot be a universal definition of religion, not only because its constituent elements and relationships are historically specific but because that definition is itself the historical product of discursive processes." Talal Asad, *Genealogies of Religion: Discipline and Reasons of Power in Christianity and Islam* (Baltimore, Md.: Johns Hopkins University Press, 1993), 29.

51. Mircea Eliade and Joseph M. Kitagawa, eds., *The History of Religions: Essays in Methodology* (Chicago: University of Chicago Press, 1959), 97–98. Although Eliade uses the term *sacred* to describe the essence of religious experience that is not employed in this project, I believe what he says concerning the distinction between manifestation and essence is certainly applicable here. It serves to clarify my intent: "We must not confuse the historical circumstances which make a humane existence what it actually is with the fact that there is such a thing as a human existence. For the historian of religions the fact that a myth or a ritual is always historically conditioned does not explain away the very existence of such a myth or ritual. In other words, the historicity of a religious experience does not tell us what a religious experience ultimately is. We know that we can grasp the sacred only through manifestations which are always historically conditioned. But the study of these historically conditioned expressions does not give us the answer to the questions: What is the sacred? What does a religious experience actually mean?" Mircea Eliade, *The Quest: History and Meaning in Religion* (Chicago: University of Chicago Press, 1969), 53.

52. Arnold Hauser, "The Scope and Limitations of a Sociology of Art," in *The Philosophy of Art History* (London: Routledge, 1959), reprinted in Fernie, ed., *Art History and Its Methods*, 205.

53. Jonathan Z. Smith, *Map Is Not Territory: Studies in the History of Religions* (Chicago: University of Chicago Press, 1993), 129, 130. It is clear that my additional work on this method will need to include attention to Susan Sontag's critique of content preoccupation and interpretation as the impetus for a lack of concern with form. See Susan Sontag, "Against Interpretation." I am interested in constructing a method of study that is sensitive to both content and form but that is weighted toward hermeneutics. How this works is not developed in this project.

54. J. Smith, *Map Is Not Territory*, 101.

55. This is the case even when "text" is defined in the broad terms provided by Wayne Proudfoot: "What are the limits within which something can validly be considered a text? Something is interpretable if it is a mes-

sage, whether its form be a written text, the spoken word, an obscure code, or the conventions of a composer or painter. In order for something to be a text in this broad but still restricted sense, it must have been coded or written by someone who intended the signs to communicate. Where no such intention can be presumed, interpretation is inappropriate." Wayne L. Proudfoot, "Interpretation, Inference, and Religion," *Soundings: An Interdisciplinary Journal* 61:3 (fall 1978): 385.

56. J. Smith, *Map Is Not Territory*, 291, 308.

SELECTED BIBLIOGRAPHY

African-Derived Religious Practices

Anderson, John Q. "The New Orleans Voodoo Ritual Dance and Its Twenti-eth-Century Survivals." *Southern Folklore Quarterly*, vol. 24 (June 1960).

Barnes, Sandra T. *Africa's Ogun: Old World and New*. Bloomington: Indiana University Press, 1989.

Bodin, Ron. *Voodoo: Past and Present*. Louisiana Life Series, no. 5. Lafayette: Center for Louisiana Studies, University of Southwestern Louisiana, 1990.

Brandon, George. *Santeria from Africa to the New World: The Dead Sell Memories*. Bloomington: Indiana University Press, 1993.

Brown, Karen McCarthy. *Mama Lola: A Vodou Priestess in Brooklyn*. Berkeley: University of California Press, 1991.

Canet, Carlos. *Oyotunji*. Miami: Editorial AIP, n.d.

Chireau, Yvonne P. "Hidden Traditions: Black Religion, Magic, and Alternative Spiritual Beliefs in Womanist Perspective." In *Perspectives on Womanist Theology*, vol. 7, Black Church Scholars Series, ed. Jacquelyn Grant. Atlanta: Interdenominational Theological Center Press, 1995.

Creel, Margaret Washington. *"A Peculiar People": Slave Religion and Community-Culture among the Gullahs*. Ithaca, N.Y.: Cornell University Press, 1988.

Curry, Mary Elaine. *Making the Gods in New York: The Yoruba Religion in the Black Community*. Ph.D. diss., City University of New York, 1991.

Fauset, Arthur. *Black Gods of the Metropolis: Negro Religious Cults of the Urban North*. Philadelphia: University of Pennsylvania Press, 1944.

Gregory, Steven. "Afro-Caribbean Religion in New York City: The Case of Santería." In *Caribbean Life in New York City: Sociocultural Dimensions*, edited by Constance R. Sutton and Elsa M. Chaney. New York: Center for Migration Studies of New York, 1994.

————. *Santeria in New York City: A Study in Cultural Resistance*. Ph.D. diss., New School for Social Research, 1986.

Haskins, James. *Voodoo and Hoodoo: Their Tradition and Craft as Related by Actual Practitioners*. New York: Stein and Day, 1978.

Hyatt, Harry Middleton. *Hoodoo-Conjuration-Witchcraft-Rootwork: Beliefs Accepted by Many Negroes and White Persons These Being Orally Recorded among Blacks and Whites*. 2 vols. (Hannibal, Mo.: Western) Washington, D.C.: Distributed by American University Bookstore, 1970.

Murphy, Joseph M. *Santeria: African Spirits in America*. Boston: Beacon, 1993.

———. *Working the Spirit: Ceremonies of the African Diaspora*. Boston: Beacon, 1994.

Pinn, Anthony B. *Varieties of African American Religious Experience*. Minneapolis: Fortress Press, 1998.

Savannah Unit, Georgia Writers' Project, Work Projects Administration. *Drums and Shadows: Survival Studies among the Georgia Coastal Negroes*. 1940. Reprint, Athens: University of Georgia Press, 1986.

Art, Art Theory, and Art Criticism

Arthurs, Alberta, and Glenn Wallach, eds. *Crossroads: Art and Religion in American Life*. New York: New Press, 2001.

Bearden, Romare, and Harry Henderson. *A History of African-American Artists from 1792 to the Present*. New York: Pantheon, 1993.

Chasman, Deborah, and Edna Chiang, eds. *Drawing Us In: How We Experience Visual Art, A Beacon Anthology*. Boston: Beacon, 2000.

Danto, Arthur C. *After the End of Art: Contemporary Art and the Pale of History*. Princeton, N.J.: Princeton University Press, 1995.

———. *Philosophizing Art: Selected Essays*. Berkeley: University of California Press, 1999.

Driskell, David C., ed. *African American Visual Aesthetics: A Postmodernist View*. Washington, D.C.: Smithsonian Institution Press, 1995.

Eaton, Marcia Muelder. *Basic Issues in Aesthetics*. Belmont, Calif.: Wadsworth, 1988.

———. *Merit, Aesthetic and Ethical*. New York: Oxford University Press, 2001.

Fernie, Eric, ed. *Art History and Its Methods: A Critical Anthology*. London: Phaidon, 1999.

Heywood, Ian, and Barry Sandywell, eds. *Interpreting Visual Culture: Explorations in the Hermeneutics of the Visual*. New York: Routledge, 1999.

Kandinsky, Wassily. *Concerning the Spiritual in Art*. Translated by M. T. H. Sadler. New York: Dover, 1977.

Lucie-Smith, Edward. *Movements in Art since 1945*. New York: Thames & Hudson, 2001.

McElroy, Guy C., ed. *Facing History: The Black Image in American Art, 1710–1940*. San Francisco: Bedford Arts; Washington, D.C.: Corcoran Gallery of Art, 1990.

Mortensen, Preben. *Art in the Social Order: The Making of the Modern Concept of Art*. Albany: State University of New York Press, 1997.

Patton, Sharon F. *African-American Art*. New York: Oxford University Press, 1998.

Southeastern Center of Contemporary Art. *Next Generation: Southern Black Aesthetic*. Chapel Hill: University of North Carolina Press, 1990.

Studio Museum in Harlem. *Memory and Metaphor: The Art of Romare Bearden, 1940–1987*. New York: Oxford University Press, 1991.

Thompson, Robert Farris. *Flash of the Spirit: African and Afro-American Art and Philosophy*. New York: Vintage, 1983.

Vlach, John Michael. *The Afro-American Tradition in Decorative Arts*. Athens: University of Georgia Press, 1990.

Christianity

Andrews, William L., ed. *Sisters of the Spirit: Three Black Women's Autobiographies of the Nineteenth Century*. Bloomington: Indiana University Press, 1986.

Angell, Steven W., and Anthony B. Pinn, eds. *Social Protest Thought in the African Methodist Episcopal Church, 1862–1939*. Knoxville: University of Tennessee Press, 2000.

Billingsley, Andrew. *Mighty like a River: The Black Church and Social Reform*. New York: Oxford University Press, 1999.

Brown-Douglas, Kelly. *Sexuality and the Black Church: A Womanist Perspective*. Maryknoll, N.Y.: Orbis, 1999.

Cunningham, Michael, and Craig Marberry. *Crowns: Portraits of Black Women in Church Hats*. New York: Doubleday, 2000.

Gilkes, Cheryl Townsend. "'Together and in Harness': Women's Traditions in the Sanctified Church." In *Black Women in America: Social Science Perspectives*, edited by Micheline R. Malson, Elisabeth Mudime-Boyd, Jean F. O'Barr, and Mary Wyer. Chicago: University of Chicago Press, 1988.

Harris, Frederick C. *Something Within: Religion in African-American Political Activism*. New York: Oxford University Press, 1999.

Hinson, Glenn. *Fire in My Bones: Transcendence and the Holy Spirit in African American Gospel*. Philadelphia: University of Pennsylvania Press, 2000.

Hood, Robert E. *Begrimed and Black: Christian Traditions on Blacks and Blackness.* Minneapolis: Fortress Press, 1994.

Johnson, Clifton H., ed. *God Struck Me Dead: Religious Conversion Experiences and Autobiographies of Ex-slaves.* Philadelphia: Pilgrim, 1969.

Johnson, James Weldon, and J. Rosamond Johnson. *The Books of American Negro Spirituals, Including the Book of American Negro Spirituals and the Second Book of Negro Spirituals.* New York: Da Capo, 1969.

Lawrence, Beverly Hall. *Reviving the Spirit: A Generation of African Americans Goes Home to Church.* New York: Grove, 1996.

Levine, Lawrence. *Black Culture and Black Consciousness: Afro-American Folk Thought from Slavery to Freedom.* New York: Oxford University Press, 1979.

Lincoln, C. Eric, and Lawrence H. Mamiya. *The Black Church in the African-American Experience.* Durham, N.C.: Duke University Press, 1990.

Paris, Arthur E. *Black Pentecostalism: Southern Religion in an Urban World.* Amherst: University of Massachusetts Press, 1982.

Paris, Peter J. *The Social Teaching of the Black Churches.* Philadelphia: Fortress Press, 1985.

Pinn, Anthony B. *The Black Church in the Post–Civil Rights Era.* New York: Orbis, 2002.

———. *Making the Gospel Plain: The Writings of Bishop Reverdy C. Ransom.* Harrisburg, Pa.: Trinity Press International, 1999.

Pitts, Walter F. Jr. *Old Ship of Zion: The Afro-Baptist Ritual in the African Diaspora.* New York: Oxford University Press, 1993.

Sernett, Milton C. *Bound for the Promised Land: African American Religion and the Great Migration.* Durham, N.C.: Duke University Press, 1997.

Sernett, Milton C., ed. *Afro-American Religious History: A Documentary Witness.* Durham, N.C.: Duke University Press, 1985.

Cultural Criticism

Anderson, Victor. *Beyond Ontological Blackness: An Essay in African American Religious and Cultural Criticism.* New York: Continuum, 1995.

Ellison, Ralph. *Going to the Territory.* New York: Vintage, 1986.

Fabre, Geneviève, and Robert O'Meally, eds. *History and Memory in African-American Culture.* New York: Oxford University Press, 1994.

Ferguson, Russell, et al. *Out There: Marginalization and Contemporary Cultures.* Cambridge: MIT Press, 1990.

Halbwachs, Maurice. *On Collective Memory.* Translated and edited by Lewis A. Coser. Chicago: University of Chicago Press, 1992.

Kirk-Duggan, Cheryl A. *Refiner's Fire: A Religious Engagement with Violence*. Minneapolis: Fortress Press, 2001.

Locke, Alain, ed. *The New Negro*. New York: Atheneum, 1986.

Matthews, Donald H. *Honoring the Ancestors: An African Cultural Interpretation of Black Religion and Literature*. New York: Oxford University Press, 1998.

Stuckey, Sterling. *Slave Culture: Nationalist Theory and the Foundations of Black America*. New York: Oxford University Press, 1987.

Wallace, Michele. *Invisibility Blues: From Pop to Theory*. London: Verso, 1990.

Wallace, Michele, and Gina Dent, eds. *Black Popular Culture*. Seattle: Bay Press, 1992. Reissued by New Press, 1999.

West, Cornel. *The Cornel West Reader*. New York: Basic Civitas, 1999.

White, Shane, and Graham White. *Stylin': African American Expressive Culture from Its Beginnings to the Zoot Suit*. Ithaca, N.Y.: Cornell University Press, 1998.

Disenfranchisement

Allen, James, et al. *Without Sanctuary: Lynching Photography in America*. Santa Fe, N.M.: Twin Palms, 2000.

Brown, Richard Maxwell, ed. *American Violence*. Englewood Cliffs, N.J.: Prentice-Hall, 1970.

Brundage, W. Fitzhugh. *Lynching in the New South: Georgia and Virginia, 1880–1930*. Urbana: University of Illinois Press, 1993.

Carby, Hazel V. *Race Men*. Cambridge: Harvard University Press, 1999.

Cutler, James Elbert. *Lynch-Law: An Investigation into the History of Lynching in the United States*. 1905. Reprint, New York: Negro Universities Press, 1969.

Fredrickson, George M. *White Supremacy: A Comparative Study in American and South African History*. New York: Oxford University Press, 1981.

Fry, Gladys-Marie. *Night Riders: In Black Folk History*. Nashville: University of Tennessee Press, 1975.

Giddings, Paula. *When and Where I Enter: The Impact of Black Women on Race and Sex in America*. New York: William Morrow, 1984.

Ginzburg, Ralph. *100 Years of Lynchings*. 1962. Reprint, Baltimore, Md.: Black Classic Press, 1988.

Harris, Trudier. *Exorcising Blackness: Historical and Literary Lynching and Burning Rituals*. Bloomington: Indiana University Press, 1984.

Howard, Walter T. *Lynchings: Extralegal Violence in Florida during the 1930s*. London: Associated University Presses, 1995.

Litwack, Leon F. *Trouble in Mind: Black Southerners in the Age of Jim Crow.* New York: Knopf, 1998.

National Association for the Advancement of Colored People. *Thirty Years of Lynching in the United States, 1889–1918.* New York: Arno Press and the *New York Times,* 1969.

Raper, Arthur F. *The Tragedy of Lynching.* Chapel Hill: University of North Carolina Press, 1933.

Tolnay, Stewart E., and E. M. Beck. A *Festival of Violence: An Analysis of Southern Lynching, 1882–1930.* Urbana: University of Illinois Press, 1995.

White, Walter. *Rope and Faggot: A Biography of Judge Lynch.* New York: Knopf, 1929.

Williamson, Joel. *The Crucible of Race: Black-White Relations in the American South since Emancipation.* New York: Oxford University Press, 1984.

Zangrando, Robert L. *The NAACP Crusade against Lynching, 1909–1950.* Philadelphia: Temple University Press, 1980.

Islam and the Nation of Islam

Austin, Allan D. *African Muslims in Antebellum America: Transatlantic Stories and Spiritual Struggles.* New York: Routledge, 1997.

Clegg, Claude Andrew III. *An Original Man: The Life and Times of Elijah Muhammad.* New York: St. Martin's, 1997.

Cuba, Prince A. *Master Fard Muhammad: Detroit History.* Stone Mountain, Ga.: The Universal Truth, 1996.

Essien-Udom, E. U. *Black Nationalism: Search for an Identity in America.* Chicago: University of Chicago Press, 1962.

Farrakhan, Louis. A *Torchlight for America.* Chicago: FCN Publishing, 1993.

———. *Let Us Make Man: Select Men Only and Women Only Speeches.* New York: Uprising Communications, 1996.

Gardell, Mattias. *In the Name of Elijah Muhammad: Louis Farrakhan and the Nation of Islam.* Durham, N.C.: Duke University Press, 1996.

Gomez, Michael A. *Exchanging Our Country Marks: The Transformation of African Identities in the Colonial and Antebellum South.* Chapel Hill: University of North Carolina Press, 1998.

———. "Muslims in Early America." *Journal of Southern History* 60:4 (November 1994), 671–710.

Haddad, Yvonne Yazbeck, and Jane Idleman Smith, eds. *Muslim Communities in North America.* Albany: State University of New York Press, 1994.

Lincoln, C. Eric. *The Black Muslims in America*. 3rd ed. Grand Rapids, Mich.: Eerdmans, 1994.

Lomax, Louis E. *When the Word Is Given: A Report on Elijah Muhammad, Malcolm X, and the Black Muslim World*. Westport, Conn.: Greenwood, 1963.

Malcolm X. *The Autobiography of Malcolm X*. New York: Ballantine, 1973.

Muhammad, Elijah. *The Fall of America*. Chicago: Muhammad's Temple of Islam, No. 2, 1973.

———. *The Flag of Islam*. Chicago: self-published, 1974.

———. *How to Eat to Live, Book No. 1*. Atlanta: M.E.M.P.S. Publications, 1967.

———. *Message to the Blackman in America*. Chicago: Muhammad's Temple of Islam, No. 2, 1965.

———. *Our Saviour Has Arrived*. Newport News, Va.: United Brothers Communications Systems, n.d.

———. *The Supreme Wisdom*. Vol. 2. Hampton, Va.: United Brothers and U. S. Communications Systems, n.d.

———. *The True History of Master Fard Muhammad*. Atlanta: M.E.M.P.S. Publications, 1996.

Muhammad, Jabril. *This Is the One, The Most Honored Elijah Muhammad: We Need Not Look for Another!* Phoenix, Ariz.: Book Company, P.O. Box 66991, 1996.

Tate, Sonsyrea. *Little X: Growing Up in the Nation of Islam*. New York: HarperSanFrancisco, 1997.

Turner, Richard Brent. *Islam in the African-American Experience*. Indianapolis: Indiana University Press, 1997.

Philosophy and Critical Theory

Bulhan, Hussein Abdilahi. *Frantz Fanon and the Psychology of Oppression*. New York: Plenum, 1985.

Camus, Albert. *The Myth of Sisyphus and Other Essays*. New York: Vintage Books, 1991.

Davis, Angela. *Women, Race, and Class*. New York: Random House, 1981.

Fanon, Frantz. *Black Skin, White Masks*. New York: Grove, 1967.

Foucault, Michel. *Discipline and Punish: The Birth of the Prison*. New York: Vintage, 1979.

Gilroy, Paul. *The Black Atlantic: Modernity and Double Consciousness*. Cambridge: Harvard University Press, 1993.

Girard, René. *Things Hidden since the Foundation of the World*. Stanford, Calif.: Stanford University Press, 1987.

————. *Violence and the Sacred.* Translated by Patrick Gregory. Baltimore, Md.: Johns Hopkins University Press, 1977.

Gordon, Lewis R., ed. *Existence in Black: An Anthology of Black Existential Philosophy.* New York: Routledge, 1997.

Kögler, Hans Herbert. *The Power of Dialogue: Critical Hermeneutics after Gadamer and Foucault.* Cambridge: MIT Press, 1999.

Morrison, Toni. *Playing in the Dark: Whiteness and the Literary Imagination.* Cambridge: Harvard University Press, 1992.

Silverman, Hugh J., and Don Ihde. *Hermeneutics and Deconstruction.* Albany: State University of New York Press, 1985.

West, Cornel. *The American Evasion of Philosophy: A Genealogy of Pragmatism.* Madison: University of Wisconsin Press, 1989.

Religious Thought

Robert H. Abzug, *Cosmos Crumbling: American Reform and the Religious Imagination,* New York: Oxford University Press, 1994.

Cannon, Katie. *Katie's Canon: Womanism and the Soul of the Black Community.* New York: Continuum, 1995.

Carson, Clayborne, ed. *The Autobiography of Martin Luther King, Jr.* New York: Warner, 1998.

Cone, James H. *Black Theology and Black Power.* 20th anniversary ed. San Francisco: Harper & Row, 1989.

————. *Risks of Faith: The Emergence of a Black Theology of Liberation, 1968–1998.* Boston: Beacon, 1999.

Cooey, Paula M. *Religious Imagination and the Body: A Feminist Analysis.* New York: Oxford University Press, 1994.

Gardiner, James J., and J. Deotis Roberts Sr., eds. *Quest for a Black Theology.* Philadelphia: Pilgrim, 1971.

Glaude Jr., Eddie S. *Exodus! Religion, Race, and Nation in Early Nineteenth-Century Black America.* Chicago: University of Chicago Press, 2000.

Raboteau, Albert J. *A Fire in the Bones: Reflections on African-American Religious History.* Boston: Beacon, 1995.

Thurman, Howard. *The Luminous Darkness: A Personal Interpretation of the Anatomy of Segregation and the Ground of Hope.* Richmond, Ind.: Friends United Press, 1989.

Townes, Emilie M. *In a Blaze of Glory: Womanist Spirituality as Social Witness.* Nashville, Tenn.: Abingdon, 1995.

Trimiew, Darryl M. *Voices of the Silenced: The Responsible Self in a Marginalized Community.* Cleveland, Ohio: Pilgrim, 1993.

Turner, Henry McNeal. *Respect Black: The Writings and Speeches of Henry*

McNeal Turner, edited by Edwin Redkey. New York: Arno, 1971.

Welch, Sharon. *A Feminist Ethic of Risk*. Minneapolis: Fortress Press, 2000.

Wells-Barnett, Ida B. *Selected Works of Ida B. Wells-Barnett*. Compiled with an introduction by Trudier Harris. New York: Oxford University Press, 1991.

West, Cornel. *Prophesy Deliverance! An Afro-American Revolutionary Christianity*. Philadelphia: Westminster, 1982.

Wilmore, Gayraud S. *Black Religion and Black Radicalism: An Interpretation of the Religious History of Afro-American People*. 2nd ed. Maryknoll, N.Y.: Orbis, 1983.

———, ed. *African American Religious Studies: An Interdisciplinary Anthology*. Durham, N.C.: Duke University Press, 1989.

Wilmore, Gayraud S., and James H. Cone, eds. *Black Theology: A Documentary History, 1966–1979*. Maryknoll, N.Y.: Orbis, 1979.

———, *Black Theology: A Documentary History, 1980–1992*. Maryknoll, N.Y.: Orbis, 1992.

Slavery and the Slave Trade

Bancroft, Frederick. *Slave Trading in the Old South*. New York: Frederick Ungar, 1959.

Berlin, Ira, Marc Favreau, and Steven F. Miller, eds. *Remembering Slavery: African Americans Talk about Their Personal Experiences of Slavery and Emancipation*. New York: New Press; Washington, D.C.: Library of Congress, 1998.

Blassingame, John W., ed. *Slave Testimony: Two Centuries of Letters, Speeches, Interviews, and Autobiographies*. Baton Rouge: Louisiana State University Press, 1977.

Curtin, Philip. *The Atlantic Slave Trade: A Census*. Madison: University of Wisconsin, 1969.

Drago, Edmund L. *Broke by the War: Letters of a Slave Trader*. Columbia: University of South Carolina Press, 1991.

Dubois, W. E. B. *The Suppression of the African Slave-Trade to the United States of America, 1638–1870*. New York: Russell and Russell, 1965.

Engerman, Stanley L., and Joseph E. Inkori, eds. *The Atlantic Slave Trade: Effects on Economies, Societies, and Peoples in Africa, the Americas, and Europe*. Durham: Duke University Press, 1992.

Ferguson, Leland. *Uncommon Ground: Archaeology and Early African America, 1650–1800*. Washington, D.C.: Smithsonian Institution Press, 1992.

Fogel, Robert William. *Without Consent or Contract: The Rise and Fall of American Slavery*. New York: Norton, 1989.

Foster, Helen Bradley. *"New Raiments of Self": African American Clothing in the Antebellum South*. New York: Berg/Oxford International, 1997.

Franklin, John Hope. *From Slavery to Freedom: A History of Negro Americans*. 5th ed. New York: Knopf, 1980.

Fredrickson, George M. *The Arrogance of Race: Historical Perspectives on Slavery, Racism, and Social Inequality*. Middletown, Conn.: Wesleyan University Press, 1988.

———. *The Black Image in the White Mind: The Debate on Afro-American Character and Destiny, 1817–1914*. New York: Harper & Row, 1971.

Fry, Gladys-Marie. *Stitched from the Soul: Slave Quilts from the Ante-bellum South*. New York: Dutton Studio Books in association with the Museum of American Folk Art, 1990.

Gathercole, Peter, and David Lowenthal, eds. *The Politics of the Past*. Boston: Unwin Hyman, 1990.

Genovese, Eugene. *The Slave Economy of the Old South: Selected Essays in Economic and Social History* (Baton Rouge: Louisiana State University Press, 1968)

———. *Roll, Jordan, Roll: The World the Slaves Made* (New York: Vintage, 1976).

Hartman, Saidiya V. *Scenes of Subjection: Terror, Slavery, and Self-Making in Nineteenth Century America*. New York: Oxford University Press, 1997.

Hoetink, H. *Slavery and Race Relations in the Americas: Comparative Notes on Their Nature and Nexus*. New York: Harper & Row, 1973.

Huggins, Nathan Irvin. *Black Odyssey: The Afro-American Ordeal in Slavery*. New York: Pantheon, 1977.

Johnson, Walter. *Soul by Soul: Life inside the Antebellum Slave Market*. Cambridge: Harvard University Press, 1999.

Jordan, Winthrop D. *White over Black: American Attitudes toward the Negro, 1550–1812*. Chapel Hill: University of North Carolina Press, 1968.

Klein, Herbert S. *The Atlantic Slave Trade*. New York: Cambridge University Press, 1999.

Mellon, James, ed. *Bullwhip Days: The Slaves Remember*. New York: Weidenfeld & Nicolson, 1988.

Owens, Leslie Howard. *This Species of Property: Slave Life and Culture in the Old South*. New York: Oxford University Press, 1976.

Patterson, Orlando. *Rituals of Blood: Consequences of Slavery in Two American Centuries*. New York: Basic, 1998.

———. *Slavery and Social Death: A Comparative Study*. Cambridge: Harvard University Press, 1982.

Phillips, Ulrich Bonnell. *American Negro Slavery: A Survey of the Supply, Employment and Control of Negro Labor as Determined by the Plantation Regime*. New York: Appleton, 1918.

Rawick, George P., ed. *The American Slave: A Composite Autobiography.* Vol. 18, *Unwritten History of Slavery: Autobiographical Account of Negro Ex-slaves.* 1941. Reprint, Westport, Conn.: Greenwood, 1972.

Reynolds, Edward. *Stand the Storm: A History of the Atlantic Slave Trade.* New York: Allison & Busby, 1985.

Rubin, Vera, and Arthur Tuden, eds. *Comparative Perspectives on Slavery in New World Plantation Societies.* Annals of the New York Academy of Sciences, vol. 292. New York: New York Academy of Sciences, 1977.

Segal, Ronald. *The Black Diaspora: Five Centuries of the Black Experience outside Africa.* New York: Farrar, Strauss & Giroux, 1995.

Smith, Abbot Emerson. *Colonists in Bondage: White Servitude and Convict Labor in America, 1607–1776.* Gloucester, Mass.: Peter Smith, 1965.

Singleton, Theresa A., ed. *"I, Too, Am America": Archaeological Studies of African-American Life.* Charlottesville: University of Virginia Press, 1996.

Tadman, Michael. *Speculators and Slaves: Masters, Traders, and Slaves in the Old South.* Madison: University of Wisconsin Press, 1989.

Thomas, Hugh. *The Slave Trade: The Story of the Atlantic Slave Trade: 1440–1870.* New York: Simon & Schuster, 1997.

Tobin, Jacqueline L., and Raymond G. Dobard. *Hidden in Plain View: A Secret Story of Quilts and the Underground Railroad.* New York: Anchor, 2000.

Vassa, Gustavus. *The Life of Olaudah Equiano or Gustavus Vassa, the African—Volume One.* London: n.p., 1789; London: Dawsons of Pall Mall, 1969.

Theory of Religion

Arthur, Linda B. *Undressing Religion: Commitment and Conversion from a Cross-Cultural Perspective.* New York: Berg/Oxford International Publishers, 2000.

Asad, Talal. *Genealogies of Religion: Discipline and Reasons of Power in Christianity and Islam.* Baltimore, Md.: Johns Hopkins University Press, 1993.

Baer, Hans A., and Merrill Singer. *African-American Religion in the Twentieth Century: Varieties of Protest and Accommodation.* Knoxville: University of Tennessee Press, 1992.

Browne, Ray B., ed. *Rituals and Ceremonies in Popular Culture.* Bowling Green, Ohio: Bowling Green University Popular Press, 1980.

Douglas, Mary. *Natural Symbols: Explorations in Cosmology.* New York: Routledge, 1996.

———. *Purity and Danger: An Analysis of the Concepts of Pollution and Taboo.* New York: Ark, 1966.

Doty, William G. *Mythography: The Study of Myths and Rituals*. University, Ala.: University of Alabama Press, 1986.

Eliade, Mircea. *Patterns in Comparative Religion*. New York: Meridian Books/New American Library/Sheed & Ward, 1958.

————. *The Sacred and the Profane: The Nature of Religion*. New York: Harvest Books/Harcourt, Brace & World, 1959.

Eliade, Mircea, and Joseph M. Kitagawa, eds. *The History of Religions: Essays in Methodology*. Chicago: University of Chicago Press, 1959.

Fowler, James W. *Stages of Faith: The Psychology of Human Development and the Quest for Meaning*. New York: Harper & Row, 1981.

Gallagher, Eugene V. *Expectation and Experience: Explaining Religious Conversion*. Atlanta: Scholars Press, 1990.

Grimes, Ronald L. *Beginnings in Ritual Studies*. Washington, D.C.: University Press of America, 1982 / Columbia: University of South Carolina Press, 1995.

Hamerton-Kelly, Robert G., ed. *Violent Origins: Walter Burkert, René Girard, and Jonathan Z. Smith on Ritual Killing and Cultural Formation*. Stanford, Calif.: Stanford University Press, 1987.

James, William. *The Varieties of Religious Experience*. New York: Collier, 1961.

Jonte-Pace, Diane, and William B. Parsons, eds. *Religion and Psychology: Mapping the Terrain, Contemporary Dialogues, Future Prospects*. New York: Routledge, 2001.

Long, Charles H. *Significations: Signs, Symbols, and Images in the Interpretation of Religion*. Philadelphia: Fortress Press, 1986.

Proudfoot, Wayne L. "Interpretation, Inference, and Religion." *Soundings: An Interdisciplinary Journal* 61:3 (fall 1978), 378–99.

————. *Religious Experience*. Berkeley: University of California Press, 1985.

Smith, Jonathan Z. *Map Is Not Territory: Studies in the History of Religions*. Chicago: University of Chicago Press, 1993.

Taves, Ann. *Fits, Trances and Visions: Experiencing Religion and Explaining Experience from Wesley to James*. Princeton, N.J.: Princeton University Press, 1999.

Trulear, Harold Dean. "A Critique of Functionalism: Toward a More Holistic Sociology of Afro-American Religion." *Journal of Religious Thought* 42:1 (spring 1985), 38–50.

Walker, Sheila S. *Ceremonial Spirit Possession in Africa and Afro-America: Forms, Meanings, and Functional Significance for Individuals and Social Groups*. Leiden, The Netherlands: Brill, 1972.

Wimberly, Edward P., and Anne Streaty Wimberly. *Liberation and Human Wholeness: The Conversion Experiences of Black People in Slavery and Freedom*. Nashville, Tenn.: Abingdon, 1986).

INDEX